HEALTH AND WELLNESS
IN THE 19TH CENTURY

**Recent Titles in
Health and Wellness in Daily Life**

Health and Wellness in Antiquity through the Middle Ages
William H. York

Health and Wellness in Colonial America
Rebecca Tannenbaum

Health and Wellness in the Renaissance and Enlightenment
Joseph P. Byrne

HEALTH AND WELLNESS
IN THE 19TH CENTURY

DEBORAH BRUNTON

Health and Wellness in Daily Life
Joseph P. Byrne, Series Editor

 GREENWOOD

AN IMPRINT OF ABC-CLIO, LLC
Santa Barbara, California • Denver, Colorado • Oxford, England

362.1
Bru

Library of Congress Cataloging-in-Publication Data

Brunton, Deborah.
  Health and wellness in the 19th century / Deborah Brunton.
    pages cm. — (Health and wellness in daily life)
  Includes bibliographical references and index.
  ISBN 978–0–313–38511–7 (hardback) — ISBN 978–0–313–38512–4 (ebook)
1. Health—History—19th century. 2. Medical policy—History—19th century.
3. Social change. I. Title.
RA776.5.B79   2014
362.1—dc23   2013032326

ISBN: 978–0–313–38511–7
EISBN: 978–0–313–38512–4

18 17 16 15 14   1 2 3 4 5

This book is also available on the World Wide Web as an eBook.
Visit www.abc-clio.com for details.

Greenwood
An Imprint of ABC-CLIO, LLC

ABC-CLIO, LLC
130 Cremona Drive, P.O. Box 1911
Santa Barbara, California 93116-1911

This book is printed on acid-free paper ∞

Manufactured in the United States of America

Contents

Series Foreword   ix

1. Factors in Health and Wellness   1
    Healthy and Unhealthy Diets   1
    Health and Hygiene   4
    Cleanliness and the Environment   7
    Climate and Health   9
    Healthy and Unhealthy Climates   10
    Exposure to Diseases and Injuries   11
    Access to Medical Care   12

2. Education and Training: Learned and Non-Learned   17
    Non-Western Medical Systems   18
    Chinese Medicine   18
    Ayurvedic Medicine   22
    Unani Medicine   23
    Western Medicine   25
    Folk Medicine   28
    The Coexistence of Medical Systems   31
    Conflicts between Medical Systems   32

3. Religion and Medicine   35

    Christianity and Healing   35
    Conflicts between Religion and Medicine   41
    Islamic Religious Medicine   42
    Buddhism and Medicine   43
    Medicine and Taoism   44
    Hinduism and Medicine   45
    Spiritual Medicine in Africa, the Americas, and the Pacific   46
    Magic and Medicine   48
    Western Views of Spiritual Medicine   49

4. Women's Health and Medicine   51

    Women's Bodies   51
    Women and Reproduction   54
    Women as Caregivers   58
    Women as Healers   59
    Midwives   60
    Women as Nurses   63
    Women as Doctors   64
    Women and Welfare   65

5. Infants and Children's Health   67

    Protecting Babies' Health   68
    Feeding and Health   68
    Protecting Children's Health   71
    Children's Illnesses   72
    Child Deaths   76
    The Rise of Pediatrics   77
    The State and Children's Health   79

6. Infectious Diseases   83

    Changing Patterns of Diseases   83
    Understanding Disease   88
    Treating Infectious Diseases   91
    Preventing and Controlling Disease   92
    Smallpox and Vaccination   95
    The Impact of Public Health   98

7. Occupational and Environmental Hazards 101
   Natural Hazards 101
   Health and the Natural Environment 103
   Environmental Cures 110
   Health and the Urban Environment 111
   Occupational Hazards 113
   Occupational Health 115

8. Surgery, Dentistry, Orthopedics 117
   Surgery Outside the West 118
   Surgical Practice 119
   Developments in Western Surgery 125
   Orthopedics 129
   Surgeons and Hospitals 130
   Surgical Exchanges 131
   Dentistry 131

9. The Brain and Mental Disorders 135
   Mental Illness in the West 135
   Therapy and Institutions 137
   The Rise of the Asylum 138
   Psychiatry and Psychiatrists 141
   Mental Illness outside the West 144
   Mental Illness in Japan and China 144
   Mental Illness in Africa 146

10. Apothecaries, Pharmacists, and Pharmacopeias 151
    The Worldwide Trade in Drugs 151
    Pharmacopeias 152
    Practitioners, Apothecaries, Druggists 160
    Patent Medicines 163
    Medical Exchanges 164
    Medicines and Patients 165
    Drug Addiction 166

11. War and Medicine 169
    Wars between Western Powers 170
    Military Medical Services 170

Battlefield Medicine 171

Civilians and War 174

Wars beyond the West 177

Non-Western Military Forces 178

Weaponry and Tactics 179

Mortality in Non-Western Conflicts 182

12. Institutions 185

Medical Institutions in the West 186

Hospitals 187

Preventative Medicine and Public Health 190

Institutions and the Medical Profession 191

Institutions outside the West 192

Traditional Welfare in China 192

Religious Institutions and Healing 193

Adapting Western Institutions 194

Adopting Western Institutions 198

13. Disease, Healing, and the Arts 201

Images and Medical Knowledge 201

Art and Spiritual Medicine 204

Healing Objects 205

Practitioners at Work 208

Portraits of Practitioners 209

Doctor as Hero or Villain 209

Patients 212

The Impact of Disease 212

Glossary 217

Bibliography 219

Index 231

Series Foreword

Communities have few concerns that are as fundamental as the health of their members. The United States' current concern for societal provision of health care is as much a political, ethical, economic, and social matter as it is a technical or "medical" one. Reflection on the history of health and medicine may help us to place our contemporary concerns in context, but it also shows how far humanity has come in being able and willing to provide for the highest levels of health and health care possible. It is a reminder, too, of the possibilities the future presents. Our culture believes in progress, but it is also aware that unforeseen challenges will continue to appear. Health and medicine are cultural as well as biological constructs, and we live each day with the constraints and opportunities that follow.

This series of seven monographs explores the courses that human health and medicine have taken from antiquity to the present day. Though far from being complete in their coverage, these volumes map out continuities and changes over time in a set of health and medical fields. Each author has taken on the same outline in order to allow the student of health, medicine, and history to discover conditions, beliefs, practices, and changes within a given period, but also to trace the same concerns across time and place. With this in mind, each volume contains chapters on, for example, healers, children's health and healing, occupational and environmental threats, and epidemic disease. To the extent possible, we authors have striven to emphasize the ways in which these have affected people in their daily lives, rather than viewing them through the lenses of the healers or their profession. These are designed not for the specialist scholar but for the younger and general student, as well as for the general public. Our hope is that these volumes constitute a small and very useful library of the history of health and medicine.

As editor, I have striven to bring on board authors who are medical historians as well as fine teachers who have the ability to transmit their knowledge in writing with the same enthusiasm they bring into the classroom. As an author, I am sharing the discoveries, the joys, and not least the challenges and frustrations that all of us have encountered in producing this series.

Joseph P. Byrne
Honors Program
Belmont University

CHAPTER 1

Factors in Health and Wellness

Throughout history, health has depended on four main factors. Diet was very important to maintaining good health. People who were hungry or lived on a very narrow range of foods were less able to resist disease and to recover from illness. Those who ate adequate amounts of a range of nourishing foods were more likely to remain well. Hygiene also played a part in preventing disease: individuals who had access to generous supplies of clean water could regularly bathe, keep their homes clean, and wash their clothes. Those who could not were exposed to "filth diseases"—infections transmitted by contaminated water or parasites. Location—where people lived—and their occupations also affected their risk of exposure to disease and injury. Finally, the ability to obtain medical care helped to ensure recovery from illness. Access to a good diet, clean water, a healthy environment, and medical care varied widely around the globe and changed radically during the century. The social, cultural, economic, and political changes associated with modern life wrought their effects on people's health and their ability to maintain their well-being in many, sometimes unexpected ways.

HEALTHY AND UNHEALTHY DIETS

Then, as now, a plentiful and reasonably varied diet was one of the keys to a long and healthy life. During the nineteenth century, most of the world's population lived by some form of subsistence farming. On all continents, peasant families or larger tribal groups worked together to cultivate crops on small areas of land, tend to grazing animals on open ground, and gather native plants and fruits. Most of the food produced in this way was eaten within the family group: any surplus was sold or exchanged to obtain items that they could not make for themselves, such as metal tools or high-quality fabrics. The diet of subsistence farmers was often monotonous, based around starchy foods such as rice, potatoes, or wheat, with some seasonal fruits and vegetables, but with only small amounts of protein from meat, eggs, and milk. Diet varied with the seasons: in the Northern Hemisphere, food was plentiful in summer and autumn but often ran short in early spring. Overall, so long as there was enough food to go around, the diet of subsistence farmers was basically healthy.

If crops failed due to bad weather or the upheaval caused by wars, then hunger and disease was the result. Famines occurred in every continent during the century, and their impact could be devastating. When the monsoon rains failed in Rajputana in India in 1869, over a million people died from hunger and disease. In China, several millions died from starvation following the Taiping Rebellion between 1850 and 1864. Even the populations of European countries, who enjoyed a moderate climate and relatively high levels of prosperity, did not escape from hunger. Ireland was devastated by famine in the 1840s. The population had grown rapidly in the early part of the century, but many were entirely dependent on growing potatoes to survive. When disease repeatedly struck the crop in the wet summers between 1846 and 1848, almost one million people died of hunger or disease, and a further million emigrated. Overall, the population fell by around a quarter.

People living in towns had to buy food. Poor workers could afford only cheap, filling foods and lived on a monotonous diet. Laborers all over Asia survived on a diet of rice. In mid-century Britain, bread with margarine and tea with sugar (providing a quick pick-me-up of calories and caffeine) was the staple diet of factory workers. Better-off families were able to buy a wider range of foods. They too ate staple foods, such as grains, that were imported from the countryside. They could afford to eat meat, from animals brought to cities for slaughter, and enjoyed a variety of vegetables grown in market gardens close to towns and cities. The wealthy classes enjoyed exotic foods that were shipped in by road, rail, and sea.

The diets of people everywhere, but especially those living in urban areas, benefited from improved transport. One of the features of the nineteenth century was the increased volume and speed of movement of goods and people around the globe, thanks to steam-driven ships and railways. In the later nineteenth century, the global trade in food brought access to a wider range of foods and brought down prices of items that previous generations had regarded as luxuries. In the 1890s, housewives in London, Paris, or Berlin bought meat shipped from South America, mutton from Australia, and tinned salmon from Canada. Bread from the local baker contained wheat from Canada, sugar came from plantations in the West Indies, and relishes contained spices from India and Java. The demand for luxury foodstuffs tempted producers and retailers to increase their profits by bulking out foods with cheap fillers or by adding materials to improve their appearance. Such adulteration could be lethal: red lead was added to cocoa, while pickled vegetables, relishes, and sweets were colored using chemicals containing arsenic and copper.

New Foodstuffs

Global travel brought new foodstuffs to populations around the world. Potatoes were introduced to New Zealand from Europe and America. A more productive crop than native roots, the potato increased the amount of food available and allowed the Māori people to trade with passing ships. Some new foods were a mixed blessing. Corn or maize had been introduced to Europe and North America from South America in the sixteenth and seventeenth centuries and remained an important part of the diet of small farmers in Italy and the southern United States in the nineteenth century. Unfortunately, the traditional method of preparing dried maize by soaking it in a solution containing lime was not transferred. This process ensured that niacin (vitamin B3), an important nutrient, was accessible to the body. In hard times, when farmers and their families were forced to rely on a diet of dried maize, they developed pellagra, a debilitating disease that caused skin lesions, weakness, and even death. Transporting food over long distances required high levels of processing to prevent it from going bad, but sometimes removed important nutrients. Polished "white" rice kept better than unprocessed "brown" rice but contained little vitamin B1. Sailors and laborers working in factories in Asia, who ate a diet based on white rice, suffered from beri-beri, a disease that caused weakness, weight loss, and heart failure.

While most of the world's population was concerned about getting enough to eat, a small section of the population in Europe and America worried about eating too well: that they ate too much rich food and as a result became ill. Many chose to follow simpler, more "natural" diets such as the one promoted by an American, the Reverend Sylvester Graham. According to Graham, eating meat irritated the digestive system and nerves, leading to excessive sexual energy and a whole range of ailments. He advocated a diet of vegetables, whole meal bread, and the fiber-rich crackers that still bear his name. The nineteenth century also saw the arrival of low-carbohydrate diets designed to reduce weight.

Toward the end of the century, food supplements were heavily marketed through advertisements in newspapers. A vast array of pills, potions, and tonics promised to protect and improve health, promoting vigor, energy, and vitality by ensuring the correct functioning of the organs and building up stores of nervous energy. Some acted on specific parts of the body, purifying the blood or stimulating the liver. Others claimed to have a more general effect. One advertisement proclaimed: "HOOD'S SARSAPARILLA which makes rich, healthy blood and thus gives strength and elasticity to the muscles, vigor to the brain, and health and vitality to every part of the body. Hood's Sarsaparilla MAKES THE WEAK STRONG."[1] Very few of these potions can have done the consumer much good, although cod liver oil was sold from 1870s as a general tonic, well before it was understood to be a source of vitamin D.

HEALTH AND HYGIENE

A second crucial factor in keeping well and avoiding disease was access to a plentiful supply of clean water for drinking and washing. Throughout the world, in Africa, Asia, Europe, and the Americas, there was a long association between dirt and disease. In rural areas, where people lived in fairly small, stable communities, they chose to site their homes close to natural sources of water such as streams and rivers. If there was no convenient natural source, householders dug wells or built tanks to store rainwater. Living quarters were arranged to ensure that water supplies were not contaminated by dirt, feces, or domestic refuse. In Indian and African villages, water was stored uphill of latrines and rubbish dumps. Zulu people collected their water upstream of villages and away from the parts of the rivers used for bathing and washing.

While access to a plentiful supply of clean water gave populations the opportunity to bathe and wash their clothes, the frequency of washing was also dictated by cultural factors. In Africa, many peoples bathed daily and took great care to keep their bodies and hair clean and free from parasites. By contrast, travelers in Eastern Europe criticized the indigenous peasant farmers for rarely bathing and for living in filthy conditions. Religious rites also affected when and how often people washed: followers of Islam washed their heads, arms, and feet before praying.

In cities, getting access to clean water was often difficult, as rapid urban growth put a great strain on traditional systems of water supply. At the beginning of the nineteenth century, there were relatively few large cities in Europe and Asia. Over the course of the century, new cities grew up around important transit points and industrial sites, and existing centers grew in size. The population of London increased

Water supplies in cities were often contaminated, leading to epidemics of diseases such as cholera. This cartoon shows Death dispensing water from a public pump to poor people who have jugs and buckets to carry it back to their homes. (Centers for Disease Control and Prevention)

from 800,000 inhabitants in 1801 to over six million in 1901. Gradually, societies moved from being predominantly rural to largely urban. In 1800, less than one-fifth of the European population lived in towns: by 1900, over half made their lives in urban areas. In Britain, over 80 percent of the population lived in towns by the end of the century. (With such rapid change, it is easy to overlook the continuities of life: at the same time, less than 1 percent of the African population lived in urban centers.)

In cities, the traditional sources of water—rivers, reservoirs, and wells—could not keep up with the demands of growing populations. In many towns, the supplies became seriously polluted by rubbish, excrement, and industrial refuse. Wealthy residents could avoid the problem by digging their own wells or by building tanks to allow water to settle and clear before use. The poor migrants to towns had no choice but to take dirty water from rivers and canals or spend time standing in line to obtain piped water from a public well.

Better-off residents of cities, who enjoyed access to plentiful supplies of clean water, could afford to follow medical practitioners' advice to bathe regularly as means of removing dirt and sweat from the skin and stimulating the body. They had servants to carry water and, later in the century, had the space and resources to build laundries and bathrooms within their homes. For the poor, who had to carry home water from a river or pump in buckets and jugs, keeping clean was exhausting and time consuming, and it is not surprising that many people rarely, if ever, bathed.

From the 1860s in Europe and America, as scientific medicine identified bacteria as the cause of many diseases, there was an increasing concern with keeping the body and the environment clean. Women took on the responsibility for keeping their homes free of germs and disease. The appearance of cleanliness was not enough to ensure that their homes were safe. "From the cellar, store-room, pantry, bedroom, sitting room and parlor; from decaying vegetables, fruits, meats, soiled clothing, old garments, old furniture, refuse of kitchen, mouldy walls, everywhere, a microscopic germ is propagating."[2] Only thorough cleanliness, proper ventilation, and disinfection would stop disease and death from visiting the home.

General levels of hygiene improved in the late nineteenth century, when city governments made enormous investments in building new reservoirs and laying pipes to bring in greater amounts of clean water. As a result, many more homes were connected to water supplies. The poorest could wash themselves at public baths and clean their clothes in public washhouses. Messages about hygiene gradually spread down the social scale through pamphlets and lectures. Schoolchildren were taught to keep their faces and hands clean. Sales of soap soared: it was one of the first branded consumer products. Regular washing must have made life healthier by cutting down exposure to bacteria and infections; it also helped reduce the incidence of skin complaints and parasites such as lice and fleas.

CLEANLINESS AND THE ENVIRONMENT

Efficient removal of refuse and waste was also important in maintaining health. Traditional forms of housing were often designed around concepts of hygiene. In African villages, houses were grouped in compounds, with each dwelling separated from its neighbors by a small patch of ground. Houses were sited on higher ground, away from animal enclosures so that no contamination reached them. Refuse was regularly removed from living areas, and feces were disposed of very carefully. In some cultures, human excrement was placed in pits and doused with boiling water. In others, all feces were buried well away from the houses, for fear that it would be stolen and used in witchcraft to cause harm to the community.

In urban areas in the West and in Asia, the large and growing numbers of people packed into small areas put strains on traditional systems of waste disposal. These relied on householders keeping their own homes clean and taking responsibility for disposing of the debris, ashes, and excrement produced in the home. Domestic refuse and excrement was often collected and sold to local farmers to fertilize their fields. City authorities were responsible for keeping the streets clean, by employing cleaners to gather refuse and by maintaining drains or ditches to carry away rainwater. As towns grew, these systems broke down. In nineteenth-century cities in Europe, India, and North Africa, refuse piled up in the streets and filled the rainwater ditches. In Beijing and other Chinese cities, travelers noted that the old drainage systems were not maintained, rubbish was not collected, and cemeteries with shallow, badly dug graves were situated close to homes. Even the air of cities became increasingly polluted by smoke from domestic fires and from factories.

Reformers, eager to whip up support for sanitary improvements, provided graphic and dramatic accounts of the levels of filth in cities. The Reverend Andrew Mearns described the slums in London:

> [C]ourts reeking with poisonous and malodorous gases arising from accumulations of sewage and refuse ... many of them which the sun

never penetrates, which are never visited by a breath of fresh air, and which rarely know the virtues of a drop of cleansing water . . . Eight feet square—that is about the average size of many of these rooms. Walls and ceiling are black with the accretions of filth which have gathered upon them through long years of neglect.[3]

In the early part of the century, the bad smells or "miasma" arising from dirt and rotting matter were blamed for producing a range of diseases. By 1900, it was understood that these complaints arose from a number of causes, but their transmission was fostered by filthy conditions. Water supplies polluted with bacteria passed in human excrement exposed town dwellers to simple stomach upsets and deadly infections such as cholera, characterized by violent diarrhea, cramps, and, in many cases, a rapid death, and typhoid that caused high fever and delirium. Crowded and dirty living conditions allowed body lice to spread from person to person, carrying typhus fever with its rashes. Epidemics of these diseases regularly struck every city, even prosperous capitals and trading centers. Other diseases were endemic or present all the time. In densely crowded housing, respiratory complaints—tuberculosis, bronchitis, and pneumonia—were readily transmitted from person to person through the air, damaging the lungs and causing many deaths. Infection rates peaked in the winter months, when urban residents huddled indoors to escape the cold. Many city children had permanently bowed legs from rickets. The disease was caused by a lack of vitamin D (manufactured in the body when exposed to sunlight) that affected bone development.

In cities, wealthy residents avoided the worst health risks by making their homes in new suburbs, built away from the densely populated slums and factories and often situated on hills. In Britain, the most desirable homes tended to be on the west side of towns, where the prevailing winds blew away smoke and pollution. In London, the upper classes lived in the fashionable West End, while the East End was a working-class area. Wealthy homes had large rooms with many windows that allowed the air to circulate and that let in sunlight. They boasted the latest sanitary facilities: bathrooms equipped with baths and showers with hot and cold running water and flushing lavatories. Over time, building regulations passed by town authorities ensured that houses built for residents lower down the social scale had similar facilities. Building codes stipulated the width of new streets (to help circulate air through built-up areas), set minimum sizes of rooms, and required all dwellings to have piped water and sinks.

Town and city authorities helped householders to keep their dwellings clean by installing drainage and sewerage systems and organizing the collection and disposal of domestic refuse. They also launched new initiatives to improve the public spaces by introducing regular street cleaning.

CLIMATE AND HEALTH

The Moving World

Nineteenth-century developments in transport, especially reliable and efficient steam engines in ships and on railways, allowed travel on an unprecedented scale. Small numbers of European and American explorers mapped the African and Asian continents, and much greater numbers of European soldiers fought indigenous peoples, bringing vast areas under the control of colonial governments. In their wake came administrators to govern the local populations, settlers to set up farms, and missionaries to spread the Christian faith. Better transport increased the numbers of settlers in older European colonies, including Canada, Australia, and New Zealand. New industries and agriculture in the colonies brought a demand for migrant labor, to tend crops for the European market such as rubber, tea, and cotton, and to labor in mines and factories. Men from the Caribbean moved to Latin America in search of work, laborers from India settled in South Africa, and over half a million Chinese and South Asians found employment in the Americas. Men from China traveled the world as sailors and settled in "Chinatowns" from Vancouver to Liverpool.

Moving around the globe or even within a region could be very dangerous. On sea voyages, ships ran into bad weather and were wrecked, or were delayed so long that supplies of food and water ran out. In the crowded conditions on emigrant ships, disease spread rapidly among the closely confined passengers. Travel on the railways too brought risks. The unprecedented speeds of over 40 miles per hour terrified many passengers, and some doctors feared that such rapid travel would damage the nervous system. The boilers on early steam locomotives occasionally exploded, killing drivers and railway staff. Trains derailed and collided, and the flimsy carriages gave passengers little protection. Rail travel even had its own medical condition called "railway spine." It was suffered by passengers who escaped apparently uninjured from crashes but later reported symptoms that were attributed to jarring. These would now be diagnosed as post-traumatic stress.

HEALTHY AND UNHEALTHY CLIMATES

Travelers arriving at their destinations were exposed to a whole new range of hazards. In Europe and America, it was generally accepted that different races were adapted to live in particular climates. White people were suited to cool, temperate climates, while black and other races of color were much more tolerant of heat and humidity. Moving to a new and unfamiliar climate therefore posed serious risks to health. For example, Bengal in India was seen as a particularly unhealthy place for Europeans. The heat, humidity, and wide variations of tempera-ture between seasons were believed to affect the blood and organs, particularly the liver, undermining the health of settlers. The forests and lakes were full of "miasma" or bad air that caused fevers and other complaints. Altitude also had an important effect on health. In Peru, Archibald Smith, a Scottish physician, concluded that the even temperatures and high humidity of the coastal regions made the immigrant population weak and subject to stomach complaints. The high mountains were also bad for new arrivals who experienced headaches, vertigo, and nausea. Although all unfamiliar climates were unhealthy in some ways, some were more dangerous than others. West Africa, where settlers and soldiers died in huge num-bers, was nicknamed the "white man's grave"; but life in the countryside of Australia or South America was relatively healthy. It was certainly more conducive to good health than living in the slums of European cities, and British charities paid for orphans to emigrate to Australia and New Zealand in part to give them the opportunity of living in healthy surroundings.

Various techniques were adopted to mitigate the effects of moving to a new and potentially dangerous climate. In the early decades of the century, new arrivals were advised to take time to acclimatize by spending some time in areas where the climate was more like that of their homeland, and only gradually moving into less healthy locations. Settlers sought to protect their health by carefully choosing the sites of their new homes. Ideally, settlers' homes should be shaded from the sun, built away from dense vegetation and damp areas, and open to breezes but not strong winds. By the middle decades of the century, doctors were losing faith in the concept of acclimatization. Instead, they recommended minimizing the time spent in the unhealthiest areas. In India, European soldiers and administrators moved away from the heat and humidity of the plains to the cooler climate of the hills for a few weeks or months each year, as a way to maintain and restore their well-being.

Similar concerns drove European families to escape the heat and polluted atmosphere of the city for a few weeks or months during the summer by traveling to the seaside, mountain resorts, or spa towns. There, the mild climate, mineral waters, and fresh air helped to build up health and strength before the winter with its colds and other minor ailments. By the end of the century, working-class families saved hard to afford a day or two in the country or by the coast, partly for pleasure, but also because they believed that the air would "do them good."

By the end of the century, climate was no longer blamed for high levels of mortality among settlers in Africa and Asia. Instead, deaths were linked to a range of "tropical" diseases associated with warm climates, such as kala-azar, sleeping sickness, yellow fever, enteric fever, and dysentery. Some hot, dry climates were even seen as healthy for Europeans. A handbook aimed at potential settlers in Queensland, Australia, claimed that "although the heat makes out-door work arduous and uncomfortable, such work can nevertheless be carried on throughout the summer without injury to men of steady and temperate habits."[4] The heat was not entirely without its dangers; settlers were warned that drinking alcohol in such a hot climate could lead to insanity.

EXPOSURE TO DISEASES AND INJURIES

Travel to a new continent, or a new country, brought people into contact with unfamiliar diseases. American and European travelers to Asia and Africa were exposed to a range of unfamiliar diseases to which they had little or no resistance. Many did not survive long: half the British soldiers sent to the Gold Coast of Africa in the 1820s died there. But there were also risks of exposure to new diseases for people traveling much shorter distances. Many rural populations suffered from a fairly small range of diseases particular to their location. For example, before the nineteenth century, the peoples of southern Africa were fairly healthy because they lived far away from ancient trade routes. With the arrival of European travelers, they came into contact with infections such as whooping cough, polio, tuberculosis, and cholera. Europeans, who moved from the countryside into towns and cities for work or to trade, had a similar experience and were exposed to infections such as smallpox, tuberculosis, and measles that were endemic in large urban populations.

Diseases moved around the globe with travelers. The increasing numbers of people making long journeys, and the greater speed of travel, allowed infections to move between continents. In the eighteenth century, someone boarding a ship while harboring an infection such as smallpox or measles would probably remain on board long enough for the disease to run its course. With steamships cutting journey times from weeks to days, passengers arrived at their destination suffering from infections that they then spread to the local population. Cholera was endemic in South Asia, but traveled around the globe in repeated pandemics during the nineteenth century. From 1855, plague moved across China and India, and as far as Australia and the United States. Diseases that were relatively mild in Europe, such as influenza and measles, had a devastating effect on unexposed populations on Pacific islands. These infections, combined with conflicts, the loss of land and resources, and social disruption, halved the native populations of Hawaii and New Zealand. Patterns of disease also shifted in response to man-made changes to the environment. In Malaya and India, the clearing of forests for the creation of sugar, cotton, and rubber plantations, and the introduction of irrigation systems, provided ideal conditions for mosquitoes to breed and resulted in the spread of malaria.

Occupations carried their own threats to life and health. Farmers working on the land risked injury from by being kicked by farm animals and from accidents when using sharp tools such as scythes. In towns, builders fell from ladders; carters and dockworkers, who moved heavy goods using muscle power, were crushed by barrels and bales. In factories and workshops, the moving parts of machines were often exposed, and women workers in particular were in danger of being caught by the hair or clothing and pulled into the mechanisms. Miners were killed and injured in rock falls and died from exposure to dangerous gases.

As if this were not enough, city life brought new threats of serious injury. Pedestrians traveling through the streets were knocked down by horse-drawn and motorized traffic. Town dwellers had to learn how to get on and off omnibuses and tramcars safely. Stress is often associated with the pace of present-day urban life, but it was also recorded in the nineteenth century. People suffered from new nervous conditions, such as neurasthenia, believed to be caused by rapid transport and the intense pace of work.

ACCESS TO MEDICAL CARE

Regardless of how carefully they guarded their health through diet, hygiene, and lifestyle, at some point almost everyone fell ill and sought medical help to cure their ailments. Although medical knowledge is usually associated with groups of experts who specialize in healing, in the past (as now), everyone had some basic knowledge of disease and remedies, called folk or popular medicine. Such medical knowledge was acquired through personal experience of ill health, from family and friends or practitioners and, increasingly over the nineteenth century, through printed books. It allowed people to deal with their own minor ailments and injuries, and those of family members. Ailments might be treated using special foodstuffs such as a nourishing soup. Local herbs or medicinal plants bought from a traveling merchant or local shop were made into infusions to be drunk or used to wash wounds. Poultices (pastes made of seeds, vegetables, or earths) were applied to encourage the healing of swellings and other injuries.

Even small communities had one or two people with a special knowledge of healing, learned through experience or from other practitioners, who provided help in return for some form of

In this late-nineteenth century photograph, a Japanese physician feels the pulse of his patient to diagnose the cause of her illness. Such highly trained practitioners charged high fees, and attended only the very wealthy. (Alinari Archives/Getty Images)

payment. They offered different types of treatment. Many were herbalists, who prepared medicines and gave advice. In many cultures
around the world, disease was often believed to have its roots in an
excess of blood. Barbers or bloodletters cut open veins to release a
controlled amount of blood and allow the body to recover its normal
functions. In cases of broken or dislocated limbs, a bonesetter would
be consulted. In many cultures in Asia, Africa, and the Americas, a
sick person could ask for help from a healer who used spiritual or
supernatural means to diagnose and treat illness caused by spirits
or by sorcery.

Wealthy members of society living in towns were able to consult
what we might recognize as a professional doctor: a healer who had
spent a long time acquiring a theoretical knowledge of how the body
worked in health and illness, and who practiced medicine as a full-
time occupation. These practitioners charged much higher fees than
local healers, reflecting the investment in their training, their sophisti-
cated knowledge, and their high social status. They visited patients in
their homes, diagnosed their ailments, and directed treatment. Over
the century, the numbers of these elite practitioners increased. More
people began to access their help, either paying for their own treatment,
or obtaining help through charities and hospitals.

Public Health

While individuals were largely responsible for looking after their own
health, over the course of the nineteenth century, governments and
other institutions played an increasing role in helping them to do so.
Particular groups of people such as members of the military or prisoners were subjected to close regulation of their diet, exercise, bathing,
and living conditions in barracks, ships, and prisons. Public health regulations protected the wider population. Regulations on the quality of
food sold by shopkeepers helped to ensure that customers did not
buy milk or meat that was unfit for consumption. Governments set limits for working hours and rules to protect workers from dangerous
machinery and from exposure to hazardous substances. They began
to improve sanitation, introducing supplies of clean water and installing drainage systems to carry away wastewater. To control outbreaks
of disease, they established quarantines, isolated and cared for the sick,
and provided immunization against smallpox. While the degree of
state involvement varied from place to place, by the end of the century,
public health regulations had begun to make an impact, helping people
to live longer, healthier lives.

The expansion of medical care to the general population was one of the justifications for colonial rule. Medicine was seen as a part of the "civilizing mission" of European governments and charities.

> I have been on horse back through the country a great deal attending to sick Natives and every where the Natives have hailed me with delight and have expressed themselves grateful to the Government for having sent me amongst them ... before ten years pass over many a savage heart will be won over to the British Government and many a Father and Mother or Husband and Wife will bless the benevolence and wisdom of that Government which entered in spirit into the sickness and sufferings of the black savage lying neglected and forlorn on the cold damp ground and suggested a remedy.[5]

NOTES

1. Takahiro Ueyama, *Health in the Marketplace: Professionalism, Therapeutic Desires, and Medical Commodification in Late-Victorian London* (Palo Alto, CA: Society for the Promotion of Science and Scholarship Inc., 2010), p. 97.

2. " 'Decomposition,' " *Sanitarian* 2 (1874), p. 316, quoted in Nancy Tomes, *The Gospel of Germs: Men, Women and the Microbe in American Life* (Cambridge, MA: Harvard University Press, 1998), p. 64.

3. Andrew Mearns, *The Bitter Cry of Outcast London* (London, 1883), p. 7, quoted in Roy Porter, *The Greatest Benefit to Mankind: A Medical History of Humanity from Antiquity to the Present* (London: Fontana, 1999), p. 400.

4. Josiah Hughes, *Australia Revisited in 1890* (London, 1891) p. 355, quoted in Helen R. Woodcock, " 'Our Salubrious Climate': Attitudes to Health in Colonial Queensland," in *Disease, Medicine and Empire. Perspectives on Western Medicine and the Experience of European Expansion*, ed. Roy MacLeod and Milton Lewis (New York: Routledge, 1988), p. 180.

5. Letter from Dr John Patrick Fitzgerald, Head of the Medical Department and Superintendent of the Native Hospital, to Colonel John MacLean, Chief Commissioner of British Kaffaria, April 13, 1856, quoted in David Gordon, "A Sword of Empire? Medicine and Colonialism in King William's Town, Xhosaland, 1856–1891," *African Studies* 60 (2001), p. 170.

CHAPTER 2

Education and Training:
Learned and Non-Learned

In the nineteenth century, many forms of medicine were practiced around the world in different cultures. The majority of the global population used some form of folk medicine—different ranges of therapies used to treat particular ailments or diseases caused by spirits or by witchcraft. These varied from simple homemade remedies for minor ailments such as colds or stomach upsets, to treatments offered by healers skilled in the preparation and use of herbal medicines or rituals to cure supernatural diseases. A smaller number of people were able to afford the services of practitioners trained in a medical system—a body of knowledge that explained how the body worked and why and how illnesses occurred, and thus gave a logical explanation of how to cure any problems. Among the most important and widely used medical systems practiced around the world were Western or scientific medicine (used in Europe and North America), Chinese medicine, ayurvedic medicine (practiced in India) and unani medicine (practiced in India and North Africa).

All systems of medicine were based on a body of texts, often dating back many centuries, but they were not ancient and unchanging bodies of knowledge. Medicine constantly developed as doctors added new observations or reinterpreted the conclusions made by earlier generations of practitioners. In the nineteenth century, this development was given a new impetus by global travel that brought about contacts between different medical systems and exposed practitioners to new approaches to medicine and different methods of practice.

NON-WESTERN MEDICAL SYSTEMS

Although each of the major non-Western systems of medicine, Chinese, ayurvedic and unani, were quite different, they shared some fundamental principles. Practitioners of all three systems believed that health reflected the smooth functioning of the body: illness occurred when there was some disruption to the body's fundamental processes—the flow of fluids or energies, or the processing of food within the body. A number of factors tipped the body from a state of health to one of illness: lifestyle (particularly diet, but also exercise and sleep patterns), strong emotions, and changes to the environment.

CHINESE MEDICINE

Chinese medicine dates back over 2,000 years. Ancient texts, written around 200 BCE, defined the central concepts of medical theory: *yin/yang* (opposing or complementary qualities) and the five phases (wood, fire, earth, metal, and water—each associated with a specific form of action or transformation within the body). Although Chinese medical theory referred to organs within the body, practitioners were concerned with the function of these organs rather than their structure. The five *yin* organs, the heart, liver, spleen, lung, and kidney, manufactured and stored *qi* (pronounced "chee")—a form of energy or spirit. The six *yang* organs, the small intestine, large intestine, gallbladder, urinary bladder, stomach, and *sānjiaō* (triple burner) were responsible for the regulation of body processes such as digestion and breathing. Health was dependent on the smooth circulation of *qi* through channels spread throughout the body. Disease occurred when the *yin/yang* balance was disrupted, affecting the flow of *qi* that could become stagnant, or blocked in a particular place. This was caused by diet, environmental factors such as cold, internal factors including emotions, or external factors including the invasion of bad *qi* arising from the environment. Disease was also widely believed to be caused by spirits or ghosts.

Chinese medicine is often portrayed as static and unchanging, but the late eighteenth and nineteenth centuries were a time of lively debate on the causes and treatment of diseases. Different schools of thought were developed by prominent scholar physicians and continued by their pupils. Doctors debated the merits of classical and modern authors, and the role of cold damage and warm pathogens in causing

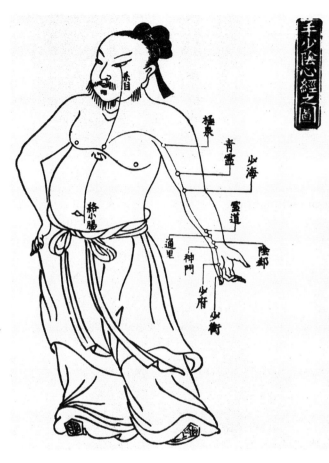

This diagram shows acupuncture points on the arm and body along one of
the channels where *qi* flowed around the body. By inserting needles at each
point, doctors stimulated specific organs or encouraged the movement of
qi. (National Library of Medicine/WHO photo)

disease. Cold Damage theory ascribed all diseases to internal, external,
or environmental factors, while Warm Factor theory claimed that some
disease was caused by pestilential *qi* entering through the mouth and
nose and attacking the body's own *qi*. Chinese practitioners also
debated the true function of internal organs. In his book *I-lin kai-ts'o*
(*Correction of Errors from Medical Literature*), Wang Ch'ing-jen complained of the contradictions in existing texts produced by earlier
writers.

> When they spoke of the lung, [they said] it is empty like a beehive and
> has no opening at its lower side. Inhaling fills it, exhaling empties it.

Now, if it is said [in one place that the lung] has no opening below, how
can it be said elsewhere that the lung has twenty-four holes pointing into
all directions as passageways for the influence of the body's depots?[1]

Wang Ch'ing-jen called for new research to achieve a better understanding of anatomy. Styles of medical practice also varied between
practitioners. Each had a particular area of expertise and style of prescribing. Some were known for their use of strong drugs to attack
the causes of disease: others favored milder remedies that supported
the body.

Treatment aimed to restore the smooth circulation of *qi*, or to get rid
of bad *qi* and to build up good *qi*, and thus return the patient to health.
Drugs were used to manipulate the functioning of the body's systems.
Each drug was categorized by its character—hot, cold, or cool—and
which organ it affected. Drugs were used to break up and disperse
blockages of *qi* or remove excess heat or cold. Practitioners also restored
the circulation of *qi* and removed blockages by acupuncture (the inser-
tion of needles at points along the channels of the body) or moxibustion
(burning small pellets of vegetable material on the skin).

Diet was an important form of therapy. Foods, like drugs, were categorized as hot, warm, cool, or cold and had particular qualities that
related to the body's internal systems. Crab, for example, was characterized as cold and salty, while mutton was hot and sweet. In hot
weather it was important to eat cooling foods—vegetables and fruits,
such as melon—and avoid hot foodstuffs such as meat and oily dishes
that would cause the body to overheat. The bad effects of eating too
much of one type of food at one meal could be balanced at the next:
so the effects of a rich dish of mutton at dinner could be countered the
next day by a meal of soup made with cool green vegetables. Some
dishes could boost health. "Guarding life soup" containing the herb
angelica and dahlia root was recommended to strengthen the body
and calm the spirits.

Chinese Practitioners

There was a wide range of practitioners in China. The elite were
learned scholar physicians, many of whom came from families who
had practiced medicine for several generations. Learned practitioners
had a deep understanding of medical theory drawn from texts. They
trained as pupils under an established practitioner, who guided their
studies and tested their developing knowledge. Pupils learned how to
diagnose illness and prescribe treatment by observing their teacher at

work. Diagnosis was made by listening to the patient's description of his or her symptoms, by feeling the pulse to read the flow of *qi*, and by close scrutiny of the face, tongue, and breathing. These signs indicated the deeper changes within the body and allowed practitioners to identify the nature of the illness, what parts of the body were involved, and whether the ailment was in its early or later stages—disease was easily cured in its early stages but at a later point required more vigorous treatment. Accurate diagnosis was vital: one symptom, such as a fever, could be caused by quite different underlying changes within the body, and the wrong therapy would make the problem worse.

Learned practitioners charged high fees: only wealthy patients could afford their services. Many specialized in treating one or more types of ailment, such as fevers or external complaints. The most common specialism was in treating children's illnesses. This required a high level of skill as children could not explain their symptoms to the doctor, so he had to rely on his ability to observe the patient and read the pulse. In the nineteenth century, the Chinese state no longer regulated medicine by requiring practitioners to pass examinations, so practitioners were ranked by their reputation for curing difficult cases. Famous doctors were praised for their skill and charged higher fees. They attracted patients suffering from complex cases, who had failed to find a cure from other practitioners.

Alongside the highly trained scholar physicians were a much larger number of other practitioners. While some made use of theoretical concepts, such as the effects of lifestyle on the body or the balance of hot and cold, they did not possess the deep understanding of medical theory of learned practitioners. For this reason, learned practitioners dismissed them as dangerous quacks, offering worthless cures and cheating their gullible patients. Street healers (*shi yi*) diagnosed illnesses, prescribed medicines, and practiced acupuncture and moxibustion. Itinerant doctors offered quick, cheap cures for diseases, especially skin and eye complaints; extracted teeth; and treated wounds. Other types of practitioners had more practical skills. Drug sellers worked in shops, making up the prescriptions written by learned practitioners and handing out medical advice, or sold simple remedies for common ailments from a stall or on the street. Midwives helped women in childbirth, using medicines and massage. Shamans and priests exorcised disease-causing demons. Knowledge of medicine was spread widely through Chinese society. Patients too had some basic understanding of medicine that they used to devise treatments for their own minor ailments and to judge the skill and ability of practitioners.

AYURVEDIC MEDICINE

Ayurvedic medicine was widely practiced in India and Asia, particularly but not exclusively among those of the Hindu faith. It too had a long history: ayurvedic medical texts dated back to the fourth century BCE. In this system, the body was believed to be composed of seven basic substances (chyle or fluid, blood, flesh, fat, bone, marrow, and semen). These were subject to the action of three *doṣas*—*vāta*, *pitta*, and *kapha* (wind, bile, and phlegm)—that regulated movement and transformations (for example, digestion) and stabilized the body by actions such as lubricating the joints. Each *doṣa* was found throughout the body, but was linked to particular organs. Thus *vāta* was associated with the large intestine, *pitta* with the stomach, and *kapha* with the heart. The *doṣas* corresponded to two of five fundamental elements: ether (or space), air, fire, water, and earth. For example, *vāta* was linked to ether and air. A natural slight imbalance of the *doṣas* affected the body shape, health, and character of each individual. Those with a *pitta* constitution were of medium height, slept lightly, and were prone to eye infections. The balance of *doṣas* was not fixed: they varied according to age (infants had more *kapha*, old people more *vāta*), the time of year, and even the time of day.

When healthy, the body, mind, and spirit were all in a state of harmony. Disease was the result of a significant imbalance within the body, usually an excess of one or more *doṣas*. Disease could be caused by many possible factors—by changes in the season and temperature; by inappropriate behavior, such as too much or too little exercise; or by eating the wrong sort of foods. Illness could also be caused by supernatural forces. Children were particularly at risk of attacks by demons and had to be protected by prayer and rituals.

When diagnosing disease, practitioners examined the body and its secretions to gain an insight into what was happening inside the body: they noted the quality of the pulse and the appearance of urine, feces, and the eyes and tongue to determine the state of the *doṣas*. Treatment aimed to remove the disease, but also to restore the body's natural healthy processes. Medicines were used to counter imbalances of the *doṣas*. Drugs were categorized by *rasa* or taste—sweet, sour, salt, pungent, bitter, and astringent—each with different effects. Sour medicines helped digestion and the healing of wounds. In addition, practitioners prescribed vomiting, laxatives, and enemas to remove toxins from the body. For example, laxatives or purges were prescribed in cases of fever, leprosy, female diseases, cholera, jaundice, and wounds. Bloodletting was used to remove an excess of blood or bad blood.

The position on the body where the blood was removed was specific to each type of ailment. Patients suffering from diseases of the ear had blood taken from the ear; in cases of madness, blood was removed from a vein on the chest. In theory, every course of treatment had to be tailored to the individual constitution of the patient; but in practice, standard preparations were often prescribed for common ailments.

As well as curing illnesses, ayurvedic medicine provided techniques to preserve health and prolong life through diet, exercise, and massage to strengthen the body and mind. Personal hygiene was very important. Texts recommended brushing the teeth twice a day, washing the face and hands, massaging the skin with oils, and exercising.

Elite ayurvedic practitioners, called *vaids*, learned medical theory by memorizing classic texts, often in the form of short rhymes. They acquired the skills of diagnosis and prescription by observing the work of established practitioners. Distinguished practitioners attracted numbers of pupils, and in the early nineteenth century, small schools of ayurvedic medicine were based in the courts of Indian rulers. In the late nineteenth century, medical students attended colleges, modeled on Western universities. Alongside learned practitioners were other, less well-educated and sometimes self-taught practitioners who possessed a basic level of knowledge and charged lower fees. Drug sellers had an understanding of medical theory to help them make up medicines. Other practitioners had practical skills. Although elaborate surgery was described in ancient ayurvedic texts, nineteenth-century surgeons carried out a limited number of procedures, including removing cataracts from the eye, bloodletting, and treating injuries. Midwives (*dais*) looked after women in childbirth.

UNANI MEDICINE

Unani medicine was derived from ancient Greek medical knowledge that spread into the Arabian Peninsula in the medieval period and was developed and elaborated by Islamic scholars. One of the central texts of unani medicine was the *Kitab al-Qunan* (*Canon of Medicine*) by Ibn Sina (known as Avicenna in the West), completed around 1025. In the nineteenth century, unani medicine continued to be practiced in North Africa, and it had spread eastward to India where it was used by the Muslim population. According to this system of medicine, health depended on a balance of four fluids or humors—*dam* (blood), *balgham* (phlegm), *safrā* (yellow bile) and *saudā* (black bile)—that were produced by digestion. Each substance displayed two of four fundamental qualities—hot, cold, wet, and dry. Blood, for example, was hot and wet. As in ayurvedic medicine, everyone had a slight natural imbalance of the humors that determined their character. The quantity of humors and their flow around the body was affected by six factors: air, food and drink, movement and rest, sleep and wakefulness, eating and evacuation, and emotions. Eating the wrong type of foods, or not getting enough sleep, or moving too quickly between hot and cold environments caused an imbalance or a blockage in the flow of humors and caused illness. Diseases caused by an excess of hot humors—blood and yellow bile—were categorized as hot; those associated with an increase in phlegm or black bile were cold complaints.

When an imbalance occurred, the body naturally tried to restore a healthy equilibrium. Practitioners aimed to support this healing process through diet, medicines, massage, and bathing. Therapies aimed to counter the effects of disease. Hot diseases, such as fevers, were treated with cooling medicines and foods including green fruits, cucumbers, and seeds. Where the flow of the humors had become blocked or corrupted humors had formed in the body, purging medicines and bloodletting were prescribed to remove them.

Unani Medical Practice

Elite practitioners (*hakims*) diagnosed illness by noting the quality of the pulse (*nabz*), the patient's breathing and general appearance, and the body's excretions, all of which gave clues to the internal workings of the body. As well as understanding the body and disease, successful *hakims* had to have a thorough knowledge of pharmacy, in order to prescribe and make up medicines for their patients. They also needed to possess patience, to be sensitive and caring, and to behave in a correct manner. Students wishing to become elite practitioners went through a formal training. They acquired knowledge of medical theory from texts, and they learned about practice by observing their teachers conducting consultations with patients. Pupils studied with established practitioners, who helped them to understand and memorize key texts that described the workings of the body and the treatment of diseases from those affecting the head to those attacking the feet. At the end of their training, their teachers certified that they had acquired the skill required of a good practitioner. One certificate (*ijazah*) from the mid-nineteenth century declared:

> I taught him many books, lesson by lesson ... Thereafter he worked on diagnosis of diseases and examination of urine and pulse, under my

supervision. I found him intelligent and skillful. He possesses wisdom as is demanded of a physician.[2]

However, there were no rules about the qualifications required to set up as a doctor, and it was possible for anyone to simply read some books and begin practice.

There were a range of practitioners within unani medicine. One traveler recorded that in the city of Hyderabad in India, there were "educated Hakeems [*sic*], following hereditary profession, uneducated quacks, the Hujams or barber caste who form the surgeons of India, herbalists of the shepherd caste, druggists, oculists, lithotomists, fakeers, midwives and leech-women."[3] While the *hakims* possessed a thorough knowledge of medical theory, the other groups possessed practical skills, in bloodletting, surgery, or making and selling medicines.

Although unani medicine had a long history, it adapted to new political and social circumstances. In India, in the early nineteenth century, unani medicine was practiced by a small elite, attached to the courts of local rulers, who learned their medicine from books written in Arabic. In the late nineteenth century, in part as a reaction against colonial rule, unani went through a revival. Old texts were translated from Persian and Arabic, languages used only by scholars, into Urdu, a language that was much more widely understood. New texts were written that retained the central tenets of unani knowledge but opened up the study of medicine. They emphasized how, by reading, anyone could learn medicine. They described practical techniques to maintain health and treat simple ailments and brought a new spiritual dimension to medicine. Allah was portrayed as a physician: through his guidance, men could learn how to be healthy. Practitioners fought back against Western criticism of unani medicine as irrational and unscientific. They pointed out that Western medicine (which they called "doctory") had a shared history with unani medicine, and that Western surgery was based on techniques described in medieval Arabic texts. They attacked Western medicine for failing to understand the fundamental processes within the body and claimed that Western medical treatments countered symptoms rather than treated the underlying causes of illness.

WESTERN MEDICINE

Western or scientific medicine, the predominant form of medicine practiced in Europe and North America, went through a radical transformation in the nineteenth century. Until the eighteenth century, practitioners followed humoral medicine. Like unani medicine, it was derived from ancient Greek ideas, and saw health as dependent on a balance of four humors—blood, yellow bile, black bile, and phlegm. In the late eighteenth century, practitioners began to abandon this system in favor of scientific or Western medicine. This was a major revolution in medical thinking: instead of seeing illness as a consequence of an imbalance of fluids, disease was now understood to be the result of malfunctions in the solid organs and tissues of the body. The new understanding emerged through anatomical research that mapped the structures of the healthy body in ever greater detail and linked symptoms in life to the effects of disease on the organs and tissues. For example, Jean Corvisart, a French practitioner and one of the leading researchers in heart disease, described the case of:

> A wheelwright [who] ... felt, after a violent effort, a sharp pain in the right side of the thorax. Immediately there ensued oppression, cough, and spitting of blood ... the pulse strong, full, regular and frequent; the strokes of the heart violent, dry and hurried, but regular ... The patient died three months [later] ... On dissection ... the inferior lobes of the lung [were] ... hard, and gorged with black blood ... the heart was twice its natural size.[4]

After 1850, research shifted from the dissection room to the laboratory. Using improved microscopes, practitioners investigated ever smaller anatomical structures, such as the nerves and muscle fibers. Through analysis and experiments they explored the chemistry of the body and the function of organs.

This new approach to disease led to new techniques of diagnosis. As well as observing outward signs—the color of the skin, the quality of the pulse, and the excretions—to understand what was going on inside the body, practitioners used instruments to see inside the body. In 1816, René Laennec, a French doctor, discovered that by applying one end of a tube of paper to the chest and pressing his ear to the other end, he could hear sounds from the lungs. Laennec's stethoscope (the name comes from the Greek word *stēthos*, meaning chest, and the French *scope*, meaning an instrument for viewing) made it possible for practitioners to visualize the changes caused by lung and heart disease in the living patient. As one contemporary put it: Laennec "placed a window in the breast through which we can see the precise state of things within."[5] By the late nineteenth century, doctors had an array of new technologies to see into the body. Ophthalmoscopes, invented in 1851, and laryngoscopes, developed in 1855, allowed them to peer into the eye and throat. Most dramatically, X-rays, discovered in 1895, graphically revealed broken bones.

Experimental techniques developed in the laboratory provided further new ways to diagnose illness. Diseased tissues were examined under the microscope to determine whether tumors were benign or malignant. Chemical analyses of blood and urine revealed problems with the kidneys or liver. Samples of body fluids could be cultured in the laboratory to identify disease-causing bacteria. Not all doctors welcomed the new array of diagnostic tests: some felt it was too easy to become reliant on technologies and that practitioners would lose the old skills of diagnosis at the bedside that relied on touch, vision, and experience.

Western Medical Training

The place of anatomy as the key to understanding the body and disease was reflected in the curriculum taught in medical schools and universities. Throughout the century, students learned in groups, through lectures, textbooks, demonstrations, and hands-on dissection. The basic shape of the curriculum remained constant: students first acquired a thorough grounding in anatomy and science before studying medical subjects, although the range of courses shifted and expanded. In the early nineteenth century, medical students began their studies with courses on anatomy, chemistry, and botany before progressing to the theory and practice of medicine and materia medica (the study of drugs). At the end of the century, students were taught anatomy, chemistry, and biology, then moved on to medical sciences such as physiology, biochemistry, and histology (the study of cells). In addition, students received clinical training in hospitals. They "walked the wards," observing patients, and the treatments carried out by hospital staff, and listening to short lectures on particular cases. Toward the end of their studies, students worked as junior staff, honing their skills in diagnosis and learning how to prescribe medicines and to apply treatments.

At the end of their training, students had to pass a rigorous set of examinations to prove their competence. In many countries, this was a requirement for them to be allowed to practice as a qualified practitioner. Most medical students went on to some form of general practice, treating the ailments of the general population. A small number specialized in a particular area of medicine, such as surgery or pediatrics. Doctors worked alongside nurses and pharmacists, who had their own forms of training, and competed for patients with unqualified quack doctors, who had no formal education and sold medicines and treatments.

Unorthodox Medicine

Not everyone welcomed the new, scientific approach to the study of health and disease. Many patients and practitioners turned to a range of new, more "natural" systems of medical practice. Homeopathy, devised by Samuel Hahnemann, a German practitioner, in the 1800s, used very small doses of drugs to produce symptoms similar to the complaint that the practitioner wanted to cure—the principle that "like cures like." Herbalism was a system of treatment based on the principle that all disorders were caused by obstructed perspiration and were cured by medicines to cause vomiting, purging, or sweating. Others argued that only water offered a truly "natural" source of healing. From 1829, Vincenz Priessnitz, an Austrian farmer, popularized hydropathy, or the "water cure." Patients drank copious amounts of water, were wrapped in wet sheets, and given cold baths and showers to balance the heat and cold within the body and to encourage natural healing processes. Hydropathy proved popular among the European upper classes: Charles Darwin went through several "water cures" to try to relieve his chronic stomach complaints. Knowledge of these systems of unorthodox medicine was spread through books, one-on-one training, and unorthodox medical schools. Homeopathic medical schools taught the usual medical curriculum and the use of homeopathic rather than orthodox therapies.

FOLK MEDICINE

Systems of medical knowledge allowed practitioners to deal with any form of illness. From the visible symptoms, they worked out what was going wrong inside the body and therefore what type of treatment would restore the body's healthy function. Folk medicine was based on repertoires of particular treatments for specific ailments. In a few cultures there were elements of a theory of body function; in southern African medical cultures, many types of swellings were attributed to an accumulation of blood, while excess bile was believed to cause stomach complaints, but in most cultures there was no overarching theory that explained the causes and cure of illness. Many forms of folk medicine were very ancient; in parts of Central America, there were elements of Aztec medicine in nineteenth-century practice. But folk medicine, like medical systems, changed in response to social and cultural developments. In Mexico, native practitioners incorporated plants and animals introduced by the Spanish into their medicines, as well as the idea of a hot/cold balance from humoral medical theory. In Kazakhstan, in the Russian steppes, native people used a mix of shamanistic medicine and Islamic medicine.

Folk medicine provided treatments for many conditions—herbal medicines for internal complaints, bone setting for injuries, drugs and massage to help in childbirth, and rituals and medicines to counter diseases sent by supernatural forces. Often, different practitioners dealt with different types of therapy. In Bantu-speaking West Africa, for example, there were *nganga mbuki* (herbalists), *nganga nkisi* (magicians or spiritual healers), *nganga ngombo* (diviners, who diagnosed disease), *nganga kilauki* (practitioners who dealt with skin complaints), and *nganga mpansu* (who treated mental illness). In Kazakhstan, shamans or *baksy* performed rituals to cast out spiritual disease, while other healers used herbal medicines, mare's milk, and saltwater baths to treat physical ailments.

The most common form of folk medicine used plant-based remedies to treat ailments. Some herbalists possessed a huge body of knowledge: in southern Africa, over 3,000 different plants were used in medicine. Herbal medicines could be drunk in the form of teas, inhaled as powders, used to bathe the skin and to cleanse wounds, or added to the water in a steam bath. For example, plains Indians in America drank yarrow tea as a tonic, took preparations containing the bark of the poplar tree as a laxative, applied poultices of poplar leaves to infected wounds, and chewed seneca root to relieve toothache. Most healers used indigenous plants gathered in the immediate area or grown in a garden, but some traded medicines over long distances. In the Andes in Bolivia, herbalists gathered medicinal plants indigenous to their area and traveled from Argentina to Peru, to practice and to trade their medicines with people living at different altitudes. Earths, minerals, and animal products, such as the fat of snakes, also had medicinal uses.

Spiritual healers dealt with illness caused by supernatural factors: by witchcraft, gods, ghosts, or the spirits of ancestors. In order to treat these patients, the healer had to diagnose the problem, and work out why it had happened, in order to affect a cure. Disease caused by sorcery might be prompted by a social dispute between individuals or families that had to be resolved before the patient could recover. Ancestor spirits might send illness if they felt neglected, and the disease would be cured by making offerings. Spiritual healers had a complex role: they were not just healers, but have been described as friends, pastors, and psychiatrists as well as doctors. Many worked to protect the health of the whole community as well as individuals, protecting chiefs from harm, or calling up rain in times of drought.

Supernatural disease was diagnosed through communication with the spirit world. Healers might enter a trance state or use various forms of divination. In Kenya and Tanzania, practitioners diagnosed illness by throwing shells or other objects from a special divination gourd or basket called an *enkidong*. The final position of each object was controlled by the spirit world and indicated the cause of disease. Among the Xhosa people of southern Africa, disease could be a sign that the spirits were trying to communicate with the living. Sufferers and their families went to an *igqirha* or diviner, who contacted the spirits and found ways to pacify them. If witchcraft was suspected, an *igqirha elinu-kayo* found out who had cast the spell and removed the material used to cause the illness by sucking it out of the patient's body. In other

Wooden *agere-Ifa* (divination bowls) were used by the Yoruba people of Nigeria to hold sixteen palm nuts used in ceremonies to determine the cause of misfortunes including illness. (Werner Forman/Corbis)

cultures, supernatural complaints were treated by rituals that often included drumming and dancing.

Skills in these forms of medicine were acquired in different ways. Herbalists, bonesetters, and midwives trained with experienced practitioners. Knowledge was passed down through families or from healer to pupil. In Africa, aspiring healers traveled long distances to train with skilled practitioners and brought back new treatments to their own communities. Spiritual healers learned how to conduct rituals and interpret divination objects from experienced practitioners. In some cultures, they acquired powers through visions or dreams. Among Plains Indians in North America, healers acquired a spirit helper who helped them to diagnose illness and to perform curing rituals through a dream or vision. The knowledge of how to use plants for healing was also passed from the spirit world through dreams. Among Xhosa healers in southern Africa, the end of the training period was marked by rituals and celebrations, during which the spirits would give some sign that they accepted the new healer.

THE COEXISTENCE OF MEDICAL SYSTEMS

Throughout the nineteenth century world, practitioners using different forms of medicine worked alongside each other. Patients were happy to turn to different forms of medicine in search of a cure. In Europe, patients tried folk remedies, and if this approach did not cure the problem, they sought help from a practitioner of Western or unorthodox medicine. Similarly in Africa, a sick person might visit a herbalist and then a spiritual healer. In the nineteenth century, the range of medical treatments on offer expanded in many countries, as Western medicine spread to Africa and Asia, where it was practiced alongside Chinese, unani, ayurvedic, and folk medicine.

In the early part of the century, practitioners of Western medicine found some common ground with other systems of medical ideas. Western and unani practitioners agreed that miasma—bad air—was the cause of epidemics. One Egyptian practitioner, trained in both unani and Western medicine, saw a common foundation in the two systems:

> Medicine is twofold, traditional (*qadam*) and modern (*jaded*). Traditional medicine consists of Greek medicine, and modern medicine comprises Greek medicine plus anatomy, pathology and some branches of mathematics, natural sciences and pharmacology, geology, physiology, botany etc.[6]

Non-Western treatments were adopted by Western practitioners. European-trained doctors working in India acknowledged that ayur-vedic practitioners possessed valuable knowledge of medicines used to cure unfamiliar local diseases. Chinese acupuncture enjoyed a brief vogue in both Europe and America, where it was used for pain relief, although practitioners were unsure how it worked.

Patients in many parts of the world called in Western doctors when their own healers failed to cure their ailments. Western surgery was particularly valued as European and American practitioners carried out a greater variety of more complex operations than their non-Western counterparts. In India and Egypt, traditional unani techniques for treating cataracts in the eye were replaced by techniques drawn from Western surgery. Some Chinese practitioners argued that Western understandings of public health were better than those of their own medicine, but their traditional medicine was better at curing most internal diseases.

Medicine on the Pacific island of Samoa shows how care could be divided between Western and indigenous medicine. At the beginning of the nineteenth century, the Samoans believed that disease was caused by the gods who had been offended in some way. They treated illness with prayers and rituals and a limited number of herbal medicines. These treatments failed to cure Western diseases such as influenza, whooping cough, mumps, and measles that were brought to the island by missionaries in the 1830s. As a result, the Samoan people redefined their medicine and split disease into two categories. Samoan illnesses (*ma'i samoa*) had existed before contact with the missionaries and were treated by indigenous healers (*fōma'i* and *fōgau*) using medicinal plants. The diseases introduced by missionaries were defined as *ma'i papalāgi* and were treated with European medicines.

CONFLICTS BETWEEN MEDICAL SYSTEMS

By the second half of the century, as Western understandings of the body and of disease completed their move away from humoral to scientific medicine, European and American practitioners became increasingly skeptical that non-Western medicine had any value. Western practitioners associated their medicine with reason, science, and progress, while Chinese, ayurvedic, and unani medicine were seen as irrational, superstitious, and unable to progress because of practitioners' reverence for ancient texts. One European doctor working in mid-nineteenth-century China described the "absurd notions of attributing diseases to wind, breath, water or sweat" and found local medical practices both laughable and dangerous.[7] There was a two-way traffic in criticisms of medical systems. Chinese practitioners generally dismissed Western medicine, complaining that the recently discovered bacteria were no different from the long-established understanding of pestilential *qi*.

The spiritual aspects of non-Western medicine came in for particularly harsh criticism from Western practitioners. African beliefs about the supernatural causes of illness were dismissed as "superstition" and indigenous practitioners seen as no better than quacks, duping their patients with useless or even dangerous medicines. Some African colonial governments tried to outlaw native medicine, punishing "witchdoctors" and banning sales of herbal medicines. Similarly, in Latin America, Western practitioners tried to get local practitioners (*curanderos*) banned from practicing, although with little success. Although many Western practitioners assumed that indigenous forms of medicine would die out and be replaced by scientific medicine, non-Western medicine not only survived, but thrived. Patients welcomed the option of consulting practitioners using different systems of medicine, and they were happy to consult the type of healer they felt best able to deal with their illness.

NOTES

1. Wang Ch'ing-jen, *I-lin kai-ts'o* (1849), pp. 177–179, quoted in Paul U. Unschuld, *Medicine in China: A History of Ideas* (Berkeley: University of California Press, 2010), pp. 213–214.

2. Tazim Uddin Siddiqui, "Nazim-e jehan Hakim Muhammad A'zam Khan," *Studies in History of Medicine* 4 (1980), p. 234, quoted in Guy Attewell, *Refiguring Unani Tibb: Plural Healing in Late Colonial India* (Hyderabad: Orient Longman, 2007), p. 133.

3. George Smith, *The Hyderabad Medical School: Its Past History and Its Present Condition* (Madras, 1859), quoted in Attewell, *Refiguring Unani Tibb*, p. 102.

4. Jean Nicholas Corvisart, *An Essay on the Organic Diseases and Lesions of the Heart and Great Vessels* (Boston, 1812), p. 80.

5. John Forbes, Preface to Rene Laennec, *A Treatise on the Diseases of the Chest and on Mediate Auscultation* (n.p., 1838), quoted in Stephen Jacyna, "Medicine in Transformation, 1800–1849," in *The Western Medical Tradition 1800–2000* by W. F. Bynum et al. (Cambridge: Cambridge University Press, 2006), p. 43.

6. *Ruznāmeh-ye 'elmi*, March 19, 1887, quoted in Hormoz Ebrahimnejad, *Medicine, Public Health and the Qājār State: Patterns of Medical Modernization in Nineteenth-Century Iran* (Boston: Brill, 2004), p. 123.

7. Ruth Rogaski, *Hygienic Modernity: Meanings of Health and Disease in Treaty-port China* (Berkeley: University of California Press, 2004), p. 94.

CHAPTER 3

Religion and Medicine

Around the globe, different cultures had different understandings of the relationship between the physical and the spiritual world that fundamentally shaped ideas about health and medicine. Some people saw ill health was the result of purely physical processes—some malfunction within the body's chemistry or damage to its structures. Others understood ill health to be caused by supernatural forces that punished individuals for breaking some religious rule, by spirits or gods associated with a particular disease, or by the ghosts of ancestors who were unhappy about the behavior of the living.

In the nineteenth century, all cultures recognized that disease had both physical and supernatural causes. In Africa, Asia, and Australia, native peoples understood the world to be full of spirits, and diseases and injuries were often, although not exclusively, caused by supernatural forces. In Christian Europe and the Americas, most disease was understood to arise from purely physical causes and was treated by drugs and surgery; however, for some religious groups, ill health was sent by God and prayers could result in miraculous healing.

CHRISTIANITY AND HEALING

In the nineteenth-century Christian West, medicine and spirituality were, in theory, clearly separated: disease and injury occurred in the physical body, and the immaterial soul had no influence on health.

The physical body was cared for by doctors and nurses, while priests cared for the soul. In practice, however, the separation between religion and medicine was by no means so clear cut. Different sects and denominations within the Christian faith had different understandings of the role of God in causing disease and of faith as a means of cure. Many doctors and nurses had a deep faith and found a model for their lives in Christ the physician.

Healing and the Catholic Church

In Catholic teaching, the body was a temple for the Holy Spirit: health was a gift from God and therefore everyone had a responsibility to care for his or her body. Pain was sent from God, possibly as a punishment and had to be accepted. If bravely borne, suffering could cleanse the soul and be a sign of grace. Injuries and illness could be cured by medical treatment or through divine intervention. Miraculous healing occurred through prayer to the Virgin Mary and to saints. Particular saints were able to intercede for specific conditions, often related to the forms of their martyrdom. People suffering from eye diseases prayed to St. Lucy, who had been blinded; those with toothache appealed to St. Apollonia, who had been tortured by having her teeth pulled out. Churches throughout Europe and the Americas displayed proof of the power of prayer in the display of ex-votos—objects left in thanksgiving for recovery from illness, injury, or danger. Votive objects took the form of a small model of the body part that had been healed—a hand, or leg, or eye—or a picture showing the patient at the moment of healing.

In the nineteenth century, many sick and injured people made pilgrimages to healing shrines in search of cures. One of the most important healing sites, at Lourdes in southwest France, was established in 1858 after a local girl, Bernadette Soubires, experienced a series of visions of the Virgin Mary. By the end of the century, hundreds of thousands of pilgrims visited the shrine every year. Lourdes was not the only new pilgrimage center set up at this time. The small town of Knock in Ireland also became a site of pilgrimage after a vision of the Virgin Mary, St. Joseph, and St. John the Evangelist appeared in 1879.

Protestant Healing

The Protestant churches saw rather different relationships between faith and healing. A few branches accepted that direct divine intervention could cause or cure illness. Disease was sign of sin and a gift of grace to improve spiritual life. For example, Charles Haddon Spurgeon, a prominent English Baptist preacher, declared:

> I venture to say that the greatest earthly blessing that God can give to any of us is health, *with the exception of sickness* [emphasis in original]. Sickness has frequently been of more use to the saints of God than health has ... A sick wife, a newly made grave, poverty, slander, sinking of spirit, might teach us lessons nowhere else to be learned so well. Trials drive us to the realities of religion.[1]

Most Protestants rejected the idea that God sent disease directly, but rather they believed that he had devised rules for healthy living, and that breaking those rules would lead to illness. A simple diet, exercise in the fresh air, a regular pattern of work and rest, and cleanliness would ensure health. ("Cleanliness is next to Godliness" was a popular proverb in the nineteenth century.) Disobeying these rules by eating to excess (especially meat), drinking alcohol, smoking, and staying up late exposed the body to infections and illness: sin thus led directly to disease. Ill health was cured by returning to a healthy and righteous lifestyle. Prayer did not cure illness but aided the healing process by strengthening the mind and spirit and giving courage.

While most Protestants called in doctors in times of illness, members of some sects opposed some or all aspects of orthodox medicine. Vaccination against smallpox caused widespread concern. Parents feared that a procedure that prevented attacks of smallpox interfered with God's right to inflict disease. Members of the Mormon, Methodist, and Seventh-day Adventist churches favored unorthodox medicine such as homeopathy and herbalism, with their simple remedies and rejection of modern excesses. The Christian Science movement rejected all forms of medicine. Followers believed that illness and pain were not real, but were produced by fear, ignorance, or sin and were cured by getting rid of these false beliefs through prayer.

Faith in the Time of Cholera

Religious faith came to the fore during the fear and panic spread by epidemics. When cholera swept Europe and the United States in the middle of the century, the new disease was widely interpreted as a punishment sent from God. While it was generally accepted that the disease was transmitted through the atmosphere (or, later, in the water supply), it was also believed that those who followed an immoral or irregular lifestyle were particularly susceptible. The disease therefore struck drunkards and prostitutes, and there was almost a sense that it cleansed society of its unproductive, criminal members. A pamphlet published in Oxford, England, on the 1854 epidemic reported:

> A woman woke in the agony of cramps with intense and sudden collapse ... in the hospital she died. Her room was cleaned out: the woman that cleaned it had next night the cholera. She and her husband were drunk in bed. The agony sobered *her*, but her husband went reeling about the room: in a room below were smokers and drinkers. Then a woman of the streets [a prostitute] in her gaudiness came to see her. They would not hear reason but drank more spirits. The victim of the disease cried out to the end that her soul was everlastingly lost; and she died.[2]

When respectable citizens fell victim to the disease, it was assumed that they must have sinned in some unknown way. Not surprisingly, respectable families often tried to hide cases of cholera that occurred in their households.

Faced with such danger, people turned to religion for help. Clergymen of all denominations visited the sick despite the risk of infection, dispensing prayers and practical advice on a healthy diet and lifestyle. Protestant churches held extra services to pray for the victims of cholera, issued special prayers, and organized fast days, when the faithful were asked to reflect on their sins. In Catholic communities, people flocked to churches to pray for protection against the disease and for help for those who were infected. Religious images were carried in processions between shrines. St. Gennaro, a fourth-century saint, was credited with bringing to an end a devastating cholera outbreak that struck Naples in southern Italy in 1884.

Christianity and Medical Care

Christian churches of all denominations played an important role in providing medical care to the poor in the nineteenth century. Even though governments began to take responsibility for the welfare of populations at this time, the number of faith-based charities increased and the scope of their work expanded.

At their simplest, churches provided care through their clergy. In rural areas, where there were few doctors, priests and clergymen provided advice to the sick poor and distributed medicines. They also organized care within their parish, encouraging members of their congregations to donate food and fuel to the sick. Members of Catholic and Protestant orders provided care to the poor on a larger scale in hospitals or though home visits. The nineteenth century saw the founding of new Catholic orders of monks and nuns, many of them dedicated to caring, such as the Sisters of Mercy, set up in Ireland in 1831, and the Little Sisters of the Poor, established in France in 1834. Protestant sisterhoods, similar to their Catholic counterparts, were also founded from the 1830s, including the Nursing Sisters of St. John the Divine and the All Saints Sisters of the Poor in London. Alongside these orders, voluntary groups such as the Society of St. Vincent de Paul, established in Paris in 1833, carried out similar work among the poor.

The services of nursing sisters were in high demand, reflecting the good standard of care they offered. In the early nineteenth century, nursing was a rather haphazard, often poor-quality service provided by working women with little medical knowledge or by convalescent hospital patients. By contrast, the nursing sisters had a strong commitment to their work: they saw nursing not as a job, but as a vocation and a way of expressing their faith. They were also well trained: the religious orders established new forms of nurse education. Trainees (often called probationers) observed the work of experienced nurses,

Members of religious orders were an important source of medical care, especially to the poor. While many nuns nursed in hospitals, they also treated patients suffering from minor illnesses such as eye infections in clinics or dispensaries. (National Library of Medicine)

and learned to carry out nursing tasks under their supervision. These forms of training were taken up by secular nursing organizations, helping to transform nursing into a profession by the end of the nineteenth century, with a distinct body of skills, recognized qualifications, and a hierarchical organization. Nursing orders provided staff for some of the most prestigious hospitals, including King's College and University College Hospitals in London and St. Mary's Hospital (the forerunner of the Mayo Clinic) in Rochester, Minnesota. Catholic and Protestant nursing sisters even served on the battlefield, tending to sick and wounded soldiers during the Crimean and Franco-Prussian wars.

Religious organizations also played an important role in organizing and delivering hospital care. For hundreds of years, churches had encouraged members to offer help to those unable to support themselves—the old, the poor, the sick, and the mentally ill. In the nineteenth century, this duty was increasingly fulfilled by donating money to hospitals and dispensaries. During this period, large numbers of hospitals were founded and run by religious institutions, both Catholic and Protestant, especially in North America. Members of religious orders provided nursing care and were responsible for all aspects of the administration of the institution, from patient admissions, to purchasing supplies, to raising funds. These institutions served the local population or particular social groups. For example, in North America, Lutheran hospitals served German-speaking immigrants from Europe. Religion played an important role in hospital life. In Catholic institutions beds were arranged so that patients could see altars and observe mass. Prayers were said and hymns sung in the wards. Chaplains or priests would talk to patients and give religious instruction; they would also administer the sacraments to the dying and baptize weak infants.

Medical Missionaries

Religion and medicine came together in the work of medical missionaries. The Catholic Church had sent out missionaries to the Americas since the sixteenth century, many of whom undertook some form of medical work. Protestant missionaries with some medical training had occasionally been sent from Europe to convert indigenous people to Christianity in the eighteenth century. In the nineteenth century, however, there was a new emphasis on medicine within mission work. Many more trained missionaries were sent out, especially to Africa and Asia, where they established hospitals and dispensaries.

Peter Parker, the first qualified medical missionary, began work in Canton in 1835. His Ophthalmic Hospital offered minor surgery such as cataract operations and the removal of small tumors, and proved popular, treating almost two thousand patients in its first year. From the 1860s, medical missionaries were sent out by both Protestant and Catholic churches to offer advanced forms of Western medical treatment. Mission hospitals grew from small affairs often staffed by a single doctor, to become large institutions with state-of-the-art equipment such as X-ray machines. Nevertheless, the numbers of medical missionaries were always small. In the 1870s, Protestant churches (who were the largest operators) sent out only 20 qualified missionaries to India and a further 15 to China. Missionaries with little or no medical training also provided free drugs and advice to local people as a means of attracting listeners and as a humanitarian gesture. As one missionary later put it, "every missionary became a quack doctor! He could not help himself. You cannot say 'poor fellow' and pass on, when you know that a dose of salts or a grain or two of quinine a day might bring back health."[3]

Medical missions were seen as a means of spreading the religious message in areas where it had proved difficult to convert local people. Missionaries held short religious services in the waiting area for potential patients and their relatives. During and after treatment, they would also talk and pray with patients. In India, where efforts to convert the male population met with limited success, female medical missionaries were employed to go into the *zenana* (the women's quarters) and treat women and children. By the end of the century, roughly half of all missionary doctors working in India were women.

Western medicine, particularly surgery, was popular among indigenous people, who recognized that it was more effective than their own medicine in dealing with some conditions. However, few abandoned their use of indigenous medicine but chose the type of medicine that was best able to help them. In China, patients went to a mission hospital as a last resort when Chinese medicine had failed, especially in cases requiring surgical treatment or difficult births. Patients were equally reluctant to abandon their religion and convert to Christianity. In 1874, one missionary society reported it had made just 12 converts from over 400,000 patients. Large numbers of converts were not made until the end of the century.

CONFLICTS BETWEEN RELIGION AND MEDICINE

Missionaries were often hostile to indigenous medicine. Those in Africa interpreted indigenous medicine as a form of religion: they called local healers "witchdoctors" and described their rituals as "pagan" or satanic. Equally, native peoples interpreted the actions of missionaries in their own terms. Missionaries in China complained that local people believed that they had magical powers and were able to ward off evil spirits and to deal with cases of "fox possession" in which the body of the patient was invaded by a spirit. The practice of baptizing very sick children led to a belief that the baptism caused their death. In Tianjin, China, in 1870, a group of Catholic nuns who ran an orphanage were massacred, following rumors that they were kidnapping children and using their body parts to make medicines.

There were also conflicts between medicine and religion in the West. In the Catholic Church, elaborate funerals, with the body on display in an open coffin, served to demonstrate piety, and burial inside the church and close to an altar was sought after as a means of helping to release the soul of the deceased from purgatory. By the mid-nineteenth century, medical practitioners condemned both practices as unsanitary and likely to spread disease. They advocated short and simple funeral rites followed by burial in a cemetery well away from populated areas.

There was also conflict over the relationship between intense religious experiences and mental illness. In North America, doctors debated whether religious experiences could be a form of mental illness, or could induce mental disturbance in susceptible individuals. The early nineteenth century saw a wave of evangelical revivals, where preachers called on congregations to confess their sins and dedicate themselves to God in readiness for the Second Coming of Christ. Such events were often highly emotional, with people wailing, singing, and dancing for hours or even days. For a few people, the heightened emotional states at these meetings were followed by bouts of mental illness, and they were confined in asylums suffering from "religious insanity." Doctors attributed their condition to nervous over-stimulation combined with an underlying mental weakness. In hindsight, the prevalence of religious insanity in the 1840s in North America was produced by a combination of the popularity of religious revivals and the building of large asylums where, for the first time, doctors saw much greater numbers of patients suffering from mental illness.

ISLAMIC RELIGIOUS MEDICINE

Religion played a central place in medicine in the Islamic world, particularly in the later nineteenth century. Allah was the supreme healer;

he had created disease, but also placed the means of curing illness in the world and given people understanding so they could seek out cures. Therefore when sick, Muslims sought the help of physicians with specialist knowledge of the body and disease. Illness could also be cured by spiritual means, through prayers and miracles. The Qur'an offered advice on how to stay healthy, especially through observing good hygiene. These parts of the text, and the sayings of the prophet Muhammad, his family, and his followers, were gradually expanded into a body of medical ideas known as prophetic medicine. It recommended simple remedies, such as honey or cumin seeds for treating internal complaints, or the use of scarification—a method of removing small amounts of blood from the body through scratches made on the skin. The Qur'an itself was believed to have healing powers—the sick benefited from hearing, reading, or reciting the text. Religious remedies were used alongside physical therapies: a nineteenth-century text on cholera, for example, contained sections on medicines and on prayers for the prevention and cure of the disease.

As well as illness arising from physical causes, the Qur'an also attributed ill health to the work of evil spirits, or *jinn*. *Jinn* were usually invisible (although they could assume the shape of animals) but bad smells were a sign of their presence. If offended in some way, they took revenge by causing illness, and large numbers of *jinn* could work together to produce epidemics. The actions of *jinn* were prevented by the use of amulets consisting of holy texts written on pieces of paper and attached to clothing. Particular substances including silver, gunpowder, and pungent herbs could also ward off *jinn*.

BUDDHISM AND MEDICINE

In Buddhist thinking, illness and suffering were facts of life. They were caused by physical factors such as diet, lifestyle, and climate, but also by spirits; or they were sent as a form of punishment for bad actions or patterns of thought. Buddhist practices, including meditation, helped to ensure good physical and spiritual health. For illnesses with a physical cause, followers sought medical advice usually from a practitioner of ayurvedic medicine. For diseases linked to the patient's spiritual condition, they had to meditate and pray to deities associated with healing. Maladies associated with evil spirits were prevented by wearing amulets: spells or Buddhist religious texts were written on slips of paper and attached to clothing, or they were burned and the ashes mixed with water and given to the patient to drink. Some Buddhist teachers and monks possessed special healing powers that were a sign of their purity and faith, and they treated illness with a combination of medicines, meditation, and exorcism.

MEDICINE AND TAOISM

Supernatural forces also played an important role in health and medicine in Chinese religions, including Taoism (or Daoism), a religious and philosophical movement popular in the nineteenth century. Illness was caused by physical factors such as poor diet, climate, or an inappropriate lifestyle and treated using medicines. Diseases were also caused by spirits or ghosts, especially the spirits of ancestors who felt neglected when families failed to venerate their memory. They possessed the bodies of the living, resulting in mental or physical illness or even death.

Divination was used to diagnose these diseases and to direct treatment: spirits were persuaded to write on a board covered in sand, or a divining stick was passed over a patient and used to produce a charm or prescription. Charms, often in the form of spells or religious texts written on slips of paper, were used to cure or to ward off supernatural disease. Spirits were also chased away by loud noises, or were persuaded to depart by offerings of food, incense and prayer. One such ceremony was reported by a Westerner in 1847. At his neighbors' house, the family:

> commence[d] beating drums and gongs, and set out a feast, in the superstitious belief that some deceased member of the family is starving in the world below, and that, in revenge of their neglect, his spirit has come to feed on the body of the sick person. Hence they seek, by the bribe of a feast, and the intimidation of sounds, to expel [the spirit].[4]

Particular gods were linked to sickness and healing. For example, *T'ou-Shen Niang-Niang* was a goddess of smallpox in China and was widely worshipped in temples and at home shrines to prevent or cure the disease. (Smallpox was also attributed to supernatural forces in Japan. A demon was believed to cause the disease, and pictures of *Tametomo*, a twelfth-century hero who was believed to have driven away the smallpox demon, were hung in the rooms of victims to help in their recovery.) The sick also prayed to healing gods, such as the Medicine King or the Empress of Heaven, to ask for relief or protection from disease. The Empress of Heaven and her associated deities were believed to be particularly effective in preventing illness among children and women. During epidemics, whole communities joined in seeking divine help. Auspicious days were chosen for prayers to halt the disease, images of gods were carried through the streets, and fireworks were set off to help drive away the illness.

HINDUISM AND MEDICINE

Particular gods were also associated with healing and with particular diseases in the Hindu religion. These included *Jvarāsura*, the fever demon, *Ghentukarna*, the god of skin diseases, and *Sitala*, the goddess of smallpox. *Sitala* was an important goddess, with many temples and shrines dedicated to her. It was believed that smallpox patients were possessed by the fiery goddess, whose presence was associated with high fevers. The disease was treated by rituals and offerings. Ritual and physical treatment overlapped—images of the goddess were washed and fanned while patients also received cooling food and drinks and were bathed in cold water.

Rituals around smallpox had a long history, but when cholera became an important cause of death in India in the early nineteenth century, new deities emerged in response to the threat. The goddess *Ola Candi* or *Ola Bibi* may have been associated with dysentery, but in the nineteenth century, she emerged as the goddess of cholera. In other areas, cholera was associated with new deities known as *kala mari* (black death). Representations of the deity were paraded and sacrifices made to try to please her and thus prevent outbreaks of cholera. During epidemics, objects or animals dedicated to the goddess were driven out of the village in the hope that doing so would also drive away the disease. In a number of areas, young women appeared, claiming to be possessed by a spirit associated with the disease. In 1818, a woman appeared:

> Her whole body and her scanty apparel were daubed and clotted with the dingy red and ochry yellow powders of the Hindoo burial ceremonies ... in one hand she held a drawn sword, in the other an earthen vessel containing fire (the one probably a symbol of destruction, the other of the funeral pyre) ... her phrenzy [*sic*] seemed beyond human control; and as she bounded along, she denounced certain destruction to all those who did not immediately acknowledge her divinity.[5]

The panic caused by cholera prompted inhabitants to reach out to more than one religion in search of some power to control the terrible disease. When cholera struck a village in Konkan, in western India, the people initially asked the Catholic priest for help. When he proved ineffectual, a Hindu ceremony was performed.

SPIRITUAL MEDICINE IN AFRICA, THE AMERICAS, AND THE PACIFIC

In many cultures in Africa, South and Central America, and throughout the Pacific Ocean, the supernatural played an important role everyday life. Gods, spirits, and ghosts were believed to influence many aspects of life—the weather, the success of crops, and the health and well-being of individual people and of groups. Every culture had a different understanding of the identity of spirits involved in health and disease, but there were some broad similarities. Many cultures recognized that disease was sent by gods or by spirits of ancestors and animals, or it was caused by magic. Native American peoples also attributed disease to soul loss and to unfulfilled desires. Certain complaints were associated with supernatural causes. In southern Africa, fevers, coughs, and diarrhea had natural causes, while spirits or ghosts were responsible for causing chronic ailments that failed to respond to herbal medicines, diseases that came on very suddenly, or illnesses that caused unconsciousness.

Different cultures had their own types of spiritual healers. Among many peoples there were diviners, who used spiritual means to diagnose the causes of illness, exorcists and shamans or "witchdoctors," who communicated and negotiated with the spirits that caused disease in order to effect a cure. Among Native American tribes, medicine men both diagnosed the spirit responsible for illness and performed rituals to cure the complaint. In some cultures, natural therapy overlapped with supernatural medicine. In New Zealand, *tohunga* healers used a mix of herbal medicines and rituals, as did the *curanderos* of Latin America. Among some indigenous American peoples, medicine men drove away disease by giving the patient bitter medicines that the spirits found unpleasant.

Healers were powerful people, often set apart in some way from the rest of their community. In some cultures, healers were "chosen" by the gods: the !Kung people of the Kalahari Desert believed that the god *Hishe* bestowed healing powers, and healers were visited by the god in dreams or visions. In *ngoma* medicine, practiced in southern Africa, people were called to become healers by illness sent by ancestral spirits. Being cured of this initial illness was the first step in becoming a healer.

Many types of healers also trained with an established practitioner, who might be a family member. Training could last for several years and involved learning about the preparation and use of drugs, the performance of rituals, and communication with the spirit world. Often training involved a purification process and required the trainee to follow special rules of diet and lifestyle. In Ghana, the first stage of training for Akan healers involved washing with infusions of herbs to strengthen their bodies and increase their spiritual powers; washing the eyes allowed them to "see" the unseen. The training process of *ngoma* healers included ritual song and dance, drumming, making medicines, and sacrifices that established a bond between healer and the ancestral spirits. Finally, the new healer's status was established by an initiation ceremony.

Diviners diagnosed illness by spiritual means. In some cultures, the diviner would enter a trance in which he or she communicated with spirits. American medicine men would contact the spirit world to discover what spirit had caused the illness—each one responded to

Spiritual healers diagnosed and cured disease caused by gods, demons or ghosts. This shaman belonging to the Dakota people of the American plains is shown communicating with the spirit world by chanting and shaking a ceremonial rattle. (National Library of Medicine)

different remedies. In many African cultures, diagnosis was performed through various forms of divination. Among Zulu-speaking people of southern Africa, people seeking help were asked to beat on the ground with sticks and to respond to a series of questions posed by the diviner. The sounds made by the sticks helped the healer to determine the cause of the disease. In other areas, healers gained information from the position of objects thrown onto the ground. The final position of each object was controlled by the gods or spirits. *Ngoma* healers diagnosed using a selection of bones or shells, each of which had a particular significance, indicating something about the cause of illness.

Treatment took many forms, depending on the problem. Rituals were used to contact the spirits and ask for a cure. Drumming, shouting and singing drove out spirits or called back lost souls. Many rituals involved 'casting out' the disease from the patient. While in a trance, a !Kung healer placed his hands on the patient, drawing out the disease and throwing it away. Illness caused by the spirits of deceased relatives or ancestors was cured by the performance of rituals or the sacrifice of animals to appease their anger.

MAGIC AND MEDICINE

Disease could also be caused by humans using supernatural forces. In Hawaii and Polynesia, sorcerers were capable of *pule 'ana'ana* (praying to death) by sending evil spirits into a victim's body. In other cultures, sorcerers would "shoot" arrows or objects into the bodies of victims, causing pain and illness. In southern Africa, witches (*umthakathis*) caused illness and death by spreading "poison" on paths used by the victim, or by using objects belonging to the victim as the base for a spell. Such cases required the intervention of a healer able to discover the source of the problem and undo the magic by rituals or counter-magic. For example, foreign objects magically implanted into a person were removed through incisions or sucking.

Slaves transported from Africa to North America and the Caribbean took with them their beliefs in supernatural disease causation and traditional forms of healing. In Haiti, "conjure" or hoodoo was used by sorcerers to cause illness. Wasting diseases such as chronic exhaustion or loss of weight were thought to come from witches eating the soul or inhabiting the body. Disease-causing charms were made from substances with special powers such as earth from graveyards, or the hair or nail clippings from the intended victim. When buried or hidden close to the target's home and activated by the spirits, they caused illness or even death. Conjurers diagnosed spirit illness by divination.

They might ask the victim to hold a silver coin: if it turned black, then this was a sign that the problem had been caused through magic. They would then hunt for the charm that had caused the illness, analyze it, and compose a counter-charm.

WESTERN VIEWS OF SPIRITUAL MEDICINE

In nineteenth-century Barbados, slaves and the descendants of slaves used "obeah" medicine, based on African traditions. Obeah healers prepared herbal remedies using local plants and provided supernatural cures. In the early nineteenth century, the plantation owners saw obeah as a threat to the health of slaves, and practitioners were punished. By the end of the century, it was dismissed as a form of quackery, practiced on gullible patients. One Western observer mockingly described:

> He [the obeah practitioner] charges a large sum, administers a large dose of powerful medicine extracted from the medicinal plants so numerous in the interior of this colony; throws the patient into a deep sleep, and then by an act of jugglery produces to the astonished and frightened relatives, a quantity of old rusty nails, glass, splinters, a dead frog or snake, and tells them that that has been the cause of the illness.[6]

As with other medical theories, ideas about supernatural or spiritual healing were not fixed; they changed in response to new circumstances. For example, in the Caribbean, conjure became mixed with evangelical Christianity. The ability to conjure was reinterpreted as a gift from God, and prayer was believed to cure illness. The similarities between evangelical religion and African rituals—the physical expression of belief through dancing and singing, and a sense of being possessed by the Christian Holy Spirit or ancestral spirits—helped in this process.

In Africa, colonial rulers attempted to control the work of spiritual healers, who presented a political problem. Healers were powerful people who had a strong influence over their communities, and they led uprisings in the Cape Colony in South Africa. But administrators faced a difficult situation. They could not acknowledge that witches caused harm by supernatural means, but they intervened when witches were condemned to death by local chiefs. They also sought to punish individuals who had murdered others by poison. In a number of colonies, colonial governments tried to ban all native healing by prosecuting and punishing healers. This simply drove the practices underground, and the rules were later relaxed.

NOTES

1. C. H. Spurgeon, *Autobiography*, vol. 2 (Edinburgh, 1973), p. 414, quoted in Timothy P. Weber, "The Baptist Tradition," in *Caring and Curing Health and Medicine in the Western Religious Traditions*, ed. Ronald L. Numbers and Darrel W. Amundsen (New York: Macmillan Publishing Company, 1986), p. 291.

2. H. W. Acland, *Memoir on the Cholera at Oxford in the Year 1854, with Considerations Suggested by the Epidemic* (London, 1856), quoted in R. J. Morris, "Religion and Medicine: The Cholera Pamphlets of Oxford, 1832, 1849 and 1854," *Medical History* 19 (1975), p. 265.

3. F. Colyer Sackett, *Vision and Venture: A Record of Fifty Years in Hyderabad 1879–1929* (London, n.d.), p. 106, quoted in Rosemary Fitzgerald, " 'Clinical Christianity': The Emergence of Missionary Work as a Missionary Strategy in Colonial India, 1800–1914," in *Health, Medicine and Empire. Perspectives on Colonial India*, ed. Biswamoy Pati and Mark Harrison (London: Sangam Books, 2001), p. 108.

4. George H. Smith, *A Narrative of an Exploratory Visit to . . . the Consular Cities of China* (London, 1847), p. 183, quoted in Linda L. Barnes, *Needles, Herbs, Gods and Ghosts. China, Healing and the West to 1848* (Cambridge, MA: Harvard University Press, 2005), p. 341.

5. R. H. Kennedy, *Notes on the Epidemic Cholera* (London, 1846), pp. ix–x, quoted in David Arnold, *Colonizing the Body: State Medicine and Epidemic Disease in Nineteenth-Century India* (Berkeley: University of California Press, 1993), p. 173.

6. Anon., *The Overseers Manual* (Demerara, 1896), p. 73, quoted in Juanita De Barros, "Dispensers, *Obeah* and Quackery: Medical Rivalries in Post-Slavery British Guiana," *Social History of Medicine* 20 (2007), p. 255.

CHAPTER 4

Women's Health and Medicine

In the nineteenth century, women's health was dominated by reproduction. Most women gave birth at some time in their lives, and many had numerous pregnancies. This was probably the most dangerous event in women's lives; they ran the risk of becoming ill or even dying from complications during pregnancy. Labor was even more dangerous, and a proportion of women died during or shortly after delivery. It was not surprising, then, that the discussion of women's health in medical texts around the world was dominated by issues surrounding reproduction—the menstrual cycle, pregnancy, and childbirth.

But women were not only patients; they were the most numerous providers of medical care. Women in every culture cared for sick family members; large numbers worked as healers and midwives, and during the nineteenth century, growing numbers entered the medical profession as nurses and doctors, which sometimes brought them into conflict with male practitioners.

WOMEN'S BODIES

In Western medicine, male and female bodies were seen to be fundamentally the same. With the exception of the reproductive system, all the organs of the body functioned in same way. In some non-Western medical systems, the sexes were understood to be slightly different. In unani medicine, all women were believed to have a natural imbalance in their humors that made their constitution colder and wetter than men. As a result they were weaker, prone to cold diseases, became ill more quickly, and could not tolerate strong medicines. In Chinese medicine, women were dominated by *yin*—the quality associated with growth—while men had *yang* constitutions. Some Chinese doctors saw women as naturally sickly and prone to poor health.

Social or cultural expectations influenced women's health in many ways. Many cultures had an ideal female form that was attractive to men. Conforming to this ideal helped to ensure that girls made good marriages. In North Africa, for example, a thin figure was not seen as desirable. Slim women sought help from healers who prescribed medicines to increase their weight. Achieving that perfect form, however, could damage the body. In some cultures in Africa and Asia, girls and women wore columns of metal neck rings to produce the appearance of a long and slender neck. The heavy rings deformed the collarbones and shoulders. In China, upper-class girls had their feet tightly bound from an early age to produce the appearance of tiny feet and a delicate, mincing walk. This very painful process displaced the bones of the feet from their normal positions and often caused ulcers and even gangrene. Opposition to the practice, led by Western missionaries and Chinese officials, led to an edict against foot-binding in 1902.

In Europe and America, women wore corsets—heavy undergarments reinforced with strips of bone or metal to compress their torsos into an attractive shape, with a small waist and a large bust and hips. At their most extreme, corsets could be used to achieve a waist measurement of just 18 inches. Most women saw nothing wrong with wearing corsets: they chose to wear them to follow prevailing fashions or to provide support to the back and waist during exercise. Corsets also had a moral meaning: uncorseted women were associated with "loose" morals and prostitution. Doctors warned that overly tight corsets were dangerous, resulting in deformed or broken ribs and causing fainting, liver damage, and even death.

Apart from complaints arising from these issues, women suffered from much the same diseases and injuries as men. Their domestic role exposed them to a higher risk of burns as they were usually responsible for cooking over open fires or on stoves. In European cities, women suffered from higher rates of tuberculosis infection, probably a consequence of poor diet and their indoor lifestyle. Women working in factories faced a particularly high risk of injury as long hair or skirts easily became caught up in the moving parts of exposed machinery,

Footbinding was widely practiced in China, although the practice was extremely painful and often resulted in infections and even death. Tiny feet and a swaying walk were thought highly erotic, and helped to ensure that girls married wealthy men. (Library of Congress)

dragging them into the mechanisms with sometimes fatal consequences.

In some cultures in Asia and Africa, elite women had limited access to medical care. They lived segregated lives, with no contact with men outside their families. If ill or injured, such women could not have a face-to-face consultation with a male doctor. Elaborate arrangements were put in place to get around the problem. Wealthy Chinese women sent a servant to describe their symptoms and consult with a doctor on their behalf. Or they sat behind a curtain and extended their arm through the material to allow the practitioner to feel their pulse but not see their face or body. If women patients were too embarrassed to describe their symptoms, practitioners gave them a small figure of a naked woman so they could mark the place where they felt pain.

WOMEN AND REPRODUCTION

When medical texts discussed women, they focused on reproduction. The lifecycle was divided into separate phases of puberty, childbearing, and menopause; and during adulthood, women's lives were punctuated by cycles of menstruation, pregnancy, and childbirth. All had the potential to undermine women's health.

Reproduction in Chinese Medicine

In Chinese medicine, the constant changes produced by women's reproductive systems posed a constant risk to their health. Blood (a term that covered all body fluids, not just the blood known to Western medicine) was the *yin* aspect of *qi*. It nourished the body and the fetus in pregnant women, formed breast milk, and was lost during menstruation. The loss of blood during the menses meant that women were at risk of a serious imbalance of *qi* and of blockages in the flow of blood, leading to a range of illnesses.

> Their monthly courses stop and go, now early, now late, [leading to] congestion and coagulation of blood, and blocking central pathways of circulation. The injuries that arise from this can't be fully enumerated. Cold and heat affect the organ systems, depletion (*hsu*) and repletion (*shih*) conditions interact, noxious blood leaks within, and the circulation vessels become worn out.[1]

Maintaining a regular menstrual cycle was crucial to both general health and fertility. Any increase or decrease in the normal flow, irregular bleeding, or pain were signs that something was wrong. Eating too much hot or cold food or exposure to cold could upset the menstrual cycle. Strong emotions were also dangerous. Anger caused barrenness, miscarriage, and blood disorders; resentment made the blood congeal, producing feelings of oppression, tightness in the chest, and loss of appetite. If blood was blocked, then it could produce a deformed fetus. "Ghost fetuses" were the result of dreams of having sex with ghosts or demons.

Books provided advice on how to deal with problems associated with menstruation. Written for a nonmedical audience and published by public-spirited laymen, they gave simple descriptions of common symptoms and explained their underlying causes. "Rushed and early menses indicate Heat. Receding and late menses indicate depletion. If Blood is stagnated, then it is proper to break it up. If Blood has dried up, then it is proper to replenish it."[2] The texts recommended medicines to treat each condition. Betel nut was recommended for late menses, and green tangerine peel for pain. The books also recommended standard remedies, such as "At ease powder" or "Menses' regulating pills."

In China, the key to a safe birth was to avoid any stagnation or blockages to the flow of the blood within the body during pregnancy. Elite doctors monitored pregnant women, giving advice and prescribing medicines to maintain a balance of *qi* and blood. They recommended that pregnant women take gentle exercise, eat moderately, avoid anxiety, and repress sexual desire. "Hot" foods such as meat and oil, and "cold" foods such as raw vegetables, were considered dangerous.

As well as using medicines, diet, and lifestyle to ensure a healthy pregnancy and safe birth, women prayed to Chinese deities. Women who wanted to conceive prayed to *Bixia Yuanjun*, the goddess of Mount Tai, and made pilgrimages to the mountain to pray for children. Or they appealed to a Buddhist deity *Guanyin*, who was also associated with fertility. During labor, women prayed to Aunty Ge, the Divine Midwife.

Childbirth left women dangerously exhausted, depleted of blood, and vulnerable to ill health. Practitioners and popular texts recommended giving medicines to replenish *qi* and blood immediately after the birth. "Producing and Transforming Decoction," containing angelica, ligusticum root and peach pit, was given to break up the old blood and prevent "noxious dew"—blood left in the body after the birth. New mothers were told to stay indoors, keep warm, and eat strengthening foods.

Reproduction in Ayurvedic and Unani Medicine

Practitioners of ayurvedic and unani medicine shared the concerns of their Chinese counterparts that reproduction was potentially dangerous to health, as well as the need for an appropriate diet and lifestyle to ensure fertility and safe childbirth. In unani medicine, regular menstruation was believed to be important for maintaining health. Irregular periods or the lack of menstruation were believed to cause the retention of menstrual blood within the uterus. This blood putrefied and moved to the heart and brain, causing hysteria. Patients fainted and experienced palpitations, and treatment included sweet smelling oils and sprinkling the patient with cold water. During pregnancy, women should follow a quiet life, pray regularly, and eat a good diet. Women who failed to conceive made pilgrimages to special springs or shrines, or sought blessings from holy men. Unani medicine recognized that men could be responsible for women's failure to become pregnant, and medicines were prescribed to increase the chances of conception.

Ayurvedic medical texts advised pregnant women to avoid heavy work and any strenuous exercise. They should eat a diet appropriate to each stage of pregnancy, with milk during the early months and later a diet rich in ghee (clarified butter). They should avoid wine, large amounts of meat, and spicy foods. Women should abstain from sex in the later stages of pregnancy. Women had to take great care as their behavior affected the unborn child. They who ate too many sweets gave birth to delicate children; those who were angry and quarreled might have an epileptic infant. After the birth, new mothers were fed nourishing foods to help recover their strength and clean out the uterus, and medicines were given to purify the blood.

Reproduction in Western Medicine

In Western medicine, although the functions of the ovaries and uterus were poorly understood, doctors believed that the reproductive organs created the feminine character. In 1848, the distinguished German medical researcher Rudolf Virchow concluded:

> The female is female because of her reproductive glands. All her characteristics of body and mind ... the development of her breasts ... the beauties of her hair ... those depths of feeling, that unerring intuition, that gentleness, devotion and loyalty—in short, all that we respect and admire as truly feminine, are dependent on the ovaries. Take the ovaries away and we get the repulsive, coarsely formed, large-boned, moustached, deep-voiced, flat-breasted, resentful and egotistic virago.[3]

Their reproductive biology determined that women were physically weak, irrational, and emotional, but with a strong moral sense and a natural instinct to care and nurture. Men's biology dictated that they were strong, rational, level-headed, and courageous, although prone to moral lapses.

Women's reproductive functions were understood to make their bodies inherently unstable and susceptible to a wide variety of illnesses. Although nineteenth-century medicine was increasingly concerned with the solid structures of the body, it retained older ideas about balance. The body was understood to contain a fixed amount of nervous energy; in women much of this energy was required to maintain the normal menstrual cycle. Any excessive demands on the supply of nervous energy produced irritation in the uterus and ovaries that spread via the spine and nerves throughout the body, and caused illnesses from hysteria, headaches, and coughs to cancer and epilepsy.

Women were particularly susceptible to poor health during periods of transition such as puberty and menopause, or immediately after giving birth. Girls at the onset of puberty fell ill with chlorosis or "green sickness." Sufferers were depressed, listless, and thin, they often refused food, and their skin was pale with a greenish tint (hence the name). Because the ovaries had a close connection to the nervous system, women were susceptible to mental as well as physical illness. One leading authority on insanity wrote that during menopause, "every care or anxiety produce a more depressing and permanent impression on the mind. There is neither so much vital nor mental energy to resist the effects of the various adverse circumstances which it is the lot of most to meet."[4] From the 1870s, as a last resort, surgeons treated some mental conditions, such as convulsions, by removing the ovaries.

The large amounts of nervous energy required for reproductive functions dictated the type of lifestyle suitable for women. According to medical authorities, women's minds and bodies were fitted for a domestic role as a wife and mother. Going out into the world of work and engaging in hard physical labor or in jobs requiring intellectual skills went beyond women's natural capacities, and threatened their physical and mental health.

> Miss C—— was a bookkeeper in a mercantile house. Like the other clerks, she was at her post, *standing*, during business hours, from Monday morning till Saturday night. Miss C—— ... believed in doing her work in a man's way, infected by the not uncommon notion that womanliness means manliness. ... When about twenty years of age, perhaps a year or so older, she applied to me for advice in consequence of neuralgia, back-ache, menorrhagia, leucorrhœa [menstrual disorders] and general debility. She was anemic, and looked pale, care-worn, and anxious.[5]

Education also posed dangers. Around the time of puberty, any mental strain drained the reserves of nervous energy, preventing the development of a healthy reproductive system and leading to menstrual disorders, depression, nervous breakdowns, madness, and infertility. Women eager to go to university argued that girls could study safely, so long as time spent with their books was balanced by rest and exercise. This image of women as delicate creatures, compelled to limit their activities in order to maintain their reproductive health, was an idealized, middle-class image of womanhood; working-class women in homes, on farms, and in factories worked long hours at tasks that required a good deal of strength without damaging their ability to have children.

Despite these perceived threats to women's fertility in Europe and North America for much of the nineteenth century, large families were the norm, with 8 or 10 children not uncommon. Many women spent a large part of their life between the ages of 20 and 40 pregnant or with a small infant. Many women did limit their family size in some way by avoiding sex for a period after giving birth or breastfeeding for long periods. Rubber condoms were available after 1850. Many women wittingly or unwittingly used drugs to induce an early abortion when their periods stopped; newspapers and magazines regularly carried advertisements for medicines to ensure regular periods or remove "stoppages." Doctors played only a minor role in looking after women during pregnancy or after birth. They simply advised them to eat a good diet of simple foods, to exercise (walking was often suggested as a suitably gentle activity), and to rest during pregnancy and for at least a month after the birth.

WOMEN AS CAREGIVERS

Throughout the world, in all cultures, women played a central role in protecting the health of their families. In most societies, they ran the household, growing and gathering fruits and vegetables, helping to raise the livestock to supply eggs, milk, and meat, and buying food. Women's ability to produce and cook food and to budget determined how well-nourished their families were. They also took primary responsibility for hygiene by sweeping out the home, collecting and disposing of refuse, and washing clothing.

Women were the primary caregivers of the sick. When family members fell ill, women nursed their children, husbands, siblings, or parents, making them comfortable by keeping their bedding clean and preparing suitable foods. Women also made simple medicines: a warm drink, a cool bath for fever sufferers, or a poultice to treat a swelling. This role in caring for family members meant that women were important consumers of medical services. All around the world, women bought remedies to treat minor ailments from a local herbalist or shop or by mail order. Buying medicines through the post was not confined to the West; by the end of the century, Western and traditional medicines were sold in this way across Africa and Asia. If these measures failed, or the case was thought sufficiently serious, it was often women who decided to seek the help of a doctor or healer.

Women were guided in this role by advice books. A reduction in the costs of paper and printing brought books and pamphlets offering advice on diet, nursing, and child care within the reach of many families around the world. In India, books of unani medicine encouraged women to take responsibility for their own health and that of their families, and advised them how to buy medicines and when to consult doctors. Books and magazine articles written by Western-trained doctors gave a new scientific gloss to the traditional role of mothers to identify, treat, and prevent illness within the family. In Europe, the United States, and many other countries where Western medicine was practiced, doctors gave out expert advice to mothers. In Egypt, for example, doctors advised women on how best to clean their houses and to prepare foods. Many manuals included advice on childrearing, encouraging women to breastfeed and to allow their children to play and exercise in the open air.

WOMEN AS HEALERS

While almost every woman cared for sick family members, a smaller but still significant number worked as healers, providing skilled services in return for money or goods. In many cultures, both men and women worked as healers using various forms of folk medicine. In American and African societies, women herbalists treated illnesses using plant-based remedies, performed bloodletting and scarification to remove blood from the body, treated wounds, and set broken limbs. In some cultures, women combined the treatment of physical ailments with work as spiritual healers. In Mexico, for example, female *curanderos* practiced among the indigenous population, curing physical ailments and illness caused by witchcraft. Sorcerers caused illness by implanting foreign objects such as beetles, feathers, and other small objects in the body. These were drawn out by massage or sucking. For physical illnesses, *curanderos* used herbal remedies and rituals that combined Christian prayers and symbols with much older practices from Aztec medicine. One *curandera* was reported to make the sign of the cross over the liver, stomach, and heart, the three important organs in ancient Aztec medicine, as part of her healing rituals.

MIDWIVES

In very few cultures, women were expected to deliver their own babies without help; but in most societies around the globe, women helped each other during labor. Female friends and family members provided physical and emotional support while midwives—women with special knowledge and experience of childbirth—supervised the birthing process. Most midwives learned through experience, by giving birth themselves, through training with an experienced midwife, and by observing births. In some parts of the world, such as Persia, midwifery was a hereditary occupation, passed down from mother to daughter. Although midwifery was a recognized specialist role, it was a part-time job for most women. In rural areas with a small population, the local midwife might deliver a few babies a year. Midwives in towns attended more births, but still combined this role with other work. In some cultures, midwives also worked as healers. In North Africa, midwives treated wounds and illnesses among women and children.

Midwives supported the mother-to-be through the labor, helped to deliver the baby, cut the umbilical cord, and often stayed to help look after mother and infant for a few days. In China, for example, midwives gave drugs to stimulate contractions, offered food and drink, and massaged the mother-to-be to help the labor progress. Once the birth was imminent, they would support the mother in a standing position and catch the infant. Native American midwives massaged the mother to help deliver the baby, to move the infant into a safe presentation, and to expel the placenta. Various plant medicines were used to increase contractions, to ease pain, and to control bleeding. After the birth, a bandage or belt was tied around the mother's abdomen to promote recovery. In the Congo, midwives tapped women on the head with a broom if their labor was prolonged: a symbolic action to sweep the child out of the womb. Iranian midwives encouraged labor by giving the mother-to-be tea made with carrot seeds and sage. Ayurvedic midwives speeded up labor by massaging the abdomen, giving drugs to induce vomiting or getting the mother to pound grain in mortar and pestle in the hope that the exertion would encourage the contractions.

Rituals were a very important means of ensuring the safety of mothers and infants at a very dangerous time. In every society, large numbers of women died when they were unable to deliver because of the size or position of the baby, or from blood loss. In the days following birth, many more succumbed to fever caused by infections usually

In many cultures, midwives encouraged delivery by getting the mother-to-be to pull downwards or by pressing on the abdomen. This illustration shows techniques used in America in the mid-nineteenth century. (Hulton Archive/Getty Images)

unwittingly transmitted by the birth attendant. Many more suffered injuries such as tears or a prolapsed uterus. Even in Europe in the late nineteenth century, where birth was relatively safe, around four in every 1,000 women died as a result of childbirth.

In many cultures, women gave birth in a special space from which men were excluded. Among the Blackfoot people of North America, birth took place in an isolated *tipi*. In India, among Hindus, birth took place in a small, warm, dark room (*āturghar*). Performing rituals was an important part of the midwives' role. In many cultures, midwives said prayers for a safe delivery. Among Australian aboriginal people, women attendants performed ritual songs to ensure a safe birth. In Persia, metal objects were attached to the bed to avert the evil eye. In Jewish homes, the key of the synagogue might be placed under the pillow to promote a safe labor. In India, Hindu midwives (*dais*) cut the umbilical cord with a knife smeared with cow dung. In Iran, the demon *Al* was kept away from women in childbirth by metal objects. Iron was thrown into the water used to wash the newly delivered infant as a means of keeping away the evil eye.

Midwives and Western Doctors

In the West, midwives had traditionally delivered babies, and they remained the main source of help for women in rural areas and for the poorer classes throughout the nineteenth century. Middle- and upper-class women increasingly chose to have a doctor present at the birth. In the case of a difficult labor, doctors could deliver the child using forceps (midwives did not, as a general rule, use instruments to help delivery) and they gave anesthetics, such as chloroform, to ease the pain. From the 1840s, surgeons could repair tears and other injuries caused by the birth, and by the end of the century, they successfully performed cesarean sections to save the lives of the mother and child.

Although doctors took an increasing role in childbirth, most women continued to give birth at home, and only the very poorest women had their babies in maternity or "lying-in" hospitals. In return for their care, medical students were allowed to observe the birth and deliver the baby under supervision. Lying-in hospitals had a dreadful reputation for high mortality, largely due to epidemics of puerperal fever after delivery. The disease killed around one in 20 patients at *La Maternité*, the largest lying-in hospital in Paris, roughly seven times the mortality rate for women giving birth at home. This institution had an exceptionally bad record: in other European hospitals, outbreaks of the disease were controlled by thorough cleansing.

Western doctors were increasingly critical of the skills of midwives all around the world. They portrayed traditional midwives as superstitious, ignorant, and a danger to both mother and infant. Indian *dais* came in for particular condemnation. Colonial doctors complained that they were dirty, clumsy, and ignorant, endangering the lives of infants and mothers by their traditional practices, such as pressing on the stomach to hasten delivery and pulling on the head or limbs to extract the baby. Such criticism was not confined to Western doctors. In China, elite practitioners complained that midwives created problems when they tried to rush the birth.

The solution was better education. By 1900, midwives working in European towns and cities were trained by attending lectures and courses at a local hospital or college. Midwives in rural areas might have had some training from a local doctor. Efforts to introduce midwives trained in Western medicine were made around the world. The National Association for Supplying Female Aid to the Women of

India, a charity set up under the patronage of Lady Dufferin, the wife of the viceroy, established programs to educate new midwives in local hospitals. In Egypt, under the Ottoman viceroy Muhammad Ali, a school of midwifery was founded in 1831. Similar initiatives were established in the Caribbean, Cuba, South America, Latin America, and Malaya. The new training strongly discouraged midwives from following traditional practices, such as delivering women in dark, over-heated rooms, or from performing rituals around cutting the umbilical cord or burying the placenta. Instead, teachers emphasized the need for fresh air and cleanliness, and for midwives to monitor but not intervene in labor. It instilled the need to follow Western practice by calling in a doctor if there were any complications.

In some parts of the world, the training brought immediate results. A program to teach midwives in Iceland to use sterile implements to cut the umbilical cord drastically reduced cases of infection. Elsewhere, women were reluctant to employ Western-trained midwives who did not follow traditional rituals or use local remedies. In Java, for example, local women disliked the way that Western-trained midwives ignored the local beliefs that an infant and his or her placenta were siblings, and that they should not cut the umbilical cord until the placenta had been delivered.

WOMEN AS NURSES

While most female healers combined caring with other work, women in the West were able to make careers in medicine as doctors or as nurses. This was part of a wider movement of women into higher education and the workplace, where they took up many of the new "white-collar" jobs, working in shops and as typists, clerks, and teachers. At the beginning of the nineteenth century, hospital nursing was provided by members of religious orders, convalescent patients or poorly paid nurses, who were really domestic servants responsible for cleaning, cooking, and laundry work, rather than providing medical care. Nursing emerged as a profession toward the end of the century as the high standards of care and training of the religious orders were transferred to a new body of career nurses.

The development of trained nurses reflected the need for more medically trained staff in hospitals to care for acutely ill patients and those recovering from surgery. In the early part of the century, training was based around the development of character and self-discipline, rather than medical knowledge. Trainee nurses absorbed a culture of order and method, keeping wards scrupulously clean, feeding and washing patients, and administering medicines. In the later nineteenth century, the nurses' role expanded to include more medical tasks. They began monitoring the patient's condition, dressing wounds, and assisting surgeons in the operating theater. Their training was expanded to include formal teaching in medicine; new recruits attended lectures on anatomy, physiology, and pharmacy. This shift was controversial; there were concerns that nurses might encroach on the work of doctors, gaining an ability to cure but losing their capacity to care.

WOMEN AS DOCTORS

Although women were free to become healers, midwives, and nurses, very few were able to access formal training in medical theory and work as learned practitioners. In China, a handful of women who belonged to medical families received an education from their male relatives. They wrote books and practiced medicine, mostly among female patients. In India, too, a very small number of women were educated in unani medicine and attended women in their segregated quarters. In Egypt, women briefly had the opportunity to enter medicine through an initiative to train midwives. Graduates from the School of Midwifery were trained not only to attend births, but as doctresses (*hakima*) providing basic medical care to communities. They treated injuries, dispensed medicines, vaccinated against smallpox, and tackled public health problems.

In Europe and North America, medicine was a male monopoly as women were excluded from medical schools and universities. In the second half of the century, women attempted to enter the medical profession, but they faced a hard battle. Although nursing fitted with the ideal of women's natural capacity for caring, the intensive study required to graduate as a doctor and the capacity to make quick, calm decisions when faced with seriously ill or injured patients was thought by many (both men and women) to be beyond the ability of women.

> Women are neither physically nor morally qualified for many of the onerous, important and confidential duties of the general practitioner, nor capable of the prolonged exertions or severe exposures to all kinds of weather which a professional life entails; nor capable of keeping the social secrets of patients, which are often dearer than life.[6]

A concerted push by women to obtain medical training began with an American, Elizabeth Blackwell, who was awarded a medical degree in 1849 from Geneva College in New York State. She inspired and encouraged women in mainland Europe to emulate her. Although elite universities in Switzerland and France began to grant degrees to women in the 1860s, in other countries, women struggled to gain qualifications. In Britain, a small group of women, headed by Sophia Jex-Blake, managed to study at the prestigious Edinburgh Medical School despite violent opposition from some staff and students. Jex-Blake and her colleagues were jeered at and jostled, and on one occasion, the male students pushed a live sheep into their classroom. At the end of their studies, although the women passed their exams, the university refused to grant them their degrees. Women did not graduate from Edinburgh until the 1890s.

Even when they had overcome the hurdles of medical training, women doctors faced further difficulties in pursuing their careers. Prestigious posts in hospitals were closed to them and few male patients were willing to go to a female doctor. Many women doctors were forced to take poorly paid posts or to work among poor women and children in small dispensaries or hospitals. Other graduates went abroad to work in the colonies where there were greater opportunities to practice.

WOMEN AND WELFARE

Middle- and upper-class women in Europe and North America played an important role in setting up charitable schemes to care for the health of the poor at home and abroad. Women had a limited role in political life in the nineteenth century—very few could vote in elections or sit on the governing bodies of institutions—and they justified these activities as an extension of their traditional caring role within the home. Women founded and helped to run charities to provide medical care to women and children, and to give advice and free or cheap baby milk and food to infants and mothers, and they organized holidays for slum children to improve their health. The Dufferin Fund in India not only trained midwives, it also provided free Western medical care to large numbers of Indian women. By the beginning of the twentieth century, Dufferin-funded institutions were treating around two million women a year.

Charities set up by women played an important role in shaping government welfare policies. In Britain, Ladies Sanitary Societies supported the public health work of local and national governments by education campaigns among the poor. They distributed pamphlets, organized lectures and employed home visitors to spread the gospel of fresh air and cleanliness among the working classes. (The word "gospel" is appropriate: their strategies were copied from religious groups.) In Argentina, elite women founded the Beneficent Society (*Sociadad de Beneficencia*) in 1823 to provide a hospital for women, care for orphans, and educate girls. The society helped to set a new agenda for social welfare and participated in running government institutions.

Women were also active in reining in governments if they felt that health policies had gone too far. In the 1870s, the Contagious Diseases Acts, designed to control venereal disease through the compulsory treatment of prostitutes provoked strong opposition among middle-class women in Britain. The Ladies National Association for the Repeal of the Contagious Diseases Acts, led by Josephine Butler, argued that the legislation unjustly targeted women, who were the victims of disease, while their male clients went free. The society played a major role in securing the repeal of contagious diseases legislation in Britain and in its colonies.

NOTES

1. *Pei chi ch'ien chin yao fang* (1849), quoted in Charlotte Furth, "Blood, Body and Gender: Medical Images of the Female Condition in China," *Chinese Science* 7 (1986), p. 50.

2. Yi-Li Wu, "Transmitted Secrets: The Doctors of the Lower Yangzi Region and Popular Gynecology in Late Imperial China" (PhD thesis, Yale University, 1998), p. 150.

3. Rudolf Virchow, *Gesammelte Abhandlunger zur wissenshaftlichen Medizin* (*Collected Essays on Medical Science*) (Frankfurt, 1856), p. 747, quoted in Chandak Sengoopta, "The Modern Ovary: Constructions, Meanings, Uses," *History of Science* 38 (2000), p. 428.

4. George Man Burrows, *Commentaries on Insanity* (1828), quoted in Joan Busfield, *Men, Women and Madness: Understanding Gender and Mental Disorder* (London: Macmillan Press Ltd., 1996), pp. 149–150.

5. Edward H. Clarke, *Sex in Education; or A Fair Chance for Girls* (Boston, 1875), pp. 76–77.

6. Editorial, *The Lancet*, August 2, 1873, p. 159.

CHAPTER 5

Infants and Children's Health

Attitudes to children in the early nineteenth century were very different from the present day. In some ways, children were treated as if they were small adults. Around the world, children worked from a very early age. Within the family, children as young as five or six looked after even younger siblings or helped to look after animals and tended crops. When a little older, they might go out to work for an employer. In Europe and North America, children were treated as adults by the legal system. The youngest convict transported from Britain to a penal colony in Australia was just 10 years old: she had stolen clothing. By 1900, attitudes had changed radically. It was widely accepted that childhood was a special period of life, when children should be allowed time to play, to be educated, and to grow and develop physically and mentally.

These two contradictory attitudes—that children were just the same as adults, and were very different—was reflected in the understanding of children's health in all cultures around the world. Babies and infants were thought to be much more delicate than adults and needed constant care to keep them in good health. Children suffered from a range of "childhood diseases" and were very susceptible to illness caused by supernatural forces. At the same time, medical systems understood children's bodies to work in the same way as those of adults. Children were therefore given the same therapies and medicines (albeit in smaller doses). Only in Western medicine, practiced by European and American physicians, did children's health emerge as a specialty by the end of the nineteenth century.

PROTECTING BABIES' HEALTH

Throughout the world, newborn babies were seen as delicate creatures, going through a massive and potentially dangerous transformation between life in the womb and life outside as an independent individual. In many cultures, infants were purified immediately after birth. Among indigenous North American peoples, babies were washed in water in which herbs had been boiled. In Europe, newborn infants were given castor oil or butter to clean any fetal material from the digestive tract. Ayurvedic texts recommended that babies should be washed then given salt and butter to cause vomiting, in order to clear out any substances in the gut left from life in the womb. In China, babies were believed to be at risk from illness caused by "fetal poison" produced by material from the womb left clinging to the infant at the time of birth. If infants inhaled any fetal matter, they suffered from conditions such as "goose mouth" or "wood tongue." Fetal poison also caused a range of illness in infants, including jaundice. If the baby was exposed to cold and dampness, the poison produced "navel wind" that caused convulsions and could kill. To help reduce the effects of fetal poison, midwives cleaned babies' mouths immediately after birth and gave them purifying tonics.

In the days and weeks after birth, infants remained at risk of illnesses caused by spiritual and physical influences. In many cultures, mothers and infants were kept isolated for a set period. In Asia, mothers and their babies remained in the birthing room for several weeks. In Persia (now modern Iran), baby girls were kept indoors for 40 days, baby boys for 90 days, to protect them from the evil eye. In the Caribbean, infants were kept indoors to protect them from witches. In China, mothers and babies were isolated for a month after the birth. Even then, infants were seen as not completely developed; over the next 18 months, Chinese children were open to all sorts of malign influences that could enter through the pores of the skin or the navel. To keep these out, babies were kept wrapped up and the navel covered.

FEEDING AND HEALTH

In most cultures, breast milk was seen as the best, most nourishing food for infants. Ayurvedic practitioners, however, recommended that the breast milk produced in the first few days after birth should not be fed to infants. Mothers should delay breastfeeding but instead feed their babies a mixture of honey and water. Mothers who breastfed their babies had to take care to ensure that their milk was plentiful and nourishing. In different medical cultures, from Europe to China, women were advised to eat simple foods and avoid rich or spicy dishes. In Asia, mothers were warned that if they ate inappropriate foods, causing an imbalance of *doṣas* within their bodies, then their milk would reflect this imbalance and cause their babies to become ill.

Emotions and behaviors were also thought to affect the quality of milk. New mothers should avoid stress and agitation as these had a bad effect on the quantity and quality of their milk. Moral qualities could be transmitted through breast milk, so mothers should not drink alcohol or have frequent sex, for fear that their children would become drunkards or prostitutes. Chinese practitioners warned against the bad effects of "ghost milk" produced by nursing mothers who became pregnant. In ayurvedic medicine, milk produced by pregnant women was believed to cause coughs and indigestion. Infant feeding was strongly influenced by culture. In most societies, mothers tried to ensure that they produced plenty of milk, but in Burma, it was traditional for pregnant women to restrict their diet to rice and dried meats and to avoid eating fresh vegetables. As a result, their babies were very small at birth, and mothers produced very little breast milk.

For women who were unable to breastfeed their infants, or chose not to because they needed to go back to work after the birth, there was the option of employing a wet nurse to feed their children. Wet nurses were usually either poor women whose infants had died or unmarried mothers, willing to place their own infants in a foundling hospital in order to earn some money by nursing another women's child—in effect, selling their milk. Women registered as wet nurses through agencies, advertised their services in newspapers, or were recommended by medical practitioners. In the Americas, slave women were often used as wet nurses. Mothers who employed a wet nurse had to be extremely careful that the women were healthy and of good character, to ensure they had a plentiful supply of good milk and would not pass on harmful influences to their infants. Wealthy women preferred to have their wet nurses live in their homes with the other servants so that they could supervise their activities. Poorer women sent their infants out to live with their wet nurses. Often this led to the death of infants, as nurses took on many children in order to increase their income and provided a poor standard of care.

The alternative to wet nursing was to wean babies on to bland, sweet, starchy foods. In Europe and North America, infants were fed cow's milk, thickened with flour and sweetened with sugar, or bread soaked in milk. In Asia, they received well-cooked rice or porridge. These diets often led to illness as they were not very nutritious. Parents often gave babies inappropriate foods, such as tea, potatoes, or beans, that they were unable to digest; and the food was often contaminated with dirt. This caused vomiting and diarrhea and in serious cases, it led to dehydration and convulsions and was a major cause of infant death. Treatments given to sick babies including purgatives (in the West) or emetics to induce vomiting (recommended by ayurvedic

Diet was crucial to the health and development of infants. When weaned, infants in all cultures were fed on bland starchy foods such as rice. (Hulton Archive/Getty Images)

practitioners) can only have made the problem worse. In the West, a better understanding of infant nutrition and of the need to keep feeding utensils scrupulously clean emerged only at the end of the century.

The stomach upsets that accompanied weaning onto a range of solid foods often coincided with the emergence of teeth. As a result, in many cultures, teething was thought to be a particularly difficult and dangerous time in an infant's life. In the West, doctors claimed that the growing teeth set up an inflammation in the gums, producing fevers, diarrhea, rickets, convulsions, and even death. They recommended cutting the gums to "release" the teeth. Ayurvedic practitioners advised applying medicines to gums to encourage the teeth to erupt.

Poor diet was a problem for older children, too. Throughout the world, children in rural areas suffered when food supplies ran short. Small children were among the first to die during famines, and lack of food permanently stunted the growth of children who survived. Urban children—middle class as well as poor—developed rickets, which prevented the bones from developing properly and left children with permanently bowed limbs. Rickets is now known to be caused a lack of vitamin D; it was prevalent among city children who rarely ate milk or eggs that contain the vitamin, and lived in streets where sunlight (which allowed the body to generate vitamin D) was cut off by the thick pall of smoke. In Europe and North America, children's diets gradually improved over the nineteenth century, reflected in a gradual increase in average height. Progress was slow and unsteady. In Britain, children's heights increased up to 1850 but then slipped back, before recovering toward the end of the century. This reflected a complex interaction between wages, the price of food, and actions to tackle disease.

PROTECTING CHILDREN'S HEALTH

Around the world, families did their best to keep their children in good health and to protect them from natural and supernatural diseases. Chinese infants were protected by *Zhang Xia*, whose arrows kept away any demons that might harm the child. The names of the Eight Immortals were embroidered on children's caps to ensure that they lived a long life, and protective spells were written on paper and pinned to their clothing. To protect children from attack by spirits or the evil eye, Iranian mothers bound a cloth over their infants' eyes for the first 10 or 15 days after birth. Children were given amulets to wear, as described by an early nineteenth-century traveler:

> They hang about the child's neck ... a bangle, the colour of a turquoise, which ... serves to annul the glance of an evil eye. They also insert paragraphs of the Koran into little bags, which they sew on the child's cap, or on its sleeve, esteeming them as great preservatives against sickness.[1]

Slave mothers hung lockets containing camphor around the necks of their children to ward off "bad airs."

Children were seen as being naturally healthy; however, some individuals, through illness, accident, or a poor constitution inherited from their parents, were delicate and needed extra care. Books on child care encouraged European and American mothers to ensure that their children had a good diet, with plenty of milk and meat, but not too much food, as this led to flabby, soft flesh. Children should sleep in well-ventilated rooms, spend time outside in the fresh air, and avoid spending long periods studying or reading. Many were regularly dosed with medicines. Mild laxatives such as castor oil or syrup of figs were given to maintain their digestive health. Similar advice was handed out to mothers in China, by practitioners who warned them not to be overprotective of their infants. Children should not be overfed, as this led to digestive upsets, or dressed in too many clothes.

CHILDREN'S ILLNESSES

Children suffered from many of the same diseases as adults. They caught respiratory infections such as pneumonia and tuberculosis; the latter was responsible for as many as a quarter of the deaths among older children. They were exposed to diseases spread through contaminated water, such as typhoid fever and cholera, and those transmitted by insects, including yellow fever and malaria. While yellow fever was not a major cause of death among children, who acquired some immunity against further attacks, malaria was a significant killer of older children, who were worn down by repeated bouts of fever.

Children were also exposed to the risks of illness and injury in the workplace. Children joined the labor force when very young, helping out in the family home. In Europe, large numbers of children worked in factories; in 1839, half of all British factory workers were under age 18. Children in Africa worked on farms, industries, and mines sometimes as slaves or unfree labor. They made up a major part of the workforce on colonial plantations. Children working on farms fell from wagons; they were kicked by animals and injured by tools. In mines, they risked death from noxious gases or roof collapses. A wide range of medical problems were associated with long working hours in cotton mills and other factories, including stomach disorders, ulcers, and deformed limbs as well as poor general health. In glass factories, for instance:

> [T]he hard labour, the irregularity of the hours, the frequent night-work and especially the great heat of the working place (100 to 190 Fahrenheit), engender in children general debility and disease, stunted growth ... Many of the children are pale, have red eyes, often blind for weeks at a time, suffer from violent nausea, vomiting, coughs, colds and rheumatism ... The glass blowers usually die young of debility or chest infections.[2]

Childhood Diseases

In addition to all this, children suffered from "childhood diseases"—a set of infectious diseases that conferred immunity to further attacks later in life, and hence were rare in adults. They included smallpox, chicken pox, measles, mumps, whooping cough, scarlet fever, and diphtheria. At the beginning of the century, most of these diseases were found in Europe and North America; by the middle of the nineteenth century, they had moved around the world with settlers and traders. Doctors struggled to understand why children caught these diseases only once. Western practitioners speculated that there was some factor in the blood that was activated by the infection and expelled during the course of the disease. Chinese practitioners believed that measles and smallpox were caused by fetal poison—material left in infants' bodies after birth. When activated by some external influence, the poison caused disease. Children suffered from measles and smallpox only once because during the course of these illnesses, the fetal poison was carried out of the body through the skin in the form of a rash.

Childhood diseases were of varying severity. Mumps and chicken pox were relatively mild diseases, although, like all these diseases, they were more serious among populations that had had no previous exposure to the infection. Scarlet fever killed many older children, breaking out in epidemics when as many as one-sixth of patients died. For reasons that are still not clear, the incidence of the disease and the number of deaths declined toward the end of the nineteenth century. Measles too killed huge numbers of children, especially those who were poorly nourished. According to one European doctor: "In healthy children among the well-to-do class the mortality is small: in the tubercular and wasted children to be found in workhouses, hospitals and among the lower classes, the mortality is enormous . . . [it] amounts to 9 or 10 percent."[3] In addition, the complications associated with measles permanently damaged the sight and hearing of many children. Whooping cough was particularly dangerous for infants, killing many young children. The initial symptoms were not serious, but patients developed uncontrollable fits of coughing, followed by a whooping sound as they gasped for air.

> To a weakly child the disease is necessarily a formidable one; the exhaustion produced by the constant muscular efforts, the frequent vomiting which prevents a proper amount of food from being assimilated . . . often reduce the child to a feeble and emaciated condition. It can easily be imagined that forty or fifty attacks of coughing every twenty-four hours produce great muscular exhaustion.[4]

When ill, children were given the same sort of care as adults. The children of wealthy families were attended by learned doctors. Most children were taken to a local healer best able to deal with their condition—a herbalist, bonesetter, drug seller, or spiritual healer. Children's bodies were thought to work in the same way as adults': they too became ill through an imbalance of humors or *doṣas*, a blockage in *qi*, a malfunctioning organ or the presence of an infection. Consequently, they received the much same treatment as adults to try to restore balance and help the natural healing process. Around the world, feverish children were sponged with cold or tepid water to make them more comfortable and treat the "hot" disease. Bathing in warm water was advised as a way of helping a rash to appear (this was seen as a positive development and part of the natural course of disease). Poultices were applied to the chest if there was difficulty in breathing or to the neck in cases of sore throat. Diet was an important part of treatment. In the West, children were given bland foods—such as rice puddings—to help build up their strength. Children were given the same types of medicines as adults. In Europe and America, children submitted to bloodletting and were prescribed purges and drugs to induce vomiting. In ayurvedic medicine, children's illnesses were treated by rebalancing the *doṣas* using vomits, purges, and bloodletting with leeches. Texts reminded practitioners of the need to use small doses of mild, astringent drugs that were often mixed with honey to make them more palatable. In unani medicine, children were given laxatives and emetics to remove bad material from the body and other medicines to help rebalance the humors.

Folk remedies were used to treat children in Africa, Asia, and the Americas. They were also popular in the West, where they were used alongside orthodox medicine well into the twentieth century. For example, children were passed under the belly of a donkey or a piebald horse to cure or prevent whooping cough. The procedure was so popular that donkey owners charged a regular fee. Alternatively, sufferers were advised to breathe in the warm air rising from the ground where a sheep had slept, or from a distillery or (a more modern version) from a gasworks.

During the nineteenth century, children were protected from the risks associated with smallpox by inoculation or vaccination. Smallpox was particularly unpleasant; sufferers developed a high fever and then a rash (or "pocks") that covered the face and hands. As many as one in 10 of all children died of smallpox, and those who survived were left with scarred and pitted skin. In the eighteenth century, children in Europe, North America, and India were protected from dying from smallpox by inoculation—deliberately infecting them with the disease. For reasons that are still not understood, the mortality from inoculated smallpox was considerably less than that from a naturally acquired case of the disease. After 1798, children were protected against catching smallpox by vaccination, infecting them with cowpox. Cowpox was a mild disease—vaccinated children had few if any symptoms—and the procedure prevented them catching smallpox. Western practitioners encouraged the use of vaccination all around the globe, but many parents were reluctant to submit their infants to the procedure. Some viewed vaccination as "unnatural" and claimed that many children suffered from side effects or even died as a direct result of the procedure. They also worried that other diseases were passed on through the vaccine. In India, Hindu parents refused to allow the use of vaccine taken from calves, as the cow was a sacred animal.

By the end of the century, Western doctors had a successful treatment for only one childhood infection: diphtheria. Diphtheria victims developed a sore throat and fever. In severe cases, a membrane developed in the throat, blocking it and leaving patients unable to swallow or breathe. Around a quarter of all patients died. In 1884, the bacterium responsible for diphtheria was identified, but further research revealed that the membrane was not directly caused by the bacteria, but by a toxin released from it into the blood. In 1890, the German researcher Emil von Behring produced an antitoxin made from the blood of horses injected with diphtheria toxin. The first ever effective specific treatment for a childhood disease, diphtheria antitoxin caused a huge sensation.

Its use spread rapidly around the world and death rates from the disease began to fall. Von Behring was awarded the first Nobel Prize in Medicine for his work.

Supernatural Disease

In many cultures, children suffered from illnesses caused by supernatural forces. Chinese babies who cried a lot were thought to be possessed by spirits. Shocks could cause "fright" (*jing*) or "soul loss" that brought on a range of problems, from irritability to convulsions. In serious cases, spiritual healers had to conduct ceremonies to call back the child's soul. In ayurvedic medicine, diseases caused by spirits and demons were recognizable by their very sudden onset, with symptoms such as fits or convulsions. They were treated with a combination of baths, prayers, and offerings. In North Africa, illness caused by the evil eye—a look from a person who wished the recipient ill luck or ill health —was cured by prayers and blessings from a holy man.

Specific demons were associated with particular illnesses. In China, smallpox was caused by the goddess *T'ou-Shen Niang-Niang*. She was believed to select pretty children as victims, so children were given ugly masks to wear, to trick the goddess into leaving them alone. Praying to the goddess provided protection from smallpox and helped victims to recover from the disease. When a child was infected, a shrine was set up within the home. Offerings were made on set days as the illness progressed. On the 14th day, when most sufferers were on the road to recovery, a ceremony was performed before the shrine. The infected child sat in front of the shrine.

> On top of his head is then put a small piece of red cloth, and . . . parched beans are taken from before the goddess and laid upon this red cloth, whence they are allowed to roll off . . . [this] indicates the strong desire that the pustules should dry up and become in appearance like the parched bean![5]

CHILD DEATHS

Despite the care of parents, doctors, and healers, in the nineteenth century, huge numbers of children died early in life. In Europe, as many as one in four or one in five children died in their first year. Such statistics are not available for non-Western countries, but the level of child deaths must have been similar and higher during epidemics or periods of social upheaval. National figures mask wide variations: well-fed infants born into middle-class families had a much better chance of survival than those born to poor mothers, and those born in the country were less likely to die than children born in densely populated cities. Infants died from injuries caused during birth, from congenital defects, or from infections caused by cutting the umbilical cord with dirty instruments. Later, they fell victim to diarrhea, convulsions, and respiratory diseases. Once children reached the age of four, they stood a better chance of survival, although they were at risk from a range of infectious diseases.

In the past, when so many children died early in life, it is often assumed that parents did not become emotionally attached to their offspring, but research shows how deeply mothers and fathers felt about child death. They were slightly less upset by the death of babies—perhaps because they had been members of the family for a relatively short time. But the death of older children, whose characters and potential were clearly established, was devastating. Even poor parents did their best to have a proper funeral for the child and to mark the site of the grave in some way.

THE RISE OF PEDIATRICS

In Europe and America, doctors had become interested in children's illnesses in the eighteenth century; however, few if any specialized in treating children until the late nineteenth century. The first area of children's medicine to emerge was orthopedics, the surgical correction of deformed limbs. From the 1830s, surgeons repaired "club foot"—a condition in which the foot turned inward so that the child walked on the side of the foot or ankle. By cutting the tendon, the foot was released into a more normal position. From the 1860s, with the development of anesthetics and antiseptic surgery, doctors were able to successfully treat joints infected by tuberculosis. Although much better known as a disease of the lungs, the tubercle bacterium also attacked skin and bones, resulting in abscesses and swellings. Surgeons cleaned away the infected bone then placed the joint in a splint to help it to heal in a more normal position and allow it to regain movement.

The establishment of children's hospitals allowed doctors to treat large numbers of children and to conduct research into the incidence, course, and outcomes of children's diseases, thus paving the way for pediatrics to emerge as a specialist field. Until the nineteenth century, children were generally excluded from general hospitals but received care as outpatients at clinics or dispensaries. The first hospital specifically for sick children opened in Paris in 1802. It was followed by hospitals in Germany and Italy in the 1830s and 1840s, and the Great

The Great Ormond Street Hospital, one of the first institutions for sick children opened in London in what had once been a grand mansion. The wards were friendly and informal, where patients were cared for and entertained while receiving treatment. (National Library of Medicine)

Ormond Street Hospital in London opened in 1855. Thereafter, these institutions spread throughout the world. Most children's hospitals were small. To deal with the huge demand for care, some opened out-patient departments or introduced home visiting schemes, where nurses treated children at home. The hospitals treated a wide range of conditions—fevers, rheumatism, skin diseases, respiratory complaints, and rickets. In these hospitals, children from poor families received care very similar to that provided to middle-class children at home. Rest, a good diet, and nursing were the basis of care. Children often stayed in hospitals for weeks or months, and some hospitals had convalescent homes, where children could continue to regain strength when they no longer needed medical care.

Although set up to treat children suffering from chronic conditions, children's hospitals regularly had to deal with outbreaks of infectious diseases. An outbreak of measles in the Benevolent Asylum in Sydney, Australia, in 1867 affected over 250 patients and killed many of those children admitted with other diseases. The solution was to create separate wards for infectious diseases and to take steps to ensure that staff members did not transfer infection. The fear of infection meant that many institutions strictly limited the number of visitors coming on to the wards; as a result, hospitalized children might not see their parents for days or weeks.

THE STATE AND CHILDREN'S HEALTH

Over the nineteenth century, governments in the Americas, Europe, and in African and Asian colonies increasingly intervened to protect the health of children. This was prompted by the introduction of accurate recording of births and deaths, which revealed the high levels of infant mortality for the first time. Governments were motivated to act by a mix of humanitarian and political concerns. Because of their age, children had little power or influence, and it was increasingly accepted in the late nineteenth century that, when exposed to unnecessary risk or suffering, it was right that the state should step in to protect them. Governments were also concerned about population size. At a time when European states were fighting over national boundaries and territory overseas, it was vital that nations had a large and healthy population to provide men for the army and a workforce to support a healthy economy. In North America, there were fears that the white, native-born population was being swamped by high immigration from southern Europe. In Latin America, new governments set up following the wars of independence saw good infant health as a measure of national well-being.

Governments and charities around the world identified the same root cause of high infant mortality: poor and ignorant mothers who were incapable of raising healthy children. The authorities took two basic approaches to the problem. In some countries, such as France, charities and local government provided a range of services to help poor mothers such as maternity benefits so they could take time off work, midwives to attend the birth, and free and cheap meals. New mothers also received advice on child rearing; their infants received free milk and free treatment from doctors and nurses. The French model inspired other governments to act, but many chose a different approach, focusing on the need to educate mothers. In Britain, classes in child care, cookery, and hygiene were offered at welfare centers. Babies were weighed and examined by nurses and doctors to check that they were developing normally, but parents had to pay for any medical treatment. The provision of infant welfare spread around the globe at the end of the century. Schemes were adopted in the newly independent states of South America and Latin America and in colonial

Africa, where the ruling powers portrayed children as the victims of malnutrition, tropical diseases, and poor mothering. Welfare schemes to teach mothers how to feed their infants and keep them clean were part of the project of bringing civilization to "primitive" peoples.

The high mortality among children sent out to wet nurses was also a cause of public concern. To ensure that the children were well looked after, and that the wet nurses received adequate payment, local governments set up official bureaus of wet nurses. In France in 1874, a national law required that all children sent to be wet-nursed had to be registered. Similarly, wet nurses were licensed in Sao Paulo, Brazil, from 1879, although the law was frequently ignored.

In the middle of the century, European governments passed a series of laws to protect children from the bad effects of factory work, and in the process defined the period of childhood as the first 13 years of life. The number of hours that children could work was gradually restricted. In Britain, under the Factory Act of 1847, children between the ages of 13 and 18 could work a maximum of 63 hours per week. The following year, the figure was reduced to 58 hours per week, and by 1870, it was accepted that children should not be employed in full-time work. Children were also banned from the most dangerous trades, such as working underground in mines; however, children working at home or in small workshops enjoyed less protection from workplace dangers or exploitation. Restricting the hours children could work did not give them free time; there was simply a shift from paid work to attendance in schools. In the 1870s, a further wave of regulation made schooling compulsory to ensure that children received a basic education and were taught norms of behavior and moral codes.

Governments throughout the world joined the effort to protect children from disease. By the late nineteenth century, doctors were required to notify local authorities of cases of childhood diseases, so that the victims could be isolated to prevent the spread of infection. Governments also joined the crusade against smallpox. In many countries, vaccination was made compulsory for all children. Laws were first introduced in the German states of Hessen and Bavaria as early as 1807, in Sweden in 1816, in England and Wales in 1853, and parts of India from 1877. While this legislation increased the numbers of children undergoing vaccination, the introduction of compulsion aroused protests in many countries, including India, Britain, Canada, and Brazil. Parents objected to governments telling them they must have their children vaccinated, and felt that these decisions should be left to the family. A small number even went to jail rather than have their children vaccinated.

NOTES

1. James Mourier, *A Second Journey through Persia, Armenia and Asia Minor ... between 1810 and 1816* (London, 1818), quoted in Willem Floor, *Public Health in Qajar Iran* (Washington, DC: Mage Publishers, 2004), p. 97.

2. Frederick Engels, *Condition of the Working Class in England in 1844* (1845; repr., London: George Allen & Unwin, 1943), p. 207.

3. Fifty-fourth Annual Report of the General Hospital and Dispensary for Sick Children (Manchester, 1883), p. 12, quoted in Elizabeth M. R. Lomax, *Small and Special: The Development of Hospitals for Children in Victorian Britain* (London: Wellcome Institute for the History of Medicine, 1996), p. 119.

4. Henry Ashby and G. A. Wright, *The Diseases of Children, Medical and Surgical* (London, 1899), p. 314, quoted in Lomax, *Small and Special*, p. 119.

5. J. Doolittle, *Social Life of the Chinese*, vol. 1 (New York, 1865), p. 15, quoted in Donald R. Hopkins, *The Greatest Killer: Smallpox in History* (Chicago: University of Chicago Press, 2002), p. 137.

CHAPTER 6

Infectious Diseases

The nineteenth century saw the most radical changes in patterns of disease in human history, driven by rapid social, political, and cultural developments. In the industrialized world, huge numbers of people moved into cities in search of work, bringing them into contact with a range of infections they might never have encountered in the countryside. Diseases began to travel in new ways; infections that had existed in particular locales for hundreds of years were spread within regions and around the globe by increasingly mobile populations traveling by steam-powered railroad and ship. European soldiers and adventurers, intent on exploring and conquering in Asia and Africa, encountered (often fatally) indigenous diseases. People from India, Africa, and the Americas moved to new countries to work in mines, on plantations, and in factories. The man-made expansion of disease prompted new efforts at control. People tried to stop the spread of diseases by religious ceremonies, cleansing of the environment, better personal hygiene, and enforced isolation of infected individuals. As a result, by the end of the century, some epidemic diseases had been brought under a measure of control.

CHANGING PATTERNS OF DISEASES

Disease and Urbanization

The nineteenth century was a century of urbanization, when populations moved from living on the land to living in the town where they found new forms of work. New cities were established and old cities expanded around the world, especially in Europe, the Americas, and Asia. Urban life impacted on the incidence of disease in many ways. Immigrants coming into cities from rural areas were exposed to new infections to which they had little or no immunity. All urban residents came into contact with large numbers of people every day, and many were exposed to contaminated food and water, allowing the rapid transmission of diseases including typhoid and cholera. Many forms of work brought particular hazards to health, such as exposure to carcinogenic chemicals.

Not surprisingly, nineteenth-century cities were unhealthy places, regularly swept by waves of infectious disease. The most common disease in early nineteenth-century urban records is "fever." Many of these cases would now be diagnosed as typhus, a bacterial infection spread by body lice that caused chills, a high fever, and a rash. Typhus had long been associated with wars, when large numbers of soldiers lived together in filthy conditions, and with famine. The disease claimed huge numbers of the Irish population when they were struck by the potato famine in 1845–1848. The disease traveled with Irish immigrants to Canada, where more than 20,000 people died between 1847 and 1848. But typhus was also a regular feature of city life. Fever broke out every few years in the poorest parts of towns across Europe and North America, often in the winter when populations rose due to an influx of agricultural laborers seeking work.

Urban dwellers also suffered from epidemics of respiratory diseases, including bronchitis, pneumonia, and influenza. Flu is still a common disease—many of us are familiar with the symptoms of chills, fever, and aching joints. The history of flu is dominated by the pandemic— the global epidemic—that swept around the world in the aftermath of the First World War, killing more people than the conflict itself. However, outbreaks of flu were closely linked to urbanization; major epidemics began in the eighteenth century with the growth of urban living. Death rates for flu were relatively low, but because the disease attacked so many people, it killed large numbers, mostly among the young and the old. Over a million people died in the 1889–1890 pandemic of so-called Russian flu (named for its origin in Eastern Europe).

Epidemics killed large numbers in short periods, and their dramatic impact means that they often dominate contemporary records. But endemic diseases—those infections that were present all the time— claimed more victims in total. Tuberculosis, a bacterial infection, was by far the biggest killer of the nineteenth century, causing up to one in four deaths in Europe, mostly among young adults. Tuberculosis commonly affected the lungs. Victims suffered from a chronic cough, fevers, and weight loss (hence the common name of the disease "consumption") over months or years. In its later stages, sufferers coughed up blood from their badly damaged lungs. In the crowded living and working conditions in cities, the infection spread rapidly. Well-fed, healthy individuals were able to fight off the infection, but anyone weakened by poor diet, bad living conditions, and long hours of work was highly susceptible to the disease.

Global Diseases

Diseases had been traveling between continents with explorers and adventurers since the fifteenth century, but the nineteenth century saw the emergence of new patterns of disease transmission. Areas of the globe were opened up to exploration and trade for the first time, particularly in Africa, exposing travelers and indigenous peoples to novel diseases. Infections spread over longer distances. With the advent of steamships, journey times decreased, and passengers incubating infections, who would previously have become ill during a long sea voyage, now disembarked still apparently healthy but carrying the seeds of disease. In addition, many more people were traveling, increasing the chances of transmitting infections.

In previous centuries, diseases from the Old World had been exported to the New World, with devastating effects. Indigenous populations, especially those isolated on islands or in mountainous and desert regions, had no previous exposure and therefore little resistance to European diseases such as influenza, measles, smallpox, syphilis, and typhus. In the nineteenth century, indigenous peoples in North and South America continued to die in large numbers from the onslaught of these diseases. Island populations in the Pacific were exposed to European infections for the first time. The population of Hawaii fell from well over 250,000 in the late eighteenth century to around 73,000 by 1853, as a consequence of syphilis (which reduced the birth rate), measles, whooping cough, influenza, and smallpox. Some commentators interpreted the decline of indigenous populations as proof of their inherent weakness and the superiority of white races.

In turn, Old World and American populations began to suffer from diseases brought from the African continent. Yellow fever had existed in Africa for centuries where it was a mild illness, mainly affecting children. In the late eighteenth and early nineteenth centuries, it spread through many parts of the Americas and southern Europe. Yellow fever is caused by a virus transmitted by mosquitoes that stowed away in the water supplies carried on ships. Victims suffered from high fever and liver damage that caused the skin to turn yellow. A letter written in 1897 describing a case of the disease recorded "the skin was a bright yellow hue: tongue and lips dark, cracked and blood oozing from the mouth and nose. To me the most terrible and terrifying feature was the 'black vomit' ... it was as black as ink and would be ejected with terrific force."[1] A series of severe epidemics struck the southern United States in the late nineteenth century and decimated some towns: Memphis was almost abandoned after serious outbreaks in 1878 and 1879 caused many of its residents to move away to healthier locations.

The mass movement of people within Africa and Asia also disturbed existing patterns of disease incidence. Travelers moving long distances within the continent, the mass migration of people seeking to escape conflicts or to find work, deforestation, the establishment of large plantations, and better transport, all helped to spread a range of diseases. Some of these were introduced from abroad, such as cholera or plague, but most were indigenous parasitic diseases that had previously been limited to specific areas. Sleeping sickness, for example, was endemic to some parts of the Congo, but spread across wide areas in an epidemic from 1900. Hundreds of thousands died in the Congo basin and Uganda. Malaria too, spread into new areas of Africa and Asia over the century.

Cholera and Plague

The most dramatic incursions of foreign diseases in the nineteenth century were the repeated pandemics of cholera and plague. Cholera spread around the globe from its roots in India in repeated epidemics throughout the century. The first cholera pandemic occurred between 1816 and 1826, affecting China, Japan, North Africa, and Russia. The second and third pandemics, from 1827 to 1835 and from 1839 to 1852, spread even further, reaching into Europe and to North and South America. Two more pandemics occurred before the end of the century. The movement of cholera graphically revealed the new global networks of trade and migration. The disease followed shipping routes, from India to China, the Persian Gulf, and the Caspian Sea. The spread of the first and fourth pandemics were hastened by international pilgrimages: the first by Hindu pilgrims traveling home from a gathering at the Ganges in India; and the fourth by Islamic pilgrims returning from Mecca in the Arabian Peninsula.

The slow, inexorable movement of cholera—it took several years for the second pandemic to travel from Asia to Europe, and then a further two years to spread across the continent—contrasted with the character of the disease itself. It struck without warning and developed at incredible speed; newspapers reported on healthy people preparing to go about their daily routine in the morning who were dead by evening. Victims suffered from violent vomiting, diarrhea, and muscular cramps, and as the body became extremely dehydrated, the face sank and the skin and lips turned blue. In the absence of good records (and the reporting of deaths even in well-administered countries broke down under the pressure of the epidemics) it is impossible to calculate accurately the total mortality from cholera, but it was clearly huge. Between 1848 and 1849, cholera claimed over 50,000 victims in Britain alone; the first two outbreaks of the disease in the United States caused around 150,000 deaths, and the toll in China, India, and Russia ran into

Honoré Daumier's image captures the horror of the 1832 cholera epidemic in Paris. A working man collapses with cramps, a woman flees, covering her nose and mouth to avoid the infectious miasma, and corpses are carried away. (National Library of Medicine)

the millions. It has been estimated that cholera killed around 15 million people between 1817 and 1865.

Just as cholera was declining, the world was hit by a pandemic of plague. Plague, or the Black Death, as it was also known, had spread to Europe in the fourteenth, seventeenth, and eighteenth centuries, but in the nineteenth century, its movement was enhanced by global travel. The outbreak of plague originated in southern China and Mongolia around 1855. From 1886, the disease moved via shipping routes to Hong Kong and India, then to Egypt, San Francisco, South Africa, and Australia by 1900, with isolated outbreaks in European ports. Victims developed fever and characteristic swellings or "buboes"; the tips of the fingers became gangrenous and turned black. The death toll was horrific: in Hong Kong, around 100,000 people died within a few months in 1894; 400,000 people had died in India by 1900. The outbreak did not end until the 1950s, killing several million people around the world.

UNDERSTANDING DISEASE

The increase in epidemics over the nineteenth century forced medical practitioners to consider how a disease could suddenly appear, infect large numbers of people, and then disappear. In China, learned practitioners had two main theories as to the cause of epidemics. Cold Damage theories blamed climatic factors, particularly excessive cold or wind, for producing a pathogenic *qi*. This entered the body via the pores, producing fevers. Warm Factor explanations, which were more generally accepted by practitioners, held that epidemic diseases including cholera and plague were caused when environmental factors came together to produce pestilential *qi* that entered through the nose and mouth.

> Then the hot qi of heaven descends, the humid qi of the earth rises, and people are stuck in the middle of these qis, and are subjected to the qi that results from the earthly and heavenly qis fermenting together. The emanation from the two qis enters through the nose, goes into the body, and results in a chaotic mixture of pure and impure, thus giving rise to cholera.[2]

Pestilential *qi* was more likely to be generated in warm air—this explained why cholera generally appeared in the summer—and in the filthy conditions found in dense, urban populations. Rats were linked to the appearance of plague; pestilential *qi* rose from the earth through their burrows and contaminated wells. When pestilential *qi* entered the body, it affected the blood (*xue*) and disturbed the healthy flow of the body's own *qi*. Symptoms varied according to where the *qi* entered the body, and where it stagnated within it.

While doctors discussed the role of *qi*, ordinary Chinese people continued to believe that epidemics were caused by supernatural beings. Armies of ghosts—the spirits of the dead who had not been given appropriate rituals at the time of their deaths—were believed to roam the land, attacking large numbers of people. They were sent by disease gods to inflict disease as a form of punishment for sin. The demons could not attack those who were honest and loyal and who gave money to the poor.

Elsewhere, medical practitioners were also divided as to whether epidemics had natural or supernatural causes, and the mechanisms by which diseases spread. In India, ayurvedic practitioners debated if the spread of cholera was linked to environmental factors, such as monsoon rains, or whether it was contagious and spread by people attending religious gatherings, or whether the pilgrims were in some way particularly susceptible to the disease. Practitioners of unani medicine in North Africa suggested that cholera was caused by celestial factors such as meteors, was a punishment sent by god, or was caused by evil spirits or *jinn*. These explanations of supernatural causes could be very elaborate, mirroring the different symptoms of disease.

> The first [*jinn*], *Aya'il*, had a list with the names of those condemned to death. Those who died barely stricken had been hit by the arrows of the second jinn *Ya'il*. Those who died on the first day after the sudden illness were hit in the heart by the arrows of the third jinn, *Haiha'il*. If an abscess appeared on the skin of the victim, it was the result of wounds from arrows of the fourth jinn, *Griha'il*. The fifth jinn, *Shaykha'il*, was armed with clubs and stones and killed by striking the victim in the heart, stomach or head, causing accumulation of blood in the mouth, altered reason, prolonged suffering, loss of speech and slow death.[3]

In parts of Africa, such as the Congo, epidemics were blamed on witchcraft.

In the West, practitioners rejected supernatural theories of disease causation but debated the mechanism by which epidemics spread through the population. Early nineteenth century practitioners understood that some diseases, such as smallpox, were contagious—they were transmitted by direct contact between infected and susceptible persons—although they did know exactly what agent was passed from person to person. Other epidemics seemed to appear spontaneously, breaking out in particular locations, and thus were linked to environmental factors. Filthy conditions were seen as a prime cause of disease: most fevers were believed to arise through "miasma"—the unpleasant atmosphere caused by rotting organic matter. Thus epidemics such as cholera were most severe in dirty urban environments. One British doctor reporting on the first epidemic in India noted "the thickly populated and close lanes of Delhi suffered more than the rectangular and spacious streets of Jaipur. And again the low and nasty town of Saharanpur more than the city and cantonment of Meerut."[4]

There was no hard and fast division between contagious and environmental diseases; the spread of a contagious disease might be enhanced by filthy conditions, or disease might arise from environmental conditions and then begin to spread from person to person. Doctors differed in their opinions as to exactly where a particular disease lay on a continuum between contagious and environmental transmission. In the 1840s, doctors in England tended to favor environmental causes for fever; their colleagues in Scotland and Ireland were more likely to believe that fevers were contagious. Western doctors also believed some groups were more susceptible to particular diseases. In the early part of the century, it was widely accepted that there was a hereditary component to the transmission of tuberculosis—a particular "constitution" handed down through the generations made some individuals more likely to succumb to the disease.

From the 1880s, a growing number of epidemic diseases were shown to be spread by bacteria. Louis Pasteur, a French chemist, had revealed the link between microorganisms and disease in the 1860s. Robert Koch, a German bacteriologist, led research into identifying the bacteria responsible for specific diseases. Koch discovered the bacterium that caused tuberculosis in 1882, and the following year, he isolated the cholera bacillus. Thereafter, the organisms responsible for major infectious diseases were uncovered at the astonishing rate of one every year for the rest of the century. In 1894, Western researchers working in Hong Kong discovered the bacterium responsible for plague was present in humans and in rodents, usually rats. The disease was transmitted when humans were bitten by an infected rat flea. Practitioners were unable to identify viruses (which are much smaller than bacteria) until the end of the century, so the agents responsible for many important diseases, including smallpox and influenza, remained mysterious.

In the past, historians believed that the so-called "germ theory"—the understanding that microorganisms caused illness—revolutionized thinking about disease causation. More recently, they have realized that doctors did not immediately switch to the idea that "germs" caused disease. Given the long association between dirt and ill health, many doctors were reluctant to believe that the environment played no part in disease transmission, and they continued to argue that it played some part in determining where and when diseases arose—especially as it was clear that bacteria were present in huge numbers and at all times. For example, it was suggested that yellow fever was spread by some "seed" or germ, but the disease would only appear if it found a suitable "soil"—dirty conditions and a humid climate. These debates over disease causation gradually declined over the last years of the century, after Koch developed a set of techniques for culturing and identifying disease-causing bacteria.

TREATING INFECTIOUS DISEASES

Although epidemics were different from other diseases in that many people were affected simultaneously, the treatment was much the same as for other ailments. Chinese practitioners believed that the pestilential *qi* responsible for outbreaks of disease had a slightly different effect on each individual depending on their lifestyle and constitution, and on where the invading *qi* came to rest within the body. As a result, individuals suffering from similar symptoms might receive quite different medicine and diet to correct the effects on the internal balance of *qi* within the body.

Unani practitioners in North Africa saw cholera as a hot disease and treated it with cooling medicines similar to those used in cases of dysentery, including herbs, honey, vinegar, and garlic. In cases of plague, they recommended bloodletting to remove the poisoned blood that had accumulated in swellings or buboes. Western practitioners treated diseases that caused vomiting or purging with medicines that mimicked this response, in the hope that clearing the digestive system of bad materials would help the natural healing process. Faced with the acute symptoms produced by cholera, Western doctors responded with their strongest treatments, including bloodletting and purgative medicines containing mercury. As it became clear that this therapy was rarely successful, practitioners switched to using milder therapies. Their treatment for the fevers associated with many infectious diseases was more successful. Quinine halted the violent shivering, while cold baths and bloodletting lowered the body temperature. Ayurvedic practitioners treated cholera with mild purgatives and later also prescribed alcohol—a medicine borrowed from Western practitioners.

Folk practitioners used specific remedies for each disease, sometimes combining natural and supernatural therapies. In the Yucatan peninsula in Mexico, shamans sought to expel smallpox from the body, but they also treated the itching associated with the rash with soothing herbs and roots. They treated the diarrhea and vomiting accompanying cholera with lemonade, herbs, and a drink made from fermented corn.

PREVENTING AND CONTROLLING DISEASE

Debates about disease causation were hugely important because they underpinned different strategies to control disease: if a disease was spread by contagion, then it could be halted by isolating infected people and destroying goods that might carry the infection; if disease was a punishment sent by gods or spirits, then only prayers and offerings would have any effect.

Individuals adopted a number of strategies in an attempt to avoid catching epidemic diseases. People left infected areas. When cholera arrived in Europe and North America, people fled from the cities to the countryside, which was traditionally thought to be healthier. People were encouraged to keep themselves and their homes clean, to eat a simple diet, and to follow a healthy regimen of moderate exercise and rest. Practitioners warned against drinking alcohol, staying up late, and eating unripe fruits. Similar advice circulated in China when the nation was struck by plague, possibly inspired by Western medicine. Individuals were advised to wear clean clothes and shoes, which helped to prevent contact with the pestilential *qi* rising from the ground. To strengthen the body against the effects of pestilential *qi*, people should eat a good, simple diet, and remain calm. Homes should be cleaned and ventilated and wells purified with garlic and other drugs. People living in the city should escape to the fresh air of the countryside. People also sought supernatural protection—they wore amulets on their clothing, placed them on their houses, and burned amulets and put the ashes into their wells. Unani practitioners recommended that to avoid plague, people should keep their blood pure by avoiding overexcitement and by inhaling sweet-smelling substances to strengthen the heart.

Collective Action

Epidemics also prompted collective responses, and the residents of villages, towns, and cities worked together to protect their communities from disease. When threatened by cholera, the inhabitants of rural communities in Finland stopped all travelers entering their villages for fear that they might bring the disease. In Chinese towns, festivals were held to ward off plague in which paper boats containing images of disease gods were burnt or floated away as a means of expelling illness from the community.

> Every spring, in the towns and countryside, people pool their money in order to hold a *Qing jiao*. They use paper to make a dragon boat, spirit mediums use red ink to paint their faces like each god in the pantheon. They seek out the fugitives [ghosts] at each household along the way in order to exorcise epidemics.[5]

Local healing gods were asked to do battle with the plague gods and keep the disease at bay. If plague arrived, gods from nearby towns and cities were invoked to strengthen the supernatural defenses. In India, too, public ceremonies and rituals were held to ward off cholera.

The arrival of cholera pandemics galvanized national and local governments to take action to protect the health of their populations. The temporary measures adopted against the disease often formed the basis for long-term strategies to deal with other diseases, and inspired the creation of public health bodies to monitor and tackle disease within communities. The authorities faced a problem, however, in deciding what measures to implement, as doctors were divided as to whether cholera was contagious or arose from environmental conditions. When cholera first appeared in Russia and Austria-Hungary in 1830, the disease was believed to be contagious, so the governments set up quarantines at their borders and outside major cities. All travelers were stopped at quarantine stations where they were held for a period of time, and their goods and belongings were cleaned and fumigated. Only those believed to be healthy were given a certificate ("a clean bill of health") and allowed to continue on their journey. When cholera broke through the cordons, governments tried to stop its further spread by forcibly isolating infected people in special hospitals and requiring all cholera victims to be buried quickly and with few funeral rites.

Countries to the west of Russia benefited from this experience and adopted a mix of strategies to deal with cholera. In Britain, ships were quarantined. Anyone infected with cholera was offered care in their own home or in cholera hospitals. (Although sufferers were not required to go to the hospital, the local authorities often effectively forced them to do so.) Infected houses were fumigated. Alongside these measures to break the chain of infection, local agencies organized massive cleaning initiatives, sweeping and washing the streets of whole towns and getting rid of accumulated refuse. This combined approach—sanitary measures plus quarantines—was generally adopted throughout Europe and beyond in the cholera outbreaks of the 1840s and 1850s.

New information about how cholera was transmitted had surprisingly little effect on these control measures. In 1855, John Snow, a British physician, demonstrated that infection was carried in the water supply. He tracked cholera cases in a London neighborhood in 1854 and showed that people whose water supply was drawn from lower down the river Thames (where it had become contaminated by sewage) were much more likely to catch the disease than those drinking cleaner water taken upstream. Snow's findings were worked into existing ideas; the British authorities interpreted his work as a demonstration of the old premise that dirt (in this case carried in water) was linked to disease and thus supported the continued use of sanitary reforms.

Even Robert Koch's discovery that cholera was spread by bacteria shed in the body fluids of cholera patients and that the bacteria could be killed by disinfection did not produce a revolution in disease control practices. Koch's discovery made it practical to reinstate quarantines in a modified form. The sheer numbers of people and quantities of goods traveling around the globe made the old system of holding all passengers impractical, so quarantines were made more focused and much shorter. Only those travelers suffering from suspicious symptoms were sent to isolation hospitals, where further infection was checked by careful disinfection. Goods that had come into contact with cholera sufferers were also disinfected.

These Western methods of prevention were widely adopted but remained controversial. Some governments were suspicious of Koch's ideas, and refused to abandon their belief that the environment played a role in the spread of cholera. Governments in India persisted with their sanitary policies, reassured by the inaccurate findings of their own experts that Koch's bacillus did not cause cholera. Unani practitioners in India were divided over the merits of measures used by British doctors against the spread of plague, such as disinfecting homes and isolating the sick. Some believed that they were necessary; others objected to the forcible isolation of the sick (especially of women) and argued that the failure of these measures to halt the outbreak was proof that Western doctors did not understand how plague affected the bodies of Indian people.

Disease controls also disrupted trade and were unpopular with the public. While European governments were able to enforce unpopular regulations on shipping, in Tunisia, Western methods of quarantine, isolation, and sanitary reforms were adopted only during cholera epidemics in the 1820s and 1830s under the leadership of a pro-Western ruler. They were abandoned in later epidemics following pressure from European traders who objected to the disruption caused by quarantines. In Europe and the United States, there were riots against the strict regulations on burial rites and the isolation of cholera patients in special hospitals. Rumors that patients would be killed and their bodies dissected prompted mobs to smash cholera ambulances and attack isolation hospitals. In Russia, government officials were accused of poisoning wells in order to kill off the peasant population.

SMALLPOX AND VACCINATION

For the vast majority of infectious diseases, sanitary measures and isolation were the only possible strategies of control. There was one exception: smallpox. Unlike any other nineteenth-century disease, it was possible to prevent smallpox by immunization. Smallpox was a horrible disease, now known to be caused by the *variola* virus. Victims were struck by a high fever and aches and pains. After a few days, the characteristic red spots began to appear, on the face and hands in mild cases, covering the whole of the body in serious ones. The spots gradually filled with a clear fluid that turned into pus. Many burst under the pressure of the patient's body, sticking the bedclothes to the skin and giving off a foul odor. It took several weeks for the spots to dry and heal. At the beginning of the century, about one in 10 people died of the disease. Those fortunate enough to survive had lifelong immunity to future attacks but were usually left disfigured with pitted skin where the spots had been.

Smallpox had become a global disease long before the nineteenth century. It had been present in Africa and Asia from ancient times, was recorded in Europe in the medieval period, and reached the Americas through European travelers in the sixteenth century. Smallpox had no respect for status; rich and poor alike suffered from the disease. In the seventeenth and eighteenth centuries, when the disease seems to have acquired a particularly virulent form, royal victims included European kings and queens and emperors of China and Japan. By 1800 in Europe, smallpox had become primarily a disease of children, except in isolated communities where it continued to attack adults.

Although smallpox posed a terrible threat, it was also a disease amenable to control. Remarkably, not one, but two forms of immunization were available in the nineteenth century. The first was inoculation or variolation. This involved deliberately infecting a child with smallpox.

Although it sounds extremely dangerous, and some recipients did die as a result of variolation, records consistently show that the death rate for inoculated smallpox was much lower than for the naturally acquired infection. (It is not clear why this should be so.) Various techniques to transmit the disease had been developed in different cultures around the world. In Asia and the near East, practitioners scratched or pierced the skin, then rubbed on some of the dried crusts from the smallpox spots; in China, patients inhaled a powder made from the scabs; in some parts of rural Europe, children simply held some smallpox crusts in the hand. Inoculation was often carried out by special groups of practitioners. In India, they were known as *tikaders*; they traveled from village to village in the spring, inoculating children, supervising their care during the bout of smallpox, and praying to the smallpox goddess Sitala to ensure a safe outcome. The use of inoculation varied around the world; the procedure was popular in India but was rarely practiced in China.

The second form of immunization was vaccination: infecting children not with smallpox but with cowpox, a related virus that conferred immunity but caused only mild symptoms. The procedure was developed by Edward Jenner, an English medical practitioner, in the late eighteenth century. Like many other doctors, he knew that women who milked cows rarely suffered from smallpox and were famous for their fine, smooth complexions. Jenner took this observation a stage further in 1796, infecting a boy with cowpox and then with smallpox. The inoculation had no effect. While Jenner proved that vaccination was effective, he did not understand how it produced immunity. He published his findings in 1798 and spent much of the rest of his life promoting vaccination through letters and publications and by sending out supplies of vaccine. This was crucial to the spread of the new procedure; cowpox was a rare disease, so new vaccine was collected from the fluid-filled spot that appeared on the arms of vaccinated children. Later, larger supplies of vaccine were produced by inoculating calves; this also ensured that the vaccine did not transmit other human diseases such as syphilis.

Vaccination spread with extraordinary speed. By 1800, it had been introduced across Europe and in America; 20 years later, vaccination had spread through the British Empire to India and Australasia, and to Spanish America. By the late 1850s, it was practiced in Japan and Asia. Initially, vaccination was used by the upper classes, who could afford to employ a practitioner to carry out the procedure. Free vaccination provided by charities and governments helped to spread the practice. States encouraged its use by passing laws to stop the older practice

Parents prayed to Sitala, the smallpox goddess to protect their children from the disease or to recover from it. The goddess is shown carrying a broom and a pot of water for ritual cleansing. (National Library of Medicine)

of inoculation that was blamed for spreading smallpox, or by making vaccination compulsory. Vaccination greatly reduced the number of deaths caused by smallpox. In Europe, the frequency of smallpox epidemics declined sharply with the introduction of vaccination, and by the end of the century, smallpox was no longer a major cause of death. Vaccination did not become popular in all countries. In India, Hindu parents objected to having their children immunized with vaccine taken from a cow, a sacred animal. Elsewhere, parents disliked taking their children to an unfamiliar (often a Western-trained) practitioner.

To overcome this prejudice, the rulers of Bhopal employed local unani practitioners to vaccinate. In some medical cultures, vaccination was rejected completely, because it made no sense within indigenous medical knowledge. In the Yucatan peninsula of Mexico, where local practitioners treated smallpox by driving the disease out of the body, deliberately inviting the infection into the body seemed a dangerous and pointless practice.

Vaccination represented a huge leap forward in disease control, but it did not immediately lead to immunization against other diseases. The new vaccines against epidemic diseases were developed around a century later, based on Pasteur's findings that the virulence of microorganisms could be weakened to the point where they could safely be injected into animals, triggering a response that protected against further attacks of disease. In 1892, Waldemar Haffkine, a Russian bacteriologist, developed a cholera vaccine that came into use in India toward the end of the century. In 1897, Almoth Wright, a British researcher, devised a vaccine against typhoid fever; however, there were doubts over its efficacy, and it came into general use only very slowly.

THE IMPACT OF PUBLIC HEALTH

The nineteenth century saw huge changes in people's experience of disease, in disease patterns and in mortality. Toward the end of the century, the number of pandemics declined and deaths from infectious diseases fell over much of the globe. As a result, life expectancy began to increase and the degenerative diseases we associate with modern life, such as heart disease and cancer, began to become significant causes of death.

The contribution of public health to the decline in epidemics has been debated by historians for many years. There is no doubt that governments around the world responded to epidemics by introducing public health policies to protect the lives of their people. But sanitary reforms were slow and patchy. While the governments of large cities could afford large infrastructure projects, such as building new reservoirs to provide clean water, the authorities in smaller towns and villages could not. The population of rural communities continued to use contaminated water from rivers and wells and the authorities had to rely on individuals to keep their villages clean.

As a result, it is difficult to be certain of the overall effectiveness of measures to control disease, even in Europe, where we have good records charting the mortality from infections and the actions taken against them. In the 1960s, historians concluded that medical treatment had done little to cure or prevent disease and that the saving of life was due to economic factors—higher standards of living and, in particular, a better diet. These arguments have, in turn, come under scrutiny as demographers have developed more sensitive analyses of nineteenth-century data. They have concluded that public health initiatives made a significant impact in reducing the number of deaths from waterborne diseases, such as cholera and typhoid fever. Efforts to reduce over-crowding in city housing, to isolate cases of tuberculosis, and to prevent infant diarrhea also helped to reduce high urban death rates. Now it is clear that the conquest of infectious disease was a slow process, affected by many factors including incomes, diet, education, and individual choices as well as public health policies.

NOTES

1. Quoted in Margaret Humphreys, "Yellow Fever: The Yellow Jack" in *Plague, Pox and Pestilence: Disease in History*, ed. Kenneth F. Kiple (London: Weidenfeld & Nicolson, 1997), p. 87 (original source not given).

2. Wang Shixiong, *Huoluan lun* (1838) part 1, 2b, quoted in Ruth Rogaski, "From Protecting Life to Defending the Nation: Tianjin 1859–1953" (PhD thesis, Yale University, 1996), p. 68.

3. E. Bertherand, *Médecine et Hygiène des Arabes* (Paris, 1855), p. 431, quoted in Nancy Elizabeth Gallagher, *Medicine and Power in Tunisia* (New York: Cambridge University Press, 1983), p. 56.

4. James Jameson, *Report on the Epidemic Cholera Morbus as it Visited the Territories Subject to the Presidency of Bengal, in the Years 1817, 1818 and 1819* (Calcutta, 1820), p. 116, quoted in Seema Alavi, *Islam and Healing. Loss and Recovery of an Indo-Muslim Medical Tradition 1600–1900* (New York: Palgrave Macmillan, 2008), p. 114.

5. *Bijiexian zhi* (1879) 7: 9a, quoted in Carol Benedict, *Bubonic Plague in Nineteenth century China* (Stanford, CA: Stanford University Press, 1996), p. 117.

CHAPTER 7

Occupational and Environmental Hazards

At the beginning of the nineteenth century, both the natural and built environment was full of hazards to health. People were at risk of injury from natural disasters, extreme weather, and wild animals. In some cultures, supernatural beings living in wild places caused disease. In all medical systems, temperature and humidity were believed to affect the normal functioning of the body, so certain climates and the changing seasons left the body susceptible to poor health. Occupations brought their own risks of injury from tools and machines or from exposure to damaging dust and chemicals.

Over the century, global travel, the expansion of cities, and the development of industry added to the numbers of people exposed to injury or illness. Settlers struggled to survive in unfamiliar climates and when exposed to new diseases. The growing population of towns and cities faced diseases that spread through the urban environment, and the expanding industrial workforce was at risk of injury from machines and chemicals used in manufacturing processes. As an understanding of the potential dangers of the workplace emerged, governments began to fight back, introducing regulations to protect workers' health.

NATURAL HAZARDS

In the nineteenth century, the natural world was full of potential danger. Around the world, farmers and people foraging for wild foods were at risk of encounters with wild animals. Large animals such as lions, bears, and elephants claimed some victims, but far more people died from the bites of poisonous snakes and insects such as scorpions and spiders. Even more suffered from diseases carried by insect vectors, including malaria and yellow fever.

Human populations were at risk from natural disasters. The eruption of the volcano Krakatoa in Indonesia in 1883 killed at least 30,000 people and disrupted weather patterns around the world for several years. In 1854, over 10,000 people died in a series of earthquakes in Japan. Although such events were dramatic, they affected relatively few people. Unusual patterns of weather—abnormally wet or dry seasons— affected far greater numbers by disrupting farming. Both droughts and floods could lead to famines. Lesthoto in Southern Africa, for example, suffered from serious droughts in every decade of the nineteenth century. These were always followed by famine, because food production was reduced and large amounts of food could not be transported into the region to make up the shortfall. Famines also arose in

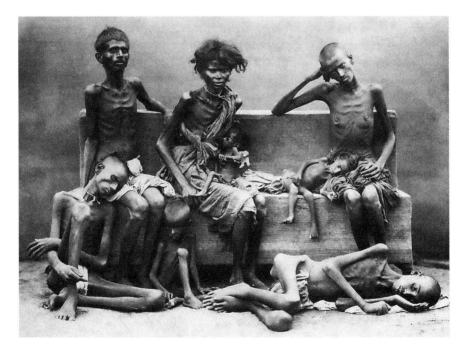

In 1876, a severe drought and crop failures resulted in a famine across southern India. Over five million people perished as a result, as the British government continued to export grain and did little to support the local population. (Sean Sexton Collection/Corbis)

the aftermath of conflicts over land and resources. The Boer people in South Africa, the descendants of Dutch settlers, fought indigenous tribes for access to farming land, killing cattle and burning crops to force them to move away.

Developments across the nineteenth century both ameliorated and exacerbated the impact of famine. Improved farming methods meant that famines became rare in Europe and North America. The last European famine occurred in Finland in 1866, when cold and wet weather led to crop failures. Global trading networks and improved transportation allowed governments to buy and ship foods into famine areas. However, in the Madras famine in India in 1877, the situation was made worse because local farmers grew grain for export: even when large numbers were starving, food continued to be shipped out to the world market.

HEALTH AND THE NATURAL ENVIRONMENT

Climate and landscapes also posed a risk to health. In all the major systems of medical knowledge—Chinese, ayurvedic, Western, and unani medicine—the body was seen as constantly interacting with the environment. Consequently, environments had a fundamental role in maintaining health and causing disease. Each medical system understood this interaction in different ways, although they identified similar factors—heat, cold, and moisture—as the main risks to health.

Environment and Chinese Medicine

In Chinese medicine, health was the product of the smooth flow and functioning of the body's *qi*: blockages or stagnation of *qi* caused disease. Disruption to the body's *qi* was often the result of eating the wrong sort of diet or an irregular lifestyle, but *qi* was also affected by six external factors—heat, cold, damp, wind, dryness, and summer heat. In warm weather, *qi* moved toward the surface of the body; in winter, it became sluggish and dormant. Thus certain diseases tended to appear at different seasons—cold diseases in winter, and hot complaints in summer.

Diseases caused by different environmental factors had their own particular characteristics. Wind diseases appeared suddenly and produced symptoms in the upper part of the body, such as shaking of the head and itching. Cold diseases were associated with feeling chilly, with excretions such as a runny nose and the stagnation of body fluids, causing pain. Damp diseases were associated with exposure to moisture from wearing wet clothes, living in damp conditions, or periods of rainy weather. Sufferers felt heavy and stiff and experienced pains in the joints, nausea, and lack of appetite. Heat diseases such as fevers were caused by exposure to sun and high temperature. In Chinese medicine, not everyone reacted in the same way to the same external factors. *Yang* helped to keep the body warm from within, and individuals with little *yang* were therefore more prone to developing cold diseases.

Pestilential or noxious *qi* was associated with environmental conditions, but there was some debate over its origins. According to one school of thought, the pestilential *qi* responsible for plague was believed to arise from the earth, finding its way to the surface through rat burrows. Other doctors claimed pestilential *qi* was generated from filthy conditions. Flies were attracted to *qi* arising from filth, hence filth and flies were present during outbreaks of disease. Some practitioners suggested that pestilential *qi* appeared spontaneously but only became active when combined with other environmental factors such as filth, warm air, or changes in the seasons.

Environment and Ayurvedic Medicine

In ayurvedic medicine the body was seen as a microcosm of the world. The three *doṣa*—*kapha*, *vāta*, and *pitta*, the fundamental factors or substances determining health—were made up of the same basic elements—ether, air, earth, fire, and water—as the rest of the world. The climate and environment thus affected the bodies of inhabitants. People living in moist, swampy areas near rivers and jungles had soft, fleshy bodies and suffered from diseases associated with *kapha* and *vāta*. In dry areas, with little vegetation and hot, dry winds, the people had thin, strong bodies. Travelers moving between areas of different climate had to take care to adjust their bodies to the new conditions by managing their diet and patterns of sleep and work.

Seasonal changes in temperature caused the *doṣas* to increase and decrease. If not countered by diet, drink, dress, behavior, and medicines appropriate to the season, this natural variation in the level of *doṣas* could become extreme, and tip over into illness. *Sushruta*, the author of one of the classic texts of ayurvedic medicine, recognized categories of disease associated with the seasons. In spring, *kapha* began to accumulate and was removed by drugs to induce vomiting. To stay healthy, diet should consist of light, digestible foods such as barley and wheat. Heavy, oily foods were to be avoided. People should take exercise and bathe in cool water. During summer, *kapha* decreased and *vāta* increased. To maintain a balance within the body, people should eat cold and bitter foods, wear light clothes, bathe in cold water, and avoid physical exertion. In winter, when the weather was cold, heat moved into the center of the body. In cold weather, the body was better able to digest rich foods, such as meats, oil, and sweets. Ayurvedic texts advised against eating light foods that increased the *vāta doṣa*. People should use hot water for washing, stay in warm rooms, and massage the head with oil.

Environment and Unani Medicine

In unani medicine, environment played a crucial role in determining health and illness. Health was a reflection of a balance of four fluids or humors (*akhlat*) within the body. These were associated with four qualities—hot, cold, wet, and dry—and the four elements—earth, air, fire, and water. Blood, for example, was hot and wet and associated with air; bile was hot and dry and linked to fire. Climate was one of the six external factors that acted on the internal balance and thus played a crucial part in maintaining health and in causing disease. Classic unani texts stressed the effects of wind, heat, cold, and moisture on the body and on health. Living in a hot climate encouraged the production of the hot humors within the body, producing diseases such as fevers. Exposure to cold increased the production of phlegm and black bile, leading to respiratory illnesses.

Environment and Western Medicine

Although Western practitioners developed a scientific understanding of the body in the early decades of the nineteenth century, older ideas about health and the environment, based on humoral medicine, coexisted with these newer ideas. Practitioners maintained a belief that environmental factors were intimately linked to body function, and thus to health and disease.

Temperate climates, without extremes of temperature, in Europe and the Americas were essentially healthy, but reckless behavior could still put the body at risk. Engaging in physical activity on a warm day then drinking cold water, or moving from an overheated room to the cold air outside without putting on warm clothes, was believed to bring on fevers and inflammation. During the early nineteenth century, doctors warned of the risks of wearing thin, fashionable silk and cotton clothing and extolled the benefits of warm wool and flannel garments. They were also concerned about the quality of air. Cool, clean, moving air, found in the countryside, was good for health; but the warm stuffy air found in homes and public buildings, heated by fires and candles and full of the products of respiration, was unhealthy.

Europeans faced much greater risks to their health when they moved from a familiar temperate climate to warmer tropical areas in Asian and African colonies. Heat was believed to affect the blood and the liver, producing a wide variety of conditions from acute fevers and dysentery to nervous disorders and chronic weakness. A combination of warmth and moisture was even more dangerous. Jungles, rivers, ponds and swampy areas in hot climates generated "miasma" or bad airs that caused fevers. These could be fatal and caused misery to travelers. One settler in the southern United States described how he "had the shakes until I was shook pretty near out of myself. I got so I did not have the strength to shake any longer: just lay and shivered outside and was burning up inside. Oh so thirsty! I felt as if I could lie and let a good sized spring branch run right into my mouth."[1] It was not until the end of the century that these fevers were recognized as attacks of malaria, spread by mosquitos that bred in warm, stagnant water. In some areas, winds were also a risk to health. Seasonal hot winds were particularly feared, such as the dust-laden *simoon* of North Africa, or the *julo* or *badé sumoon* of India that was reputed to kill. Even if settlers survived the heat, fevers, and wind, they still could not escape the deleterious effects of foreign climates: the children born to settler parents were weak and prone to illness.

Unhealthy environments could be improved by agriculture. Initially, cutting trees and leaving them to rot down added to the amounts of miasma, but once planted with crops, the air became clear and healthy. Draining swamps helped to get rid of miasmas. Planting trees, especially varieties of eucalyptus, was recommended as a means of removing moisture from swampy, saturated soils and releasing it into the air.

The climate of particular areas produced specific local forms of disease. Fevers were common diseases in Europe and the Americas, but in India their symptoms were particularly violent and they did not respond to the usual treatments. As a result, doctors named diseases after their location, such as "Bengal fever" found in northeastern India. Local practitioners used this geographical specificity to claim a special competence to treat local diseases. Archibald Smith, a Scottish doctor working in Peru, engaged in a debate with José Manuel Valdés, a local practitioner, over the merits of bleeding in the treatment of dysentery. Smith claimed that bloodletting was unsuitable for patients from coastal cities, but could be used on the strong indigenous people of the Andes. Valdés was scornful of Smith's knowledge, claiming that although Andean people could resist the cold and carry out hard physical labor, their constitutions were naturally weak and they could not bear such strong therapies.

Coping with Unhealthy Climates

In the early nineteenth century, doctors were optimistic that settlers could adapt to their new surroundings through a process of "seasoning" or acclimatization. New arrivals should arrive in the coolest season, when the climate was similar to that of their homeland, and move into hotter and wetter areas very slowly. Justus Post, who moved from Vermont to the Mississippi Valley in the 1810s, warned:

> Emigrations to this or any other country should be made in the fall ... otherwise the arrival would be made in the heat of summer, when even the fatigues of travelling in the heat of the sun would be sufficient to produce disease. You must not place your heart on a farm at the mouth of the Ohio [River] ... —you must come to that point by degrees—it is in too low a latitude (37°) for a man of 45° north to strike the first dash—you will find the country above the Missouri to suit you and the people of your country best.[2]

As part of becoming acclimatized, newcomers expected to suffer from one or more bouts of fever, after which their bodies were able to come to terms with the new environment. To help the process, settlers were advised to eat a bland diet, avoid raw vegetables, get regular hours of sleep, and avoid alcohol. Frequent doses of quinine helped to ward off fever.

By the middle of the century, such optimism had evaporated. Doctors became convinced that different races were adapted to living in particular climates. The ill health suffered by Europeans settling in the tropics came about because their bodies were naturally adapted to a temperate climate. The bodies of people indigenous to tropical regions, such as African slaves and Indian laborers, were physiologically different from whites. A slave of African descent was able to tolerate heat because:

> His head is protected from the rays of a vertical sun by a dense mat of woolly hair, wholly impervious to its fiercest heats, while his entire surface, studded with innumerable sebaceous glands, forming a complete excretory system, relieves him from all those climatic influences so fatal, under the same circumstances, to the sensitive and highly organized

white man. Instead of seeking to shelter himself from the burning sun of the tropics, he courts it, enjoys it, delights in its fiercest heats.[3]

It was widely believed that black people were immune to the fevers associated with warm climates but were more susceptible to diseases associated with unfamiliar cold weather. Thus they suffered from high rates of respiratory infections in winter. In retrospect, some African slaves had a degree of genetic immunity to malaria, but many had to go through the same "seasoning" to develop tolerance of the local strains of the disease as white settlers. Slaves in the West Indies and southern United States, and Indian laborers on plantations in Indonesia, actually suffered from much the same diseases as Europeans—malaria, fevers, dysentery, and cholera.

Now practitioners recommended that the best way for Europeans to survive in hot climates was to limit their exposure to dangerous heat and miasma. In the southern United States, settlers avoided living and working on low-lying swampy land, preferring to set up their new homes on drier slopes. In summer, plantation owners moved away from their mansions to the sea or to the hills, where the climate was cooler and they could enjoy fresh breezes. They were unconsciously imitating Native American people living around the Mississippi who moved away from rivers during the summer season. In India, British administrators and soldiers were periodically moved to "hill stations" where, it was hoped, the more agreeable climate would counteract the effects of the heat during the rest of the year. Even this was not sufficient to protect the health of children, and many were sent home to attend schools in Europe.

In an effort to work out which areas were suitable for European settlement, doctors gathered data on a wide range of environmental factors in the new colonies. Almost every aspect of the landscape was relevant to the issue. Investigators exhaustively described:

> [T]he surface and elevation of the ground, the stratification and composition of the soil, the supply and quantity of the water, the extent of marshes and wet ground, the progress of drainage; the nature and amounts of the products of the land; the condition, increase or decrease, and prevalent diseases of the animals maintained thereon; together with periodical reports of the temperature, pressure, humidity, motion and electricity of the atmosphere.[4]

Another strategy was to adapt the European lifestyle to a new context. John Dudgeon, a Scottish doctor who lived and worked in China, joked: "Europeans come to China, and they eat, and they drink, and they eat, and then they die, and afterwards wire home that the climate killed them."[5] A typical European diet included plenty of meat and alcohol. Both of these foodstuffs were believed to heat the body and predispose it to fevers. Dudgeon argued that Europeans should follow the example of the Chinese people and eat a diet of beans, rice, and vegetables, with no meat or alcohol. Other doctors disagreed; different diets were suited to different races. European settlers should modify their diet, eating less meat and more vegetables, rather than make radical changes. They should also adapt their clothing and wear light, loose garments rather than the usual heavy European dress, and rest during the heat of the day. Regular bloodletting, especially at the change of seasons, helped to keep the body healthy.

The connection between environment and disease was not broken until the end of the century, when doctors working in the new field of tropical medicine began to identify the organisms responsible for the diseases previously linked to the climates of India and Africa. In 1898, Ronald Ross proved that malaria was not the result of miasma, but was caused by a parasite spread by mosquitoes. In 1900, the transmission routes of elephantiasis and of yellow fever were also described. As a result, the diseases of tropical regions were no longer seen as an inevitable consequence of living in hot climates, but were a set of illnesses that could be prevented by appropriate sanitary measures.

Environment and Folk Medicine

Folk medicine did not have explanations for how aspects of the natural world influenced the internal functions of the body, but indigenous people in Africa and America still identified risks to health originating in their environment, both natural and supernatural. Native American peoples believed that the world was full of spirits, many of which could cause disease if not shown respect. A fisher who wasted his catch or a hunter who did not ask the spirits for permission to kill animals by praying or making ritual offerings might be struck down with illness. In southern Africa, Zulu people refused to go into forests that were reputed to be inhabited by witches. As forests were inhabited by tsetse flies, this taboo provided protection against sleeping sickness.

People also had cultural practices that helped to protect against environmental disease. Native American people moved away from rivers in the summer, when mosquitoes were prevalent. Zulu people built their settlements well away from swampy ground. Their houses had floors made of cow dung and smoky fires were used for cooking; both these practices helped to repel insects. Houses that became infested with insects were burned. The people disposed of excrement in pits in the ground well away from living quarters, or covered it with boiling water.

ENVIRONMENTAL CURES

While some environments produced disease, in every culture, particular climates and natural products were used to heal the body. A wide variety of natural substances were used in therapy. Mud and earths were collected to make poultices to treat injuries and skin complaints, and many minerals had medicinal uses. Plants formed the main source of drugs in every culture. Hot springs and waters impregnated with minerals had long been used as a form of therapy by indigenous peoples in Africa and the Americas; this is the origin of the place name "Indian Springs" still found in North America. Mineral waters were believed to be particularly effective in curing diseases of the liver—a frequent problem in hot climates—and settlers bathed in the water of mineral springs used by local peoples. On the island of Guadeloupe in the Caribbean, thermal mineral springs traditionally used by indigenous peoples became sites for hydropathic bathing establishments for

Bathing in water naturally impregnated with minerals was believed to cure diseases and to improve health and well-being. These patients bathing in water from a sulphur spring might have been seeking relief from skin diseases or rheumatism. (Rykoff Collection/Corbis)

settlers. There, soldiers and administrators spent time recovering their health by drinking and bathing in the waters. Mineral waters were also used in nineteenth-century Europe to treat a variety of ailments, especially skin complaints. Natural springs became centers for spa towns—therapeutic resorts where the sick came to drink and bathe.

European and American people, wealthy enough to be able to travel freely over long distances, sought out healthy climates to cure their ailments. Coastal resorts were initially built to allow the sick to bathe in saltwater and to breathe sea air. Over time, they became sites primarily for leisure, although they never entirely lost their therapeutic identity. A seaside holiday was a chance to take in sea air and provided a chance to relax and "recharge the batteries." Living in a sunny, dry, airy environment was recommended as a cure for tuberculosis. Sanatoria were set up throughout the world in appropriate situations—on the coasts of California, on Pacific islands, and on European mountains where the resinous smell given off by pine trees was believed to add to the therapeutic qualities of the air.

HEALTH AND THE URBAN ENVIRONMENT

Around the globe, towns and cities were seen as inherently unhealthy. In Western medicine, dirt was seen as a direct or indirect cause of disease, and nineteenth-century cities were filthy places. Huge amounts of refuse were generated by homes and businesses. In small communities with a fairly static population and active local government, these could be removed efficiently. Sweepers carted away street and household refuse from built-up areas. Privies and cesspools were emptied by night-soil men and the contents used as manure on nearby fields. However, when urban populations expanded rapidly, these mechanisms broke down. There was too much excrement to use on the land, and old rubbish dumps were quickly filled. Householders began to deposit their refuse on the streets, in empty spaces, and in rivers, often polluting water supplies. In the early part of the century, doctors warned that rotting refuse generated miasmas that caused fevers and other diseases; by the end of the century, they understood that dirt helped to spread infections via contaminated water or dirty living conditions.

City dwellers were also exposed to the danger of air pollution. Coal was used to fuel industrial processes (tall factory chimneys dominated the skyline of many towns) and to heat homes. The resulting smoke pollution was visible to all; it blocked out sunlight, so that plants could not grow, and children developed rickets. The air of towns smelled of smoke, and people's eyes stung from the sulfur released from the coal. Every surface became coated with particles of soot, so much so that the industrial north of England was nicknamed "the Black Country." Constant exposure to smoke pollution increased deaths from respiratory diseases; bronchitis was the most common cause of death in industrial areas in the late nineteenth century. Even more dangerous was smog, when smoke and fog combined to make a dense, choking atmosphere, sometimes lasting for days. In Britain, such smog was called a "pea-souper" after a type of thick, yellowish soup. During periods of smog, the numbers of traffic accidents rose and deaths from respiratory complaints rocketed.

Certain spaces within cities were associated with pollution and disease, especially graveyards. As the population of urban areas expanded, so did the numbers of bodies requiring burial within churches or their adjoining cemeteries. These became overcrowded, with new bodies crammed into shallow graves on top of older burials. The custom of visiting the graves of recently deceased relatives so as to stay close to the body was increasingly seen as a health hazard.

In the second half of the century, urban authorities throughout Europe and the Americas began to tackle the health hazards associated with urban life. Reformed systems of street sweeping and refuse collection reduced the amount of rubbish on the streets. New sewer systems removed excrement beyond the city limits for processing and disposal. Large cemeteries were built away from town centers, and from the 1880s, a growing number of people chose to have their bodies cremated after death. City authorities could do little to reduce smoke pollution; burning coal was vital to many industries, and factory owners were reluctant to take any measures that might reduce the efficiency of their operations. Smog and smoke remained health hazards for urban dwellers well into the twentieth century.

Other cities around the world were equally filthy, but local doctors did not necessarily see this as a source of ill health. Western observers complained of the filthy conditions in Chinese cities, and were surprised that the inhabitants nevertheless seemed to be healthy. Although some Chinese practitioners believed that filth was associated with pestilential *qi* and disease, the inhabitants of Chinese cities were apparently fairly tolerant of dirt. Indeed, they valued excrement as a fertilizer and collected it from homes and the streets to sell to local peasant farmers. They probably escaped some urban diseases through the practice of treating water to make it pleasant to drink. Water collected from wells and rivers was stored for some days so that dirt or sediment collected in the bottom of the vessel. It was then treated with alum (potassium aluminum sulfate) to make it clear and was boiled before use.

OCCUPATIONAL HAZARDS

In addition to the hazards posed by the natural world and the built environment, workplaces brought their own sets of dangers. In every culture, certain occupations were known to carry risks.

Agricultural Hazards

By far the most common set of dangers was those associated with agriculture. Subsistence farmers, growing crops to feed themselves and perhaps to trade, used simple tools. Even so, they received cuts, bruises, or even broken bones from sickles, axes, and plows. Animals were an essential part of many farms: they provided meat and milk and the motive force to pull carts or plows. But even well-trained animals could be dangerous and unpredictable; riders fell from horses and camels, workers were trampled by cattle and run over by carts. Where farmers lived in close proximity to their animals, they were likely to pick up parasites and diseases such as anthrax.

The risks of injury increased when farming became industrialized. Where farmers could sell to a big market, they began to use machinery to till the soil and raise crops. Steam engines or "traction engines" were used on large farms in Europe and North America to pull plows and run threshing machines. Smaller machines, such as reapers to cut grain crops and mills to process vegetables, were powered by horses. Both large and small machines presented new dangers as it was all too easy for fingers, hands, or whole limbs to be caught in the moving parts and cut or torn off.

In addition, agricultural workers suffered from spending long hours outdoors. In cold climates, a large proportion of farm laborers developed chronic ear infections that led to deafness. Workers on rice, cotton, rubber, and coffee plantations in tropical parts of Asia and Africa endured very poor health. Many of these plantations were worked by indentured laborers from India, who signed up for a period of two or three years. Little money or attention was given to building good living quarters for them. Workers were packed into huts or barracks, working long hours with few rest periods. They suffered from high rates of tuberculosis, from cholera and dysentery spread through contaminated water supplies, from parasitic infections such as hookworm picked up from the damp soil, and from deficiency diseases such as beri-beri from a poor diet. Not surprisingly, mortality rates were high.

Industrial Hazards

Diseases and injuries were known to be associated with particular occupations throughout the nineteenth century. The first occupational disease, a form of cancer found among chimney sweeps, was identified as early as 1775. Workplace hazards to life and health were found not only in the industrialized West. Mining for minerals, metals, coal, and precious stones took place around the world. Regardless of the depth of the mines, and whether hand tools or cutting machines were used, all miners faced the risk of lung disease from inhaling dust. "Miner's lung" was first recorded in Europe in the early 1830s. Workers developed a chronic cough, breathlessness, and chest pains, and many died. The disease was characterized by the black phlegm coughed up by victims, full of particles of dust. Postmortem examinations revealed the damage.

> When cut into, both lungs presented one uniform black carbonaceous colour, pervading every part of their substance. The right lung was much disorganised, and exhibited in its upper and middle lobes several large irregular cavities ... The cavities contained a good deal of fluid, which, as well as the walls of the cavities, partook of the same black colour.[6]

While "black lung" was associated with miners, especially coal miners, many other groups of workers suffered from similar illnesses. Stone masons, bakers, and textile workers all labored in dusty conditions and experienced high death rates from respiratory illnesses. Workers in the metal industries breathed in dust and grit from machines used for sharpening and grinding. Many went blind from small particles of metal that became lodged in their eyes.

Industries exposed workers to a variety of toxic substances. Women working in match factories developed "phossy jaw," a disease that ate away at the bones of the face due to contact with phosphorus. Mercury compounds, used in the hat and fur trades and in silver mines as an agent to separate metal from ore, caused damage to the nerves. One of the most common occupational diseases was lead poisoning. Lead was used in many manufactured goods such as batteries and paint. Workers suffered from "lead colic"—an acute form of poisoning that caused severe stomach pains and seizures. Those who came into contact with lead over long periods suffered chronic poisoning that damaged the kidneys and blood, and left them unable to fight off infections.

Many workers employed in occupations requiring physical strength, from farmers to builders, coal miners, dockworkers, and general laborers suffered from injuries. They were crushed by falling objects. Strenuous physical effort resulted in hernias, when part of the internal organs bulged through the muscular wall of the abdomen. Trusses—special bandages to support the injury—allowed sufferers to continue to work.

OCCUPATIONAL HEALTH

Tracing out the links between diseases and occupations was far from straightforward. Workers often developed symptoms years after exposure to toxins. Workers handling the same chemicals might fall ill after a short time or remain unaffected for long periods. Nevertheless, by the end of the century, doctors in the West had described many of the most common industrial hazards, and governments—particularly those in Europe—had begun to pass legislation to limit the dangers. Regulation had little effect, however. Many of the new laws advised factory owners to take action but did not require them to install ventilation or provide special clothing. Workers did not always welcome measures to protect their health. Safety goggles, gloves, or masks might protect their eyes, hands, and lungs, but they were uncomfortable to wear for long periods and slowed the pace at which they could work and thus reduced their wages. Given the lack of effective treatment for most occupational illnesses, many workers chose to take the risk and to earn high wages in dangerous workplaces for a limited time, then change jobs if they became ill.

NOTES

1. James F. Keefe and Lynn Morrow, eds., *A Connecticut Yankee on the Frontier Ozarks: The Writings of Theodore Pease Russell* (Columbia: University of Missouri Press, 1988), pp. 122–123, quoted in Conevery Bolton Valenčius, *The Health of the Country: How American Settlers Understood Themselves and Their Land* (New York: Basic Books, 2002), p. 83.

2. Letter from Justus Post to John Post, August 23, 1816, quoted in Valenčius, *The Health of the Country*, p. 32.

3. John H. Van Evrie, *Negroes and Negro "Slavery"* (New York, 1861), p. 256, quoted in Todd L. Savitt, "Black Health on the Plantation: Masters, Slaves, and Physicians," in *Sickness and Health in America: Readings in the History of Medicine and Public Health*, ed. Judith Walzer Leavitt and Ronald L. Numbers (Madison: University of Wisconsin Press, 1978), p. 316.

4. James Martin, *The Influence of Tropical Climates on European Constitutions* (London, 1856), p. 99, quoted in David Arnold, *Colonizing the Body: State Medicine and Epidemic Disease in Nineteenth-Century India* (Berkeley: University of California Press, 1993), p. 27.

5. John Dudgeon, *The Diseases of China, Their Causes, Conditions and Prevalence, Contrasted with Those of Europe* (Glasgow, 1877), p. 36, quoted in Shang-Jen Li, "Discovering 'The Secrets of a Long and Healthy Life': John Dudgeon on Chinese Hygiene," *Social History of Medicine* 23 (2009), p. 28.

6. James Gregory, "Case of Peculiar Black Infiltration of the Whole Lungs, Resembling Melanosis," *Edinburgh Medical and Surgical Journal* 36 (1831), pp. 389–394, quoted in Alan Derickson, *Black Lung: Anatomy of a Public Health Disaster* (Ithaca, NY: Cornell University Press, 1998), p. 5.

CHAPTER 8

Surgery, Dentistry, Orthopedics

In the present day, surgery is a specialist branch of medicine, concerned with repairing injuries to the body and treating disease by the removal of malfunctioning tissues. Surgeons enjoy high status within the medical profession and work exclusively in hospitals. This modern form of surgery emerged in the nineteenth century in Europe and North America. In 1800, in many medical cultures, manual procedures were carried out by groups of healers (called surgeons in the West but with a variety of names in non-Western cultures). They treated complaints on the outside of the body—injuries, skin diseases, and abscesses—and performed various procedures aimed at curing internal diseases, such as bloodletting and acupuncture. A few carried out major operations, such as the removal of bladder stones, but only as a last resort when patients' lives were in danger.

While these forms of surgical practice continued in non-Western cultures throughout the nineteenth century, in Europe and North America, surgery underwent a revolution. Scientific medicine saw illness arising from some problem within a particular organ, and it allowed practitioners to develop new procedures to treat illness by the removal of diseased tissue. The discovery of anesthetics and the development of antiseptics enhanced these developments, ensuring greater levels of success. As a result, surgery moved onto center stage in medicine and surgeons became medical heroes, no longer dealing with minor complaints but treating serious, acute disease.

SURGERY OUTSIDE THE WEST

Surgical Practitioners

In many (although not all) cultures, medical practice was divided between healers, who dealt with internal diseases, and surgical practitioners, who treated injuries and ailments that affected the surface of the body. In Chinese, unani, and ayurvedic medicine, learned practitioners, trained in medical theory, diagnosed disease and prescribed medicines and other therapies. They regarded any form of manual work as demeaning to their status as learned men, and left the application of mechanical treatment to surgical healers. In unani medicine, for example, bloodletting might be prescribed by a learned *hakim*, but because touching the patient's body (except to take the pulse) was not appropriate behavior for an elite practitioner, the bloodletting was performed by a *jarrāh*—a surgical practitioner. In systems of folk medicine, there was no distinction between learned and surgical practitioners. Many healers diagnosed, prescribed, and carried out surgical treatments, although some, such as diviners and spiritual healers, did not perform manual therapies.

Surgical practitioners could specialize in a single form of treatment or offer a range of therapies. In Costa Rica, for example, most practitioners were barber-surgeons or bloodletters (*sangradores*). (At first glance, this seems an odd combination of occupations, but both barbering and bloodletting required the use of sharp instruments.) Bloodletting was a popular therapy and was the mainstay of their work, but some practitioners also lanced abscesses, extracted teeth, cauterized wounds, and practiced bonesetting. A few forms of surgical therapy were highly specialized. The removal of bladder stones, small masses of material that formed in the urine and irritated the bladder, was a very dangerous operation requiring great skill. The condition was relatively rare and was treated by a small number of specialist itinerant practitioners, who traveled over large areas to treat patients.

Surgical practitioners acquired their skills and knowledge by observing the work of experienced practitioners and learned to practice under their supervision. In Costa Rica, they were called *empíricos* (a term with the same root as the English word "empirical"), reflecting the importance of experience and observation, rather than theory, in their practice. Although surgical practitioners were distinguished by their mechanical skills, many often possessed some basic knowledge of medical theory. In China, acupuncture was prescribed by a learned doctor but was carried out by healers skilled in the techniques of inserting the needles and with some understanding of the actions of *qi* and a knowledge of the points to use in order to achieve the desired effect.

Practitioners carrying out surgical procedures had an uneasy relationship with practitioners formally trained in medical theory. Learned physicians frequently complained that surgical practitioners did not confine their practice to the exterior of the body but attempted to take over their role by diagnosing illness and prescribing treatment. Given their limited understanding of how the body worked, this often had disastrous results. In many places, physicians tried to impose some form of regulation on surgical practitioners, by requiring them to have evidence of their training and limiting their practice to manual procedures. These efforts rarely succeeded. Usually, surgical healers who dealt with simple cases were ignored or tolerated by the local authorities, unless their practices were dangerous to patients. In times of emergency, such as during epidemics, local governments sometimes employed surgical healers to treat patients under the supervision of formally qualified practitioners.

SURGICAL PRACTICE

Surgical practitioners provided a wide range of therapies. These included manual procedures to treat injuries, by cleaning and closing wounds and setting broken and dislocated limbs. They cured lesions on the exterior of the body, lancing or applying medicines and poultices to swellings, and carried out therapies such as bloodletting, cautery, or acupuncture to treat internal complaints. Finally, some surgical practitioners dealt with eye diseases, operated for stones in the bladder, removed teeth, and carried out smallpox inoculation and later vaccination

Wounds and Broken Bones

When confronted by wounds to the skin and flesh, surgical healers around the world used broadly similar treatments. They first cleaned the injury by washing it using plain water or water in which herbs had been boiled, or by sucking to remove any blood and dirt. Various substances were applied to stop bleeding, including spider's webs, the spores of puffballs and other fungi, and the roots and leaves of plants. Injuries were then bandaged with cloth or bark. If the wound was serious, practitioners in some cultures closed it by stitching the skin using sutures made of plant fiber or animal hair. In Africa, travelers described how biting ants were used to close a wound. The insects were encouraged to clamp their jaws over the edges of the skin and then the ant's body was twisted off, leaving the mouthparts in place.

A range of medicines were used to help healing. Minor wounds were allowed to heal spontaneously, but in the case of deep or complex injuries, practitioners often deliberately tried to induce infection as the formation of pus was seen as a necessary part of the healing process. Healers tried to prevent the surface of the wound from healing, while infection remained within the body. Ideally, wounds should heal from the bottom upward to achieve a complete cure. To encourage this, Native American healers blew a powder made from roots into wounds. In other cultures, healers prevented wounds from closing by inserting small pieces of reed, bark, or cloth into the flesh. This technique was particularly important in cases in which arrows or bullets remained in the body. If the object was close to the surface, it was removed using a knife or a magnet. If it was out of reach of instruments, healers induced infection to push the foreign object out of the wound.

In some cultures, medical theories were used to guide what medicines should be used in the treatment of injuries. In unani medicine, the treatment of wounds drew on the principle of opposites. Weeping wounds should be treated with dry medicines. The wound should be "pressed so that the fluids ooze out. Then medicine should be applied on the wound with cotton wool wrapped on a slim rod ... it should be allowed to dry ... [then] medical ointment [*marham*] mixed with egg white is put on it. The wound should be washed with water boiled with fruits and herbs like dried pomegranate."[1]

Broken or dislocated bones were treated using very similar techniques around the world. The damaged limb was straightened and massaged so that the ends of the bones moved back toward their normal alignment and then held in place with bandages and splints made of thin strips of wood or bones. In southern Africa, broken bones were supported with a cast made of clay, and in North Africa, gypsum plaster was used to make a cast. Medicines were used to help the healing process. Poultices or ointments were applied to help the bones to heal. In southern Africa, herbal medicines were rubbed into incisions above the damage to encourage the ends of the bone to unite.

Skin Diseases and Abscesses

Skin conditions such as rashes and insect bites were treated with soothing applications. Native American peoples used bear's oil to prevent and to cure a variety of skin diseases. The rash caused by contact with poison ivy was treated with bruised leaves applied directly to the skin or with a lotion made from leaves boiled in water. Localized infections that produced swellings called boils or abscesses were treated with hot poultices. The heat was soothing, and the poultice encouraged the abscess to burst, letting the pus flow out. Alternatively, healers cut open the swelling or applied a caustic substance to make it burst. Ayurvedic texts applied medical theory to direct the best course of treatment. As tumors, boils, and ulcers developed under the skin, they were believed to reflect an imbalance of *doṣas* within the body. Different imbalances produced different types of skin lesion: abscesses caused by an excess of *kapha* were white, and with a copious discharge; those associated with *pitta* were yellow and burning. They were treated with a combination of external treatments, such as poultices, and internal medicines to deal with the underlying imbalance within the body.

Bloodletting and Cautery

Bloodletting—removing a controlled amount of blood from the body—was widely practiced around the world. In ayurvedic and unani medicine, the procedure was used to remove bad blood, or excess amounts of blood associated with a range of illnesses. Bloodletting was also used to treat local pain, and as a general tonic. Many people chose to be bled at the end of winter or at the change of seasons to remove "worn out" or stagnant blood. In some forms of folk medicine, such as those practiced in southern Africa, bloodletting was used to remove accumulations of blood that were believed to cause swellings. Only Chinese practitioners rarely used bloodletting. Learned practitioners argued that bloodletting was pointless, as bad and good blood were released at the same time. Patients with too much blood should be treated with medicines to tackle the causes of the excess.

The techniques of bloodletting were very similar across all cultures. Cupping was used to remove small amounts of blood. The skin was scratched or rubbed, then blood was drawn through it using pressure. African folk practitioners applied a vessel such as a cow's horn to the skin and sucked air out through a hole in the narrow end. In India, a glass or pottery vessel was heated and put on the skin. As it cooled, a vacuum formed, drawing out some blood. Small quantities of blood could also be removed using leeches. This technique had several advantages. The operation was relatively painless as when it bit, the leech injected a form of local anesthetic and an anticoagulant. The quantity of blood removed from the body was easily controlled by varying the number of leeches; each would suck out around a table-spoonful of blood, and then drop off. Leeches could be applied to particular parts of the body and they were often used to remove blood around swellings. When a larger amount of blood needed to be removed, in cases of serious internal illness, bloodletters cut open a vein, allowed the blood to flow until a sufficient amount was removed or until the patient fainted, and then applied pressure to stop the bleeding. The site chosen for bloodletting depended on the condition. When treating localized conditions, bloodletters opened a vein close to the site of the problem; so for headaches, blood would be taken from the head. For generalized conditions, such as fever, the practitioner would open a vein at any convenient point, usually on the arm.

Like bloodletting, cautery or localized burning of the skin was used to treat various ailments, including stomach complaints and skin lesions such as ulcers, and to stop bleeding. In unani medicine and in some systems of folk medicine, it was also performed to relieve pain. In North America, indigenous healers used a burning reed, placed over a piece of thin wet leather, to produce a burn. In other tribes, practitioners placed a small piece of burning fungus or plant directly on the skin. In North Africa, surgical practitioners used a hot knife to lightly touch the skin over a painful joint or over the stomach to treat gastric pains.

Acupuncture and Moxibustion

In Chinese medicine, health was the product of a regular, smooth flow of *qi*, and blockages to the flow caused illness. Acupuncture was used to influence the flow of *qi* and cure internal diseases. Practitioners inserted fine needles into the skin along channels running throughout the body. The exact position of the needles stimulated different pathways or organs, and different combinations of points were used to treat conditions including pain, fevers, colic, and headaches.

Chinese medicine also made use of heat to stimulate the movement of *qi*, a process called moxibustion. Small pellets of moxa, dried material from the mugwort plant, were placed on the skin above the channels through which *qi* flowed. They were lit and allowed to burn, producing heat and a small burn or blister. The substance used for the moxa pellets was important—it needed to burn quickly so as to stimulate the body but not to cause serious damage to the skin.

Traditional Surgical Operations

Outside Europe and North America, surgical operations that required deliberately cutting open the body were not a major form of

In many cultures, a group of practitioners specialised in carrying out eye surgery, including operations for cataracts. This image shows an Indian eye surgeon at work, with his instruments and pots of medicines (Wellcome Library)

nineteenth-century medical practice. Although accounts of a range of operations appeared in ancient and medieval Chinese, ayurvedic, and unani texts, the evidence suggests that relatively few were regularly performed. Historians have suggested that these descriptions of operations may have been written to show off the skill and knowledge of the author, rather than to provide a practical guide for surgical practitioners.

In the nineteenth century, operations were carried out for a handful of very serious conditions, when treatment using medicines had failed. Operations to remove cataracts from the eye, and thus preserve sight, were carried out by specialist eye doctors in many cultures. In China, India, and North Africa, they used very similar techniques. A lancet or needle was inserted slowly into the eye, and the damaged lens pressed downward to push it out of the line of vision. In some cases, the lens was pierced to allow the fluid to flow into the eye. While the operation was often successful in restoring some sight, Western travelers reported that many patients later lost their eye to postoperative infections.

Operations on the internal organs were much more dangerous and were performed only as a last resort. Bladder stones caused acute pain and, if they prevented urination, could prove fatal. Patients usually tried taking medicines to break up the stone and allow the pieces to pass out naturally with the urine. Only if this failed were specialist practitioners called in to operate. Ayurvedic texts described how the patient was given alcohol before the procedure to dull the pain. A skilled surgeon located the stone by massaging around the bladder area. He then made a small incision through the abdomen and into

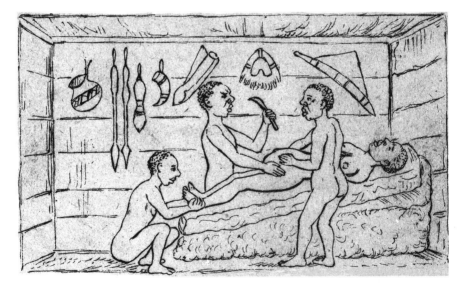

This drawing, made by a European observer in 1879, shows a group of indigenous practitioners in Uganda about to perform a caesarean operation. Although extremely dangerous, the procedure was successful. (Wellcome Library)

the bladder, removing the stone with a hooked instrument. The surgeon had to be very precise in making the incision—cutting into the urethra or uterus caused dangerous complications.

Cesarean sections to save the life of an infant when the mother could not deliver it naturally were attempted only when the mother had died or was close to death. The operation seems to have been performed occasionally in many cultures, but was rarely successful. A handful of nineteenth-century travelers reported seeing cesarean sections carried out by indigenous practitioners in Africa. In 1879, a British traveler witnessed the operation in Uganda in East Africa. He reported that the healer gave the patient alcohol to dull the pain before making the incision. Cautery was used to stop the bleeding and massage to make the uterus contract. The incision was dressed with a paste prepared from roots.[2] Reports of similar operations came from Rwanda in Central Africa.

DEVELOPMENTS IN WESTERN SURGERY

Outside the West, practitioners continued to use this traditional repertoire of procedures during the nineteenth century; by contrast, in Europe and North America, surgery was revolutionized, going from a set of techniques to deal with a limited number of fairly minor conditions to procedures capable of treating a large number of serious or life-threatening diseases. In 1800, surgeons in the West performed procedures similar to those performed in the rest of the world: they treated injuries, dealt with diseases affecting the surface of the body, and let blood. They operated on cataracts in the eye and for bladder stones. Unlike non-Western surgical practitioners, they also routinely amputated diseased and damaged limbs.

In the early part of the century, the success of all surgical procedures was limited by pain, blood loss, shock, and infection. Even simple operations had a high mortality rate, and all were traumatic for the patient. Fanny Burney, the English novelist, recorded the experience of undergoing a 20-minute operation for breast cancer in 1811. The opium and alcohol she was given to reduce the pain clearly had only a limited effect.

> When the dreadful steel was plunged into the breast—cutting through veins—arteries—flesh—nerves—I needed no injunctions to restrain my cries. I began a scream that lasted unintermittingly [*sic*] during the whole time of the incision ... when again I felt the instrument—describing a curve—cutting against the grain ... while the flesh resisted ... I thought I must have expired.[3]

The early decades of the century saw a number of improvements in surgical techniques. The treatment of broken limbs was helped by the development of bandages impregnated with plaster of Paris to make a secure and durable cast. Better tourniquets helped to reduce blood loss in cases of serious injury or during amputations. Survival rates after amputation increased as surgeons reduced blood loss and shock by operating more quickly. Amputation of the leg at the hip took around 20 minutes at the beginning of the century; by the 1830s, James Syme, a London surgeon, performed the same operation in 90 seconds.

New understandings of disease—that illnesses were often localized within one organ or tissue—developed in the early part of the century encouraged Western doctors to explore the possibility of treating these conditions by removing the malfunctioning part of the body. An operation to remove diseased tonsils was first carried out in 1828. Two American physicians Ephraim MacDowell and James Marion Sims pioneered the successful removal of ovarian tumors and the repair of tears in the vagina following childbirth in 1809 and the late 1840s, respectively. Nevertheless, it required a series of breakthroughs in the control of pain and infection before surgery could become a highly successful method of treating disease.

Anesthesia

From the early nineteenth century, practitioners knew that inhaling nitrous oxide (laughing gas) or the fumes from diethyl ether (usually called simply "ether") produced mild euphoria and reduced pain. Doctors had experimented with ether as an anesthetic in the early 1840s, but its use was established by a public demonstration in October 1846, when William Morton, an American dentist, removed a small tumor from the neck of an anesthetized patient. Word quickly spread. Ether anesthetic was used in Paris two months later, and shortly afterward, a leg amputation, the first major operation under anesthesia, was performed in London before an audience of medical students and practitioners. Ether presented a great advance on earlier attempts to control pain. When they breathed the fumes from an ether-soaked cloth, it brought a blessed unconsciousness to the patient. It also made the surgeons' job much easier, as they no longer had to operate on a screaming, struggling patient. The drug was not without its hazards. Ether was highly inflammable, unpleasant to inhale, and caused nausea and vomiting when the anesthetic effect wore off.

Practitioners therefore looked for other chemicals with similar effects. Just one year later, James Young Simpson, a Scottish obstetrician, tried inhaling chloroform, another organic chemical, and passed out. Within days, he began using the drug in his own practice and later published his findings. Chloroform was quickly adopted by European practitioners to ease the pain of childbirth and for surgical operations. Chloroform had the advantage of acting more quickly than ether, and patients did not go through a period of exhilaration before becoming unconscious. On the other hand, a slight overdose of chloroform was highly dangerous, as patients suffered fatal heart attacks. This problem was solved by developing inhalers that precisely controlled the amount of anesthetic given to the patient.

Both ether and chloroform induced general anesthesia. Local anesthetics, which dulled pain in a part of the body while the patient remained conscious, were first used in the 1880s. The numbing effect of chewing leaves of the coca plant had been known for centuries. Cocaine, the chemical responsible for this effect, was isolated in 1859, but not until 1884 was the drug applied to control the pain of eye operations and dental work. However, the problems associated with its use —several patients died, and more became addicted to the drug—meant that it quickly fell out of favor, and local anesthesia was not routinely used until new compounds such as procaine were developed in the early twentieth century.

While anesthesia freed patients from excruciating pain, it was not without controversy. Doctors believed that pain was a natural response to injury and a stimulus to healing, and worried that incisions made under anesthesia would not heal properly. As a result, not all patients received anesthetics. A study of operations conducted in American hospitals in the decade after the introduction of anesthetics showed that men, especially soldiers, black men, and Irishmen, were believed to be able to stand the pain of operations and were less likely to receive anesthetics than women and children. Patients too had their concerns: would surgeons be tempted to carry out unnecessary procedures or experiment with new and unproven techniques on their unconscious subjects? Surgeons were optimistic (to modern eyes, hopelessly overoptimistic) about the benefits of the removal of organs. In the 1870s and 1880s, many women had their healthy ovaries taken out in the hope of curing nervous conditions such as hysteria.

Antisepsis and Asepsis

While anesthetics made operations safer and more bearable, patients were still at risk of developing fatal wound infections after surgery. Surgical wounds were exposed to contamination from many sources. Procedures were carried out in operating theaters, often in front of an audience of medical students, or on hospital wards or in patients' homes. These spaces were clean, but not scrupulously so. Surgeons expected to be spattered with blood during surgery, so they operated wearing old clothes. Often they wore the same coat for many operations. Surgical instruments were wiped or washed, but not sterilized. Sometimes infection became so prevalent that it affected the wounds of every patient in a hospital ward. The only way to deal with these outbreaks was to shut the ward and under-take a thorough cleansing, sometimes even stripping the plaster from the walls.

From the 1840s, some surgeons adopted a "cold water and cleanli-ness" strategy to combat infection, ensuring that instruments, the sur-geons' hands, and the operating area were thoroughly scrubbed before each operation. In 1867, Joseph Lister, a Scottish surgeon, pub-lished the results of using antiseptic techniques—an approach that attempted to kill all germs in and around the wound. Lister's work was based on Louis Pasteur's observations that bacteria were respon-sible for putrefaction. He began to systematically disinfect everything that came into contact with a wound using carbolic acid. Lister experi-mented on cases of compound fractures that routinely became infected. Wounds were cleaned with carbolic acid and dressed with bandages soaked in the chemical. The surgeon's hands and all instruments were disinfected; even the air was disinfected using a fine spray of carbolic. Lister's results were spectacular. Compound fractures healed without infection, avoiding the need for amputation of the limb, and the death rate following amputations fell from 45 percent of all cases to just 15 percent.

Lister's methods were not immediately adopted by all medical prac-titioners. Some doubted whether invisible bacteria were really the cause of infection. Others found that Lister's procedures were difficult to use, and that the carbolic acid disinfectant irritated the skin of sur-geons and their patients. Over the following decades, his techniques were adapted, moving from antisepsis to asepsis (working in a germ-free environment). Operating theaters were redesigned: wooden floors and cabinets gave way to tiled or glass surfaces; windows and sky-lights were replaced with electric lights, and simple tables removed in favor of specialized operating tables. Steam was found to be a more effective means of disinfecting instruments than carbolic acid. Surgeons began to wear sterilized gowns, caps, and gloves, and students were banished from the operating room to enclosed viewing galleries.

The Rise of Surgery

The combination of anesthetics, antisepsis, and asepsis allowed surgeons to safely open up all parts of the body without risk of infection, to operate slowly and carefully, to remove the minimum of diseased and damaged tissues, and to control blood loss by clamping vessels. Improved suturing techniques allowed surgeons to reconnect the cut edges of skin and tissues inside the body. These techniques allowed surgeons to devise a range of new operations in the late nineteenth century. In the 1860s, surgeons mainly repaired limbs and dealt with superficial tumors. By the end of the century, they were carrying out complex operations to remove diseased tissue from the internal organs, and thereby treat diseases such as appendicitis and duodenal ulcers. Surgeons could take out gallstones and kidney stones and remove tumors anywhere in the body, even from the brain and spinal cord. Often, new operations carried a high mortality rate, but as surgeons refined their skills and understanding, death rates fell. Mortality from removal of goiter (an enlarged thyroid gland) fell from 14 percent to less than 1 percent in around a decade.

Surgery offered the hope of a cure in previously untreatable conditions. Until the late nineteenth century, cancers of the breast and uterus had inevitably caused lingering and painful deaths. Early attempts to remove tumors usually proved unsuccessful—the patients either died as a direct result of surgery, or the cancer returned within a few years. Toward the end of the century, surgeons began to have some measure of success, as they realized the need to remove tissues around the tumor. However, survival rates rose only slowly. In 1870 in Vienna, one of the best centers for surgery, only eight of 170 women operated on for breast cancer were cured.

The number of patients undergoing surgery increased, not just as a result of the availability of new operations to treat a wider range of conditions. More patients were seen as suitable cases for surgical treatment. Prior to the introduction of anesthetics, women had been less likely to undergo operations because doctors feared that they were unable to stand the pain. Ether and chloroform removed this barrier, and many more women underwent surgery. Patients suffering from serious disease or injury, who had previously been expected to die and therefore were not operated on, could now be saved through prompt surgical intervention.

ORTHOPEDICS

Developments in surgery further advanced the creation of orthopedics as a new area of specialist practice. From the eighteenth century, a few doctors specialized in the treatment of deformed limbs and joints. They mainly practiced on "crippled" children, suffering from deformities such as curvature of the spine or club foot—a condition in which one or both feet were pointed inward or down, leaving the patient unable to place weight on the sole of the foot. A combination of splits, plaster casts, bandages, and massage were applied to gradually push the affected joint back into a more normal configuration.

Surgery opened up new possibilities for treating these conditions. From the 1830s, doctors developed an operation to treat club foot by cutting the Achilles tendon, thus allowing the foot to fall into a better alignment. With improved infection control, surgeons began to operate on bones. Limbs that had become bowed as a result of rickets, a deficiency disease linked to lack of vitamin D, were treated by cutting through the bone and allowing it to heal in a straighter form. Infections within bones and joints, often caused by tuberculosis, were now cured by opening the abscess and allowing pus to drain out. Surgery did not displace older, nonsurgical methods of treatment. The two were combined to treat many conditions, such as congenital hip displacement.

SURGEONS AND HOSPITALS

Developments in surgery had profound effects on the status of surgeons. Traditionally, surgeons, with their practical training in surgical procedures acquired through apprenticeship, had a lower status than university-educated physicians. Over the course of the eighteenth and nineteenth centuries, the relationship between the two groups changed radically. In the late eighteenth century, the training of the two groups came together. Surgeons began to attend lectures in medical schools, and physicians were taught anatomy and surgery. Gradually, a standardized curriculum covering both medicine and surgery became the norm in all medical schools. While most practitioners performed basic surgical procedures such as cleaning and stitching wounds as part of their medical practice, surgery emerged as a specialty within medicine. Following basic training, students wishing to become surgeons received further training in hospitals. As surgery became an option for the treatment of previously incurable diseases, the status of surgeons rose. By the end of the nineteenth century, surgeons were godlike figures, commanding respect, admiration, and high fees.

The rise of surgery also had a dramatic effect on the work of hospitals. In 1800, they were places of care, treating chronic disease among the poor with medicines, diet, and basic nursing. By 1900, hospitals had become centers for surgery, taking in patients suffering from acute illnesses and serious injuries. The role of nurses changed, too, as they began to assist in operating theaters and to care for very sick patients recovering from surgery.

SURGICAL EXCHANGES

New surgical techniques developed in Europe and North America were taken to non-Western cultures by colonial practitioners, especially medical missionaries. The superiority of Western surgery over the procedures traditionally used in Asia and Africa, in terms of both the range of conditions that could be treated and the success of operations, was quickly recognized. Patients flocked to hospitals and dispensaries offering Western surgery. In China, where indigenous practitioners performed very little surgery, medical missionaries attracted patients suffering from eye diseases and large tumors. In India, dispensaries treated broken bones, carried out amputations, and treated eye diseases and skin lesions. British surgeons taught Western techniques of cataract surgery to local eye doctors. Not all Western techniques were welcomed. Patients in many countries feared the use of anesthetics that seemed to produce a deathlike state.

There was a two-way traffic in surgical techniques: acupuncture was adopted from Japan and China by European practitioners in the early nineteenth century. However, European doctors struggled to understand the rationale behind the practice. Initially, they assumed acupuncture was a form of bloodletting. Instead of using the procedure to treat internal disease by manipulating *qi*, European practitioners used it to treat pain by inserting needles over painful joints in cases of gout or rheumatism.

DENTISTRY

At the beginning of the century, all around the world, dentistry was largely concerned with the treatment of toothache by the removal of painful teeth or application of medicines. Indigenous American peoples used hot poultices applied to the cheek or chewed the prickly ash bark to ease the pain. One traveler reported that a healer treated toothache by performing ritual songs, then scratching the skin over the aching tooth and sucking out the spirit that had caused the pain. In North Africa, toothache was attributed to worms inside the teeth, and it was treated by holding the mouth open to expose the painful tooth to the smoke from burning henbane seeds. If the pain became intolerable, the rotten tooth was extracted. In all cultures, this was performed by knocking out the tooth using a stick, or by pulling it out using some form of tool.

More elaborate forms of dental treatment developed in Europe and North America in the late eighteenth century. As the upper classes grew more conscious of the appearance of their teeth, practitioners devised wire braces to pull displaced teeth back into line. Around the same time, practitioners developed artificial teeth to replace missing ones. Teeth, made of bone or ivory or taken from corpses on battlefields, were used in these primitive dentures. Teeth were taken from dead soldiers in huge quantities; they were shipped from the battlefield of Waterloo by the barrel. The use of soldiers' teeth was so common that all false teeth became known as "Waterloo teeth." These dentures were purely cosmetic; the plates were not firmly anchored to the jaw and had to be taken out when eating. Attempts were made to transplant teeth from the jaws of the poor into those of wealthy patients but failed.

For much of the nineteenth century, filling decayed teeth was a painful and expensive option affordable only to the middle and upper classes. It usually required several visits to remove the decayed material. Gold foil was then pounded into the cavity or an amalgam of mercury and silver pressed into the hole and then heated. In the late nineteenth century, filling teeth was made quicker and easier by improved drills; first by a foot-operated drill (based on the treadle mechanism used to power sewing machines), and later by more powerful electric machines. It became a routine practice following the discovery of local anesthetics.

Taking out a rotten tooth was a cheaper, simpler option. From the 1860s, it was also painless, as patients inhaled nitrous oxide anesthetic before the procedure. The inhalation of nitrous oxide (laughing gas) started as a form of entertainment. Horace Wells, an American dentist, was among many to note that it appeared to dull pain, and he had a tooth extracted by one of his students under nitrous oxide anesthesia in 1844. The problems of ensuring that patients received a standard dose—enough to kill the pain, but not kill the patient—meant that the use of nitrous oxide did not become a routine part of dental practice for another two decades.

As patient demand for dental services grew, dentistry emerged as a new profession. In 1800, dentistry was practiced in the West by a few medical practitioners and by a larger number of people with little or no formal training. With the development of more complex equipment, dentists moved from working on the street to practicing in offices.

Dental schools were established to train students in knowledge of the mouth and teeth, techniques of filling and extraction, and giving anesthetics. The world's first dental school was established in Ohio in 1828 and the first dental college in Baltimore in 1840. Dentistry gradually took on the features of other professions, with standardized qualifications, professional societies, and journals where dentists exchanged information.

NOTES

1. Hakim Hadi Husain Khan, *Zakhirah-I-Khwarzmshahi* (*Thesaurus of the Shah of Khwarzm*), vol. 2 (Lucknow, 1878), p. 1258, quoted in Seema Alavi, *Islam and Healing: Loss and Recovery of an Indo-Muslim Medical Tradition 1600–1900* (New York: Palgrave Macmillan, 2008), p. 213.

2. R. W. Felkin, "Notes on Labour in Central Africa," *Edinburgh Medical Journal* 20 (1884), pp. 922–930.

3. Roy Porter *The Greatest Benefit to Mankind: A Medical History of Humanity from Antiquity to the Present* (London: Fontana Press, 1997), p. 365 (original source not given).

CHAPTER 9

The Brain and Mental Disorders

Mental illness (commonly called "madness" in the nineteenth century) was recognized around the world. The mentally ill displayed strange behaviors; madmen and women were unruly, were suicidal, ignored social codes by not dressing properly or by shouting, neglected their family responsibilities, or wandered about. However, different cultures understood mental illness in different ways. In Europe and North America, madness was thought to be fundamentally different from other diseases. Mental illness was seated in the mind and the brain. It was believed to be caused by a number of factors: disruption to the circulation or the functioning of nervous system, physical damage to the brain, or psychological trauma. All forms of mental illness were treated by specialist practitioners in institutions using medical and psychiatric therapy. Outside the West, the mind and body were perceived to be more closely linked. Mental illness was caused by the same factors as all other ailments—both physical and supernatural—and was treated with the same type of therapies, by healers who dealt with other diseases. Patients were cared for at home, not in special institutions.

MENTAL ILLNESS IN THE WEST

Theories of Mental Disorder

Within Western medicine, mental illness was defined by its symptoms. Sufferers displayed bizarre, irrational behaviors such as delusions, hallucinations, removing their clothing, wandering about, singing and shouting, aggression, and failure to deal with family or work responsibilities. In mild forms, such behaviors were tolerated by families and communities, who thought of them as simply odd or eccentric. If individuals became violent or unruly, families would conclude that he or she was mad and seek medical help. For example, in 1835, a mentally ill patient admitted into a hospital was described as being "restless melancholy, violent towards his life [*sic*], wandering about the country leaving his work & crying 'lost man.' [He] . . . refused food, and would have destroyed his wife and himself."[1] A woman who entered an asylum in 1881 was reported to be "violent in word and action: never asks after her child; incessant talking, most absurdly singing."[2]

During the course of the century, the definition of madness was extended to include idiocy and imbecility (in modern terms, forms of learning disability), nervous complaints, and even behaviors such as masturbation and homosexuality. Among women, strong sexual desires were labeled as nymphomania. Even high intellectual ability (again, especially among women) became suspect; genius and madness were seen as close allies.

It was generally accepted in the West that there was a clear division between the mind and the body, and thus a split between illness that afflicted the body and mental disorders that arose in the brain and affected the mind. In the eighteenth century, madness was interpreted as a loss of reason; the mad were like children or animals. The only means of cure was to force them to recover their rationality through punishment and restraint. The nineteenth century saw the emergence of new ideas about mental health and a debate over the causes of mental illness. There was little doubt that direct injury to the brain from a blow or a tumor produced mental illness. Puerperal insanity was acknowledged to follow childbirth.

For most physicians madness was rooted in the brain and nerves and caused by the same basic phenomena as other ailments. In his 1812 book on diseases of the mind, Benjamin Rush, a Philadelphia physician and one of the founders of psychiatry in America, proclaimed: "the cause of madness is seated primarily in the blood-vessels of the brain, and it depends upon the same kind of morbid and irregular actions that constitute other arterial diseases."[3] Other practitioners believed that the problem lay in irritation to the nerves and brain. Whether based in the circulation or the nerves, the triggers of mental illness were the same: exposure to extremes of heat or cold or prolonged mental or physical strain. Toward the end of the century, practitioners increasingly stressed the role of heredity in mental illness and mental disability.

Brain damage accumulated down to the generations: parents with nervous conditions or suffering from alcoholism produced children and grandchildren who exhibited criminal behaviors and mental disorders.

Some physicians, led by J. C. Heinroth in Germany, believed that madness was a psychological, rather than physical, phenomenon. Extreme emotions or traumatic experiences such as bankruptcy, disappointment in love, or bereavements permanently disordered brain function. Those with a healthy constitution and regular lifestyle could bear such shocks; people with a family history of mental illness or lacking emotional control, drunkards, and gamblers were more likely to succumb to mental illness.

THERAPY AND INSTITUTIONS

In the eighteenth century, nearly all mad people were cared for at home; they were looked after within the family, and they received little medical treatment aimed at curing their condition. A tiny proportion of the mentally ill was confined in institutions, often called "madhouses." In the nineteenth century, while wealthy patients and people suffering from mild forms of mental illness continued to be cared for at home, a much greater number were treated in a new type of institution—the asylum. Rather than an institution of confinement and punishment, the asylum (as its name suggests) was a place of refuge and cure. The institution itself was seen as having a curative influence. It took patients away from the setting, lifestyle, and surroundings that had provoked their illness. The ideal asylum was located in the calm of the countryside, away from the stresses and bustle of the town:

> [It should be a] spacious building ... airy, and elevated, and elegant, surrounded by extensive and swelling grounds and gardens. The interior is fitted up with galleries, and workshops and music-rooms. The sun and air are allowed to enter at every window, the view of shrubberies and fields, and groups of labourers, is unobstructed by shutters or bars; all is clean, quiet and attractive.[4]

Within the asylum, patients were subjected to a treatment regime. "Moral therapy" was developed at the end of the eighteenth century by a number of doctors and laymen; by Philippe Pinel in France, the Tuke family in England, and Vincenzo Chiarugi in Italy. It recognized that the harsh treatment meted out in early institutions was likely to provoke violent responses from inmates, and it took an optimistic view that most patients could be cured. Moral therapy was based on the idea that the mentally ill were not wholly irrational but capable of recovering their self-control. Asylum patients were not restrained (except in extreme circumstances, to prevent harm to themselves). Quiet entertainments, work, and an ordered routine were intended to divert the mind from irrational thoughts and behaviors. Patients were encouraged to return to conventional standards of behavior: to dress and converse normally, adopt hobbies, and take exercise. Good behavior was praised. In the asylum:

> The inmates all seem to be actuated by the common impulse of enjoyment, all are busy, and delighted by being so ... There is in this community no compulsion, no chains, no whips, no corporal chastisement, simply because they are proved to be less effectual means of carrying any point than persuasion, emulation, and the desire of obtaining gratification.[5]

In practice, asylum staff used fear as well as a desire for praise to keep their charges in line: patients who persisted in displaying irrational behaviors were punished by scolding, loss of privileges, or confinement. Under such regimes, it was confidently predicted that most mad people would be cured, especially if they were admitted to the asylum in the early stages of their illness.

In many asylums, psychological therapy was combined with medical and physical treatments aimed at restoring brain function. For much of the century, tried-and-trusted therapies were applied. Bloodletting, medicines to induce vomiting and purging, and hot and cold baths were used to stimulate the circulation throughout the body, including the brain, and to reduce the excitement exhibited by unruly patients. Mechanical treatments were also used to affect the circulation. Benjamin Rush's "tranquillizer" was a chair in which the patient was completely immobilized, to stop any muscular movements and thus reduce the circulation. On the "gyrator," the patient was whirled around, the circular motion forcing blood to the head. When none of these therapies proved successful, doctors turned to new drugs, including cannabis, amyl nitrate, and digitalis, along with mild electric shocks, to calm agitated or violent patients and to stimulate the morose.

THE RISE OF THE ASYLUM

The nineteenth century saw a huge increase in the numbers and size of asylums. In Europe and North America, local and national governments and charities funded institutions to treat the poor. In England

In the early nineteenth century circulating swings were used to treat mental illness. The patient was strapped in and the chair or bed rotated rapidly to force blood to the head and restore normal brain function. (National Library of Medicine)

and Wales, the number of publicly funded asylums rose from 23 in 1849 to 87 in 1904. At the same time, the average number of patients in each institution rose from fewer than 350 to almost 1,000. Some asylums were even larger: Colney Hatch Asylum had over 2,000 patients by 1860. In other countries, the boom in numbers came rather later; in Italy and Germany, public asylums grew rapidly in the last two decades of the century. Private asylums continued alongside the public institutions, serving a class of patients able to pay for care. They were always much smaller, sometimes with only a handful of patients.

Despite this building boom, there was never enough asylum accommodation. As fast as asylums expanded, so did the number of patients requiring treatment. The reasons for the rise in the numbers of the mentally ill were not clear. Contemporary commentators believed that mental illness was becoming more common due to a rise in alcohol abuse and to the stresses of industrial and urban life. Others suggested that more of the mentally ill were ending up in institutions as a result of changing attitudes among the public: families were less willing to care for the insane, or they were less able to look after a family member displaying awkward and disruptive behavior if they lived in cramped accommodation in a city and worked long hours in factories. On a more positive note, it was claimed that with improved treatment on offer in asylums, relatives were happy for patients to be admitted in the hope of finding a cure for their illness. There was also a perception that asylums were simply filling up with incurable patients as the initial optimistic estimates of the proportion of cases who could be cured by asylum therapy were never realized. In fact, recent studies by historians have shown that while some patients were institutionalized for many years, around a third were discharged within 12 months of their admission. In many cases, the extreme behaviors that had led to their committal had diminished, so patients could return to the family home. In some cases, families took their relatives out of the asylum even if they had shown little or no improvement. In addition, a substantial number of patients died within a year of entering an asylum, often from the conditions underlying their irrational behavior such as old age, syphilis, brain tumors, or strokes.

The growing size of asylums made it more difficult to treat patients. While active treatment was pursued in the smaller private asylums that cared for better-off patients, in huge state-funded institutions, there were too few staff for doctors or attendants to develop a relationship with their patients. As a result, asylums increasingly became places to confine the insane:

> Many asylums have grown to such a magnitude, that their general management is unwieldy, and their due medical and moral care and supervision an impossibility. They have grown into lunatic colonies of eight or

nine hundred, or even of a thousand or more inhabitants, comfortably lodged and clothed, fed by a not illiberal commissariat, watched and waited on by well-paid attendants, disciplined and drilled to a well-ordered routine.[6]

While a small number of patients worked within the asylum, helping with cleaning or in the laundry, the remainder had little to do with their time. Organized entertainments, such as dances and concerts, were few and far between, and visitors reported that wards of patients simply sat doing nothing. The large proportion of incurable patients seemed to prove that mental degeneration was the cause of madness in many cases. If asylums could not cure these patients, they could at least incarcerate them and prevent them from having children and perpetuating the problem.

One exception to the rule was the treatment of puerperal insanity. A form of mental illness that developed in the weeks following birth, it was attributed to the associated trauma and linked to poverty. The symptoms and treatment varied: women who became depressed were cared for at home or in maternity hospitals. Manic cases, in which women shouted, sang, or were violent, were more likely to be admitted to asylums. In the mid-nineteenth century, treatment took the form of supportive therapy—rest, a nourishing diet, and stimulating medicines. Later, doctors treated the disease more aggressively, with drugs and force feeding. Most patients recovered within a few months.

PSYCHIATRY AND PSYCHIATRISTS

The asylum provided the arena for the emergence of a new specialty within medicine, concerned with the treatment of mental illness. In the early nineteenth century, patients suffering from mental illness were cared for by family, by laymen, by ministers of religion, and by doctors. As it was increasingly accepted that madness was a form of illness, medical men became the acknowledged experts in dealing with the condition. Although initially the opinion of family members was influential in deciding who should enter the asylum (and families also chose to take back their relatives), over time, the views of medical staff based on observation of patients became the main criteria for diagnosing mental illness. Patients were admitted to and discharged from asylums on the certification of one or two doctors. Once inside the asylum, medical superintendents were responsible for prescribing their treatment.

In the asylum, doctors had an opportunity to observe patients with a range of conditions, to identify patterns of symptoms, and thus to divide cases of mental illness into different types so as to allow better treatment. However, madness defied easy categorization. All doctors recognized a few broad classes of mental illness, such as mania, melancholia, dementia, idiocy, and epilepsy, but not all defined these forms of madness in the same way; individual doctors might label the same patient as suffering from idiocy or from melancholia. Different doctors subdivided these classes in different ways. Some categorized cases by the circumstances that provoked the illness, such as "wedding night psychosis" or "religious mania," others by the major symptom, as in "delusional disorder." Mental illness was extremely complex. While puerperal insanity was a clearly defined syndrome, doctors concluded that there were four types and followed a course of six distinct stages. Attempts to classify different forms of mental illness by tracking the signs of mental disease in damage to the nerves and brain also proved fruitless, although neurologists did succeed in identifying the areas of the brain responsible for particular functions, such as speech and movement of the limbs. A new taxonomy of mental illness was finally developed from clinical observations by Emil Kraepelin in the 1880s and 1890s. He argued that forms of mental illness should be identified by typical patterns of symptoms, rather than their cause, and for the first time defined manic depression (now known as bipolar disorder) and schizophrenia.

The asylum also provided a career ladder for doctors wishing to specialize in the treatment of mental illness. The first asylum superintendents were trained in general medicine and had some interest or experience in dealing with madness. Later practitioners received formal teaching in the subject at medical school, and they worked their way up a hierarchy of asylum posts. Alienists, as members of this new group called themselves (since they treated mental alienation), formed professional societies and founded journals to advance research into mental illness and to increase the status of their specialty.

The nineteenth century saw the rise of public concern about asylums. There were criticisms of the quality of care offered to patients. Autobiographies of former asylum patients complained about the brutal treatment inflicted by staff. Poor patients were particularly vulnerable, and in the United States, Dorothea Dix led a campaign for better care after discovering a group of patients confined in an unheated room in an asylum. In Britain in the mid-nineteenth century, there were a number of notorious cases of wrongful incarceration in which families used the asylum to control unruly relatives. In many of these cases, the patients did display erratic behavior, but it was not clear if they were genuinely mad. Rosina Bulwer Lytton, wife of a famous English author, was briefly sent to an asylum after she launched a campaign of harassment that included sending obscene letters against her estranged husband. Ironically, her family probably hoped that keeping her out of the way would avoid a public scandal, but the case was widely discussed in the newspapers of the day. In another *cause célèbre*, Louisa Nottidge's family forced her into an asylum after she joined a highly unorthodox religious sect and gave away substantial sums of money to its leader. There was also public concern that patients who had recovered (or thought that they had recovered) from mental illness struggled to leave the asylum system. John Perceval, son of a British prime minister, was admitted to an asylum following a severe mental breakdown. After three years, he recovered, but he initially failed to persuade his doctors to release him. Once outside the asylum, he wrote two books, condemning the treatment he had received, and helped to found the Alleged Lunatics' Friend Society.

Nervous Disorders

Asylums were places of care mainly for those with severe forms of mental illness, or for patients with no family able to take care of them. Milder forms of mental illness were diagnosed as "nervous disorders" and were treated at home or in private clinics. In North America, neurasthenia was a common diagnosis. Identified by George Beard in 1869, it was a form of nervous disorder brought on by excessive mental effort or a serious shock, such as involvement in a road or rail accident. Women were believed to be prone to hysteria; the condition was particularly common among middle-class women who had little to do and suffered from unstable emotions. Patients diagnosed with hysteria and neurasthenia displayed a wide range of symptoms, from ringing in the ears, headaches, and indigestion, to paralysis, claustrophobia, and exhaustion.

Silas Weir Mitchell, an American neurologist, devised a "rest cure" to treat nervous disease. He prescribed an extreme form of bed rest (patients were not allowed to get up, wash, read, or have visitors), a milk diet, and massage for several weeks or months to allow the overworked nerves to recover. In Europe, many patients with nervous conditions went for treatment at spas, where they drank and bathed in natural mineral waters in the hope of restoring the health of their nervous systems. Hand-cranked machines were used to give small electric shocks to the head or other parts of the body to stimulate the nerves. In the 1890s, Sigmund Freud developed psychoanalysis as a new therapy for hysteria. Trained in neurology, Freud rejected theories that located these diseases in the nervous system, arguing that nervous diseases resulted from a conflict between the conscious mind and unconscious desires and were ultimately rooted in traumatic (often sexual) experiences in childhood.

MENTAL ILLNESS OUTSIDE THE WEST

Non-Western medical cultures, in Africa, Asia, and the Pacific recognized remarkably similar forms of mental illness to those described in Europe and North America. Mad people displayed strange, socially unacceptable behaviors: they were violent, went about naked (even in cultures where people normally wore very minimal clothing, refusing to wear anything was seen as very odd), or wandered about ignoring their familial responsibilities. However, cultures outside the West saw mental illness arising from the same causes as other diseases, so healers who dealt with other diseases provided treatment, not any special group of practitioners.

In most cultures, the mentally ill were kept at home, rather than in special institutions. People with violent forms of madness were restrained in some way—often chained up or locked in a small room—and given food and water. Care was often very limited. Missionaries in China reported that mentally ill patients lived in squalid, filthy conditions in sheds or other buildings close to the family home. The exception to home care was found in North Africa, where charitable *bismaristans* (or *maristans*)—hospitals for the sick and the mad—had been founded from medieval times. Early records show that mentally ill patients admitted to a hospital were treated using drugs and other remedies. By the nineteenth century, however, all efforts to cure seem to have stopped. Travelers reported that the *bismaristans* were simply places of confinement for patients who were likely to harm themselves or others. After a short stay, they were released back onto the streets.

MENTAL ILLNESS IN JAPAN AND CHINA

From ancient times, physicians in China and Japan (where a version of Chinese medical theory called *kampo* medicine was used) had recognized different forms of mental disorders. These included imbecility, hysteria (*yi zheng* or *yi bing*), madness (*kuang*), and epilepsy (*dian*). Doctors knew that women were susceptible to bouts of mental illness after giving birth. As in the West, people suffering from mental illness displayed unusual behaviors. A Japanese text of 1807 described the symptoms of madness (*kan*):

[Sufferers] are frightened by the slightest sound and are suicidal. They try to hide to avoid persecution. They cannot sleep because of anxiety or they sleep badly, often having nightmares. They talk grandiosely and behave arrogantly. They wash their hands or clean up their room many times, because they hate dirt ... They do one thing over and over again and cannot stop themselves. They feel guilty and suffer from regret and grief.[7]

Japanese practitioners also described cases of anorexia nervosa in which patients refused to eat or ate very little. If forced to eat, they vomited.

Unlike doctors in the West, Chinese and Japanese physicians did not see mental illnesses as different from other physical ailments. Chinese authors ascribed mental illness, like other diseases, to climate, lifestyle, or strong emotions that in turn produced a disturbance in the *yin/yang* balance and in the circulation of *qi*. Madness was associated with an increase in *yang*, and epilepsy with increased *yin*. By the nineteenth century, doctors had largely abandoned the ancient belief that madness was caused by ghosts or demons, although such ideas still circulated among ordinary people. Practitioners debated exactly how the disease was produced, whether it was a cold or warm disease, and if it affected the heart, liver, or spleen. Since mental illness was caused by the same mechanisms as other diseases, the same therapies—drugs and acupuncture—were used to restore balance, to relieve the symptoms, and to help restore control over the emotions.

Japanese practitioners also held that mental disorders had the same roots as other diseases, and they too debated the seat of mental illness and the processes that produced mental disorder. Some attributed madness to stagnant *qi*; others to poisons produced within the body that became active following a traumatic experience. The poison or *qi* formed a hard accumulation that could be felt by palpation and affected the organs linked to thought. Practitioners were divided as to the seat of thought within the body; some believed it to be the heart, while others located it in the stomach. Physicians exposed to Western medical ideas that were introduced to Japan in the seventeenth century believed that the poison acted on the brain. Some practitioners also accepted the view held by many laypeople that madness could be caused by supernatural means, such as possession by a demon or fox.

Treatment was aimed at dispersing the stagnant *qi* or poison by moxibustion (burning small amounts of fiber on the skin to warm the *qi*) and drugs to provoke vomiting or sleep. Some doctors also recommending a form of psychotherapy (*isei-henki*):

A 59-year old widow had been depressed since losing her eight children in a series of epidemics. She kept grieving over her misfortune, and wept night and day ... Wada [a physician] was called in to examine her ... he was unable to find any signs of physical disease. When Wada scolded her, with the intention of shifting her attention from the disease to him, the woman opened her eyes. Then Wada talked to her patiently. He said that her life and death were determined by Heaven's will, that everyone is destined to die sooner or later, and that it was pointless to be so upset ... His psychotherapy ... was effective, and the patient's fear of death disappeared.[8]

Mental Illness in Ayurvedic Medicine

In ayurvedic medicine, madness was thought to be seated in the heart, the organ associated with thought. Mental disorders shared the same basic cause as physical illness: they arose from an imbalance of *doṣas* caused by the wrong diet, lifestyle, or strong emotions. Such an imbalance could cause many types of illness: mental illness occurred when there was some predisposing factor that drove the excess *doṣa* toward the heart, causing malfunctions in the vessels carrying the *doṣas*. Epilepsy, for example, was caused by a sudden blockage in these channels. Imbalances in the different *doṣas* produced different types of madness: mental illness arising from *pitta* had symptoms such as anger, violence, sleeplessness, and obstinacy. The imbalance was treated with the same therapies as for physical illness: drugs, diet, and bathing with decoctions of herbs all helped to reduce the excess *doṣa*, to purify the body and strengthen the nerves.

MENTAL ILLNESS IN AFRICA

In Africa, people saw madness in similar ways to those in the West. Mental illness was defined by a set of strange behaviors: hallucinations, disordered speech, going naked, or wandering about. Healers identified a range of types of mental illnesses including melancholy, fits, and epilepsy. However, where Western medicine associated mental illness with the mind and brain, African healers saw no division between the body and mind. Mental illness arose from a same range of causes as other ailments, responded to the same therapies, and was treated by the same healers. Madness could be caused by natural means and treated with herbal medicines. Some forms of mental illness were understood to be hereditary, or to develop in old age. Sufferers might be confined in their homes to prevent them from wandering off or doing harm to themselves or to others. Mental illness could also be brought on by supernatural means—by sorcery, by spirit possession or sent by the gods as a punishment for breaking taboos. In these cases, after diagnosis through some form of divination, the complaint was cured by rituals and by sacrifices of animals to appease the supernatural being responsible for the illness.

Just as physical disease moved between cultures, so did mental illnesses. In Zululand in southern Africa, a new form of disease appeared in the late nineteenth century. *Indiki* possession was introduced from areas further north. Initially, it was supposed to be caused by the spirits of warriors killed in battle that had not received proper burial rites and affected both men and women. Later it was predominantly found among women and was associated with the spirits of dead male relatives. Sufferers displayed symptoms such as twitching, weeping, fits, and numbness. It was treated with medicines (some of them poured into the ear), rituals, and the animal sacrifices.

Western Views of Mental Illness in Africa and Asia

Many Western writers claimed that mental illness was almost unknown in isolated indigenous societies in Africa and the Pacific region. They suggested that indigenous people lived simple, stress-free lives, and as a consequence, very few people succumbed to nervous diseases. Alternatively, they claimed that the brains and nerves of native peoples were less developed than those of Europeans, and therefore not susceptible to the irritation that caused madness. Mental illness was believed to become more common following contact with Europeans as a result of exposure to new diseases, alcohol, and new lifestyles. Such an analysis fit with colonial ideas of indigenous people as "primitive" and unable to survive within the modern world. In fact, Western travelers did occasionally report instances of madness among indigenous people. One author reported that insanity was not uncommon among old male Australian aborigines. While family members were rather afraid of those elders who suffered from mental illness, they looked after them.

Madness was a problematic category for Western travelers. To some observers, the trance states that diviners used as a means of diagnosing illness were a form of madness. The colonial authorities associated *indiki* possession with witchcraft, but administrators were unable to decide if sufferers were displaying the symptoms of a nervous disorder such as hysteria, were the victims of witchcraft, were the gullible dupes of people claiming to be witches, or were fraudsters who feigned possession in order to demand animals for sacrifice. In 1910, in an effort to control the outbreak of *indiki*, 11 women suffering from possession were put on trial for practicing witchcraft.

The Colonial Asylum

There were occasional suggestions that the *indiki* sufferers were mad and should be sent to an asylum for treatment. Asylum accommodation became available in European colonies in Africa and India from the early nineteenth century as part of the drive to civilize and to improve the lives of the indigenous population. The development of the asylum system followed the same pattern as in Europe and North America. In the later nineteenth century, colonial governments built asylums for the care of the poor Europeans—white soldiers, sailors, and workers—and for indigenous peoples. Over time, the number of asylums increased, and the institutions grew larger. Despite this, the number of asylum places relative to the population was tiny. Kissy Asylum in Sierra Leone took in patients from all over West Africa, but in 1887, it had only 70 beds.

In other respects, the colonial asylum was different from that in the West. There was much less demand for asylum accommodation from the families of the mentally ill. Relatives preferred to treat the mentally ill at home using traditional remedies. Indigenous patients were

The Lunatic Asylum at Kissy in Sierra Leone offered care to a small number of patients suffering from mental illness across West Africa. Only the most difficult patients, unable to find care within their families, entered such institutions. (Wellcome Library)

usually admitted to an asylum by the police or through the law courts, after they had been arrested for some act of violence or had been found wandering and unable to look after themselves. Diagnosis was often based on the testimony of police officials and other white people. In asylums in New Zealand, for example, few if any doctors spoke Māori, and translators were often not provided.

Asylum organization mirrored colonial society. Patients were segregated by race and class. White Europeans were believed to succumb to mental illness as a consequence of living in an alien culture. "In England and other cold countries, attacks of Insanity generally arise from sudden reverses of fortune, keen disappointments, and other causes of deep mental depression, but in this country it is otherwise; here the attack may at almost every instance be traced to exposure to the sun; hard living and other irregularities."[9] Asylums took European patients away from these dangerous influences, but if they failed to respond within a year, they were sent back to Europe and more familiar surroundings where, it was hoped, they might be cured. European patients were generally given good accommodation within asylums, often in rooms rather than large wards. In the Bombay Lunatic Asylum, the wing for Europeans had "cheerful and pleasing views . . . of the entrance to the harbour, bay, Malabar Hill and the adjacent country."[10] Treatment was tailored to the colonial situation. European patients resented being restrained by Indian attendants, so staff resorted to older forms of physical restraint such as strait jackets and manacles. Recreational facilities such as magazines, board games, and bowling were provided for patients, and they were rarely expected to undertake any form of work as part of their therapy.

Relatively few asylum places were available for indigenous people, and those were reserved for the most serious cases. The causes of mental illness diagnosed in indigenous patients were broadly similar to European inmates, although their condition was sometimes linked to the colonial situation. In midcentury, madness in Māori patients was linked to the loss of land to white settlers. Accommodation in native asylums was not as good as that provided for European patients. Indigenous patients were accommodated on large and often crowded wards, and sometimes slept on mats, or on the floor, rather than in beds. Inmates were separated according to their symptoms—whether they were quiet or violent, or recovering. This caused conflict in Indian asylums, where diagnosis took priority over the important distinctions of social group (caste) and religion. Like their European counterparts, indigenous asylum patients were encouraged to undertake activities. They were more likely to be prescribed some form of work than

Europeans, and their pastimes were tailored to local tastes. Indian asylum inmates were allowed to play active sports, such as cricket and shooting with a bow and arrows, and to keep a variety of pet animals. In Delhi Asylum, the patients formed an orchestra and were taken to religious festivals. In New Zealand asylums, however, there seems to have been little attempt to fit asylum life to Māori culture, and many patients were reported to have become mute, passive, and withdrawn.

NOTES

1. "Memorandum upon Admission of Patients into Bethlem Hospital for John Bool," quoted in Akihito Suzuki, "Framing Psychiatric Subjectivity: Doctor, Patient and Record-keeping at Bethlem in the Nineteenth Century," in *Insanity, Institutions and Society, 1800–1914*, ed. Joseph Melling and Bill Forsythe (New York: Routledge, 1999), p. 119.

2. A Campbell Clark, "Clinical Illustrations of Puerperal Insanity," *Lancet* 21 (1883), p. 98, quoted in Hilary Marland, " 'Destined to a Perfect Recovery': The Confinement of Puerperal Insanity in the Nineteenth Century," in Melling and Forsythe, *Insanity, Institutions and Society*, p. 146.

3. Benjamin Rush, *Medical Inquiries and Observations upon Diseases of the Mind* (1812), quoted in *The Faber Book of Madness*, ed. Roy Porter (Boston: Faber and Faber, 1991), p. 41.

4. W. A. F. Browne, *What Asylums Were, Are, and Ought to Be* (Edinburgh: Adam and Charles Black, 1837), p. 229.

5. Ibid., p. 230.

6. John Thomas Arlidge, *On the State of Lunacy, and the Legal Provision for the Insane* (n.p., 1859), quoted in Porter, *Faber Book of Madness*, p. 365.

7. Kagawa Shutoka, *Ippondo-Gyoyo-Igen* (*My Extra Medical Commentary*), quoted in Hiruta Genshiro, "Japanese Psychiatry in the Edo Period," *History of Psychiatry* 13 (2002), p. 134.

8. Wada Tokaku, *Syosou Zatsuwa* (*Small Talks by a Window Facing a Japanese Banana Plant*), quoted in Genshiro, "Japanese Psychiatry in the Edo Period," p. 136.

9. India Office Records, London, Medical Board to Government, November 30, 1818, quoted in Waltraud Ernst, "Colonial Lunacy Policies and the Madras Lunatic Asylum in the Early Nineteenth Century," in *Health, Medicine and Empire: Perspectives on Colonial India*, ed. Biswamoy Pati and Mark Harrison (London: Sangam Books, 2001), p. 148.

10. Asylum Superintendent to Medical Board, February 28, 1850, quoted in Waltraud Ernst, "The European Insane in British India, 1800–1858: A Case Study in Psychiatry and Colonial Rule," in *Imperial Medicine and Indigenous Societies*, ed. David Arnold (New York: Manchester University Press, 1988), p. 35.

CHAPTER 10

Apothecaries, Pharmacists, and Pharmacopeias

Drugs were the cornerstone of medical treatment in almost every culture in the nineteenth-century world. They were used in all systems of medicine and in folk medicine. A huge range of substances—plants, animal parts, minerals, metals, even earths and precious stones—were prescribed to cure illness, either singly or in combination. Drugs were available from a wide range of sources. Families made their own remedies in the home using plants or foodstuffs from the family garden or local countryside. The sick obtained medicines directly from their healers, from specialist traders such as druggists and pharmacists, from general retailers, and even by mail order. The nineteenth century saw a boom in sales of medicines: people with a little spare cash were increasingly eager to buy remedies to cure illness or to preserve health. As a result, drugs were traded around the world in ever greater quantities to satisfy this demand.

THE WORLDWIDE TRADE IN DRUGS

Locally sourced plants, animal products, and minerals were the backbone of medical preparations worldwide. Healers gathered indigenous plants growing in forests and open areas, and cultivated native plants in gardens. Practitioners were not limited to making use of local plants; seeds were bought and sold around the world, allowing healers to grow exotic species for use in medicines. Cultivation took place on both large and small scales, by individuals and by large companies. Cinchona trees, the source of quinine, were native to South America; but seeds were transported to India, Sri Lanka, and Java where plantations were established. Asia became the major center of quinine production.

Preserved plant material and other medicinal substances had been traded over long distances for hundreds, possibly thousands of years, carried by people, on pack animals, and by sailing ships. Traditional trading routes remained in use during the nineteenth century. In Africa, for example, traders gathered, dried, and carried plant and other materials for hundreds of miles, from mountainous areas down to the plains, or from the coast to inland communities. New methods of transport made possible the shipment of much larger quantities of drugs within and between continents, and to ensure that they arrived quickly and in good condition. The raw materials for medicines flowed into Europe and North America from around the world. Aniseed, camphor, gamboge (the fruits and sap of a tree), rhubarb, china root, and green tea came from China. Nux vomica, belladonna, asafetida, senna, camphor, and castor oil were imported from India. Chinese traders brought asafetida and putchuck (the roots of a plant) from India, ginseng from the United States and Turkey, and mercury from Europe and North America. As the manufacture of pharmaceuticals became industrialized, prepared and packaged medicines were exported from Europe and North America back to Africa and India.

New plant-based drugs were also discovered in the nineteenth century. European and American botanists explored many regions of Africa and Asia, bringing home new plants for use in gardens and in medicines. In 1859, a botanist connected with David Livingstone's expedition in Malawi collected the seeds of the *kombe* plant. This was used by local peoples to prepare poisoned arrows used in hunting. Analysis of the seeds revealed a chemical that slowed the heart, which became the basis of strophanin, a heart medicine, marketed from 1885.

PHARMACOPEIAS

All the world's systems of medical knowledge—Western, Chinese, ayurvedic, and unani medicine—contained explanations of how drugs acted within the body to cure disease. Books of materia medica (medical substances) or pharmacopeias provided lists of drugs and medicines classified according to their source, action in the body, methods of preparation, and uses. Often these texts were illustrated with drawings showing the plant or animal source of the drugs, helping practitioners to identify plants growing in the wild or to check that they were being sold the correct dried or preserved materials and were not duped into purchasing an inferior substitute.

Chinese Medicines

Chinese pharmacopeias dated back thousands of years. The classic Chinese text on medicines was the Shen nung *Pen ts'ao ching*, written around 2700 BCE. Later books followed the same format but included many more medicinal substances, as the Chinese empire expanded and practitioners made contact with healers in other cultures. For example, *Dongchong xiacoa*, a fungus that attacked caterpillars, was

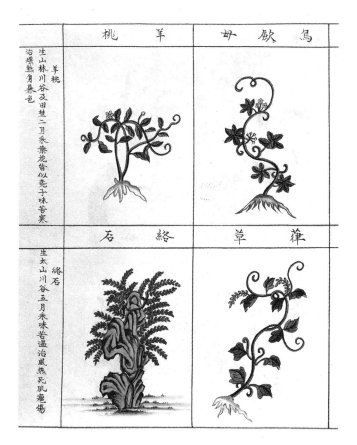

Illustration from a *Pen ts'ao*, a Chinese pharmacopeia, showing medicinal plants. Although published in the nineteenth century, this book follows the form and layout of ancient texts. (Societe Asiatique, College de France, Paris, France/Archives Charmet/The Bridgeman Art Library)

probably adopted into Chinese practice from Tibetan medicine in the eighteenth century. Drugs were used to manipulate the circulation of *qi* around the body and hence to restore health. Medicines could remove blockages in the flow of *qi*, nourish the *qi*, warm the body, or reduce heat. All drugs were classified by five "tastes"—acrid, sweet, bitter, sour, and salty—and their nature, whether hot, cold, warm, or cool. These factors determined the effect they had within the body. Sour medicines stopped discharges such as diarrhea. Bitter drugs had a drying effect; they were used to treat diseases caused by dampness and to clear heat from the body. Licorice root, for example, was sweet and promoted *qi*. Abalone shell was salty and cold; it nourished *yin* and was used to treat liver diseases. Pharmacopeias described medicines by these principles and the type of conditions they cured, rather than giving very specific uses or exact doses because in Chinese medicine, every patient was an individual. Disease was a product of their natural constitution, age, lifestyle, and circumstances, and medicines had to be tailored to take account of all these factors. In practice, Chinese practitioners and their patients did use standard remedies to treat common conditions, such as the "Strongly Replenishing Infusion of Ten Ingredients" or the "Powder for Arousing the Pulse." Drugs were usually taken in the form of pills, powders, or decoctions (medicines boiled in water, then cooled and strained).

Chinese medicine made use of a huge number of materials, usually in combinations in order to exert exactly the right effect within the body. Strong drugs were mixed with other substances to moderate their effects, or with materials to help strengthen the body. Some drugs could help to direct medicines to particular organs, to ensure that they produced the maximum effect. Minerals and animal materials, such as sea horses, bones, and even excrement such as bat dung, had medicinal properties. Plants were a common source of medicines, and a single plant could have multiple uses. The leafy tops were prescribed for illnesses affecting the head and the roots for complaints in the lower parts of the body. A single drug could be used to treat different ailments. Licorice root (*gancao*) replenished *qi* in the spleen but also moisturized the lungs and stopped coughs, counteracted the fire poison that caused ulcers, relieved cramps, and was an antidote to toxic substances.

Ayurvedic and Unani Medicines

Ayurvedic and unani medicine, like Chinese medicine, saw disease as an individual phenomenon. Medicines were categorized by a set of principles that defined their effect within the body. In ayurvedic medicine, illness was caused by imbalance in three *doṣas*—*kapha*, *vāta*, and *pitta*. Diet, behaviors such as sleeping or exercise, heat, and cold all affected the *doṣas* and could cause illness or be manipulated to restore balance to the body. Diet was the first means of curing disease; medicines were prescribed for more serious complaints. Ayurvedic practitioners mainly used plant-based medicines with a few animal and mineral substances. They were categorized by their qualities and effect on the *doṣas*. Castor oil (extracted from the seeds of the castor oil plant) was heavy, hot, and sweet. It had a laxative effect and was used to treat a number of conditions, including hiccups, asthma, and gout. Urine was light, sharp, and hot, reduced *kapha*, and was used to treat colic, parasitic infections, and skin diseases. The types of medicines prescribed by practitioners varied across the country, taking account of the local climate and making use of plants found in the area.

Unani medicine, like ayurvedic medicine, saw balance as the key to health and disease. However, rather than three *doṣas*, unani practitioners sought to control a balance of four humors. These had four essential qualities—hot, cold, wet, and dry—and drugs were also categorized by these qualities and by their potency, if mild or strong. For example, garlic was hot and dry and was prescribed in cases of fever, colic, or forgetfulness. The bruised bulbs were also used in ointments and poultices. The root and wood of the barberry shrub was hot and moist, acted on the spleen, and was used to treat dysentery. The oil of the camphor tree was cold and dry and was a brain tonic given to cure headaches. Unani medicines included a large number of animal and mineral substances alongside plant-based drugs. Musk, obtained from the glands of deer, was used as a tonic for the heart and brain, to combat inflammation, and to cure coughs. Drugs were taken singly or combined into medicines for a stronger effect. They were taken in the form of syrups, pills, powders, or decoctions.

Medicines in the West

In Europe and North America, knowledge of the body and disease was revolutionized during the nineteenth century. Research demonstrated that disease was not caused by changes in the humors but by malfunctions of the organs or tissues. While theories of the body changed rapidly in the early part of the century, a new understanding of the action of medicines developed more slowly. Doctors and their patients were reluctant to abandon tried-and-tested medicines that had been used for hundreds of years. For much of the nineteenth century, doctors continued to prescribe medicines that affected the body's excretions—by inducing sweating or vomiting—or controlled the symptoms of disease with the aim of making the patient feel better and allowing the body to heal itself. Practitioners were well aware that many of their medicines were of limited efficacy. Oliver Wendell Holmes, a distinguished American practitioner, reflected practitioners' cynicism when he concluded:

> [T]hrow out opium ... throw out a few specifics which our art did not discover, and it is hardly needed to apply; throw out wine, which is a food, and the vapors which produce the miracle of anesthesia, and I firmly believe that if the whole materia medica, *as now used*, could be sunk to the bottom of the sea, it would be all the better for mankind,— and all the worse for the fishes [emphasis in original text].[1]

Over the century, practitioners gradually reduced their use of strong medicines such as mercury and antimony and replaced them with milder drugs given in smaller doses.

The uncertainty over the curative action of medicines was reflected in the organization of pharmacopeias. At the beginning of the century, medicines were listed by their effect on the body's excretions and secretions. Drugs were classified under categories such as sudorifics (inducing sweating), emetics (provoking vomiting), or purgatives (laxatives). Other drugs were listed according to their uses, such as carminatives (to combat flatulence), sedatives (to calm the nerves), and emollients (to soothe or soften the tissues). By the middle of the century, when practitioners had abandoned their belief in the importance of the body fluids in disease causation, authors shifted to producing alphabetical lists of drugs or classifications based on the diseases that they cured.

Many texts also provided detailed instructions on how to prepare drugs, revealing the long, arduous, and complex tasks required in making medicines. For example, the *British Pharmacopeia* for 1867 described how to make extract of opium, a relatively simple process.

> Take of
>
> Opium in thin slices. . . . . . .1 pound
>
> Distilled water. . . . . . .6 pints
>
> Macerate the opium in two of the pints of water for twenty-four hours, and express the liquor. Reduce the residue of the opium to a pulp, macerate it again in two pints of the water for twenty-four hours, and express. Repeat the operation a third time. Mix the liquors, strain through flannel, and evaporate by a water-bath until the extract has acquired a suitable consistence [*sic*] for forming pills.[2]

Pharmacopeias also included recipes for medicines used to treat common minor complaints. European and American pharmacopeias were unusual in that they often included the appropriate dose for each drug. Unlike other systems of medical knowledge, Western medicine saw each case of a particular disease as fundamentally the same, and so each should be treated by standard amounts of a particular drug, adjusted according to the patient's body weight.

New Drugs

Before the nineteenth century, new drugs were discovered by rather haphazard means. Interested doctors experimented with substances often taken from folk medicines. In the 1780s, William Withering, an English doctor, proved the effectiveness of a traditional herbal medicine in the treatment of dropsy—fluid retention caused by heart failure. Withering worked out that the active ingredient in the medicine was derived from the foxglove plant. We now know that foxgloves contain digitalis that stimulates the heart. The nineteenth century saw the arrival of the pharmaceutical industry, bringing together large-scale production of medicines and research in company facilities or in universities to discover new drugs and systematically test their effects. German pharmaceutical companies set new standards of quality, introducing much greater standardization—they routinely tested the quality of each batch of medicines. Industrialized production also led to the introduction of new forms of medicine. Instead of the traditional liquid medicines and large, hand-rolled pills, pharmaceutical companies produced small machine-made pills and capsules that were much easier to swallow.

In these laboratories, the active ingredients within traditional medicines were isolated and identified for the first time. Preparations based on the bark of the cinchona tree had long been used to treat fevers, but the active substance, quinine, was not isolated until 1820. Similarly, opium was a traditional painkiller, produced from the dried sap of the opium poppy. Research into the chemistry of the plant revealed two painkilling chemicals, morphine (discovered in 1804) and codeine (isolated in 1832). Similar compounds were also discovered in other plants. Atropine, a drug used to treat gastric upsets, was isolated from deadly nightshade, and cocaine from the coca plant of South America.

In the late nineteenth century, research yielded completely new drugs, or synthetic forms of existing medicines. The discovery of the anesthetic effects of ether and chloroform prompted research into the medicinal effects of organic chemicals. Chloral hydrate, the first synthetic medicine to induce sleep, was created in 1869; and veronal, the first barbiturate drug, in 1903. The painkilling chemical in willow bark had been identified as early as 1826, but when isolated, it proved unsuitable as a medicine as it irritated the stomach lining. In 1899, Felix Hoffman synthesized a related compound, acetylsalicylic acid, that showed fewer side effects. Marketed as aspirin, it became one of the most popular medicines of the twentieth century. Chemical dyes were an unlikely but fruitful source of new medicines. In 1856, an English chemist tried to synthesize quinine, but succeeded in producing the first chemical dye used to color cloth. From 1880, dyes became the starting point for new drugs. Antipyrine, a drug similar to quinine, was produced in 1884 from a chemical used to make yellow dyes. Phenacetine and paracetamol came from similar sources and were used to reduce fevers and kill pain.

Unorthodox Medicines

Many of the medicines used in nineteenth-century Europe and North America produced extreme reactions. Vomiting after taking an emetic was reassuring (it was clear that the medicine was having an effect on the body), but it was uncomfortable and unpleasant. Even pure forms of drugs could have unpleasant side effects. A French traveler observed in 1850: "Quinine . . . does relieve fever quite rapidly, but when you have recovered from the disease, you still have to recover from the remedy . . . quinine inflames your bowel, blurs your vision, and causes so much hearing disorder that it sounds as though you could hear 36,000 bells in the ears."[3]

It is perhaps not surprising that many people turned to alternative or "unorthodox" forms of medicine that used simpler, more natural therapies. Thompsonian medicine sought to cure all illness using a small range of medicinal herbs to regulate the heat within the body. These caused purging and vomiting but were perceived to be milder and more natural than the medicines prescribed by orthodox practitioners that contained poisonous substances such as mercury. Homeopathy, another popular unorthodox system of medicine, had no such unpleasant effects. Practitioners did use some strong, mineral-based drugs, but in a very dilute form to stimulate the body's own healing responses.

Folk Medicine

Folk medicine, unlike systems of medical knowledge, did not have an underlying theory of body function, and thus no explanation of the effect of medicines on the body. Instead, practitioners prescribed specific treatments for particular ailments. Many materials were used in medicines. Remedies incorporated local and exotic plants, earths, minerals, and animal products. In some cultures, healers made use of several hundred medicinal substances. Plants were a rich source of drugs, and all parts—roots, leaves, bark, and seeds—had their uses. Each was used in a variety of ways. For example, the leaves of trees or plants could be boiled in water to make an infusion, pounded to a paste with water or fat to make an ointment, squeezed to extract juice, rubbed directly on the skin, chewed, added to hot water in a steam bath, or burned and the smoke inhaled. In many cultures, plants were gathered at a specific time of year, in particular weather, and even at an exact stage of the lunar cycle to ensure their potency. Herbs were prepared in very precise ways; they could be dried quickly over a fire or in the sun, or more slowly in the shade. Many medicines must have been discovered by a process of trial and error, but the medicine men of North American tribes received information about the use of drugs in dreams from spirit guides. In other cultures, the appearance or qualities of substances suggested their use. Zulu healers used plants with a red sap resembling blood to treat bleeding. The cause of ailments could also suggest a cure: medicines made from the flesh of snakes were applied to snakebites.

Indigenous people made use of local plants to treat disease. In the southern United States, the indigenous tribes used angelica root, a tender herb that grew only in warm areas, to treat stomach disorders. Among northern peoples, the buds and resin of pine and spruce trees that flourished in the cold climate were given for colds and respiratory ailments. Sometimes a single plant could cure several complaints. Preparations of the raw roots of butterfly weed were taken by native peoples in cases of respiratory diseases, and the dried and powdered roots were applied to wounds. Different groups of Native Americans used different plants for the same purpose. The Rappahannock prescribed wild ginger tea or bruised plantain leaves to treat fevers, while the Teton Dakotas used the root of little rattlepod. Equally, the same medicine was applied for different purposes by different peoples. The Cherokees used wild cherry bark during childbirth, the Ojibwas applied it to sores and for chest complaints, and the Poncas used it to treat diarrhea.

The use of medicines varied between cultures. Herbal medicines were the keystone of medical care throughout Africa and Asia, but Western travelers to the Pacific islands and in New Zealand reported that the indigenous people used only a few medicines. Māori people treated common digestive complaints, such as diarrhea or constipation, with plant juices, and they prepared ointments and salves containing extracts from leaves, berries, and bark to treat external complaints. Their limited use of medicines reflected their belief that most disease was caused by spirits, and as a result, they relied on rituals rather than drugs to treat illness.

PRACTITIONERS, APOTHECARIES, DRUGGISTS

Around the world, the nineteenth century saw an expanding market for medicines, which could be obtained through a variety of channels. Learned practitioners trained in Chinese, ayurvedic, or unani medical theory prescribed medicines for almost all their patients, tailored to their illness and designed to suit the constitution and lifestyle of each individual patient.

Prescribing was the key outcome of a medical consultation with an elite Chinese practitioner; patients were given a written prescription, which they took to a drug seller to be made up. Practitioners constantly adjusted their prescriptions to follow the course of the illness, sometimes changing them every day. When treating the Chinese emperor for smallpox in 1874, his doctors began by prescribing cooling remedies. As the disease ran its course, these were replaced by a mix of warming and cooling medicines to help replenish *qi*. The drugs prescribed for the emperor included milk vetch, magnolia bark, bamboo shavings, plantain, and ginseng. Patients often negotiated with practitioners over their prescriptions: they asked for medicines they did not like to be removed or for drugs that they believed were suited to their case to be included.

Ayurvedic physicians (*vaids*) and unani *hakims* were trained in pharmacy and made up medicines as well as prescribing for their patients. Practitioners produced medicines in small amounts, with the dosage and composition adjusted to the age and strength of the patient. In Europe and North America, all doctors received training in the use of medicines as part of their education. Elite physicians prescribed, but did not prepare, drugs for their wealthy patients. Practitioners who served middle- and lower-class patients often kept a supply of commonly used drugs on hand and would make up their own prescriptions.

While textbooks stressed the need to prescribe for individual patients, in practice, physicians working in all medical systems often turned to standard medicines or favorite remedies. The composition of these medicines was often handed down from teacher to pupil: one Chinese remedy was called the "Ointment Medicine Secretly

Transmitted by Master Feng." Even standard remedies were not rigidly specified. *Nushkas*, prescriptions written by famous unani practitioners and sometimes published, could be made up with alternative ingredients, allowing the medicines to be adjusted to the individual patient.

Folk healers, too, provided medicines as part of a consultation. As well as knowing the identity of the raw materials for medicines, healers had to know where to find them, what parts to use, and how to store and prepare drugs so as to maximize their potency. Not surprisingly, in many communities it took several years to learn the preparation and uses of medicines.

Drug Vendors

Specialist drug sellers made up the medicines prescribed by Chinese and Western practitioners and sold standard remedies. Drug vendors were found in every medical culture and went by a variety of names. In India, *attars* prepared and sold unani medicines; in the West, drug sellers were known as apothecaries (this was a traditional name that fell out of use during the century), chemists, pharmacists, herbalists, or druggists. They had some training in medical theory, but they learned the practical skills of preparing medicines through apprenticeships. The best druggists' shops carried a huge stock of drugs. One Western traveler wrote:

> The drug shops of China are large, and are commodiously fitted up. They have a great array of drawers and jars. Arranged much in the same way as in England; glass vessels are very rare. Different departments are allotted to separate classes of medicaments; care is taken to keep things in order; and there is a great degree of neatness and method in their appearance which would not be discreditable to a London laboratory.[4]

Ordinary medicines were wrapped in paper, with instructions written on the outside. Expensive medicines, such as ginseng, were wrapped in red paper. Drug sellers had a comprehensive knowledge of the preparation and uses of medicines. Not surprisingly, many also offered medical advice as well as selling medicines. At the other end of the scale from the druggist in his well-stocked shop were street traders, who had a limited knowledge of medicine and sold a few herbs or a handful of general remedies.

As well as making up prescriptions, druggists made and sold standard preparations, such as laudanum, a medicine made of opium in

The mid-nineteenth century saw a boom in pharmacy in the West, when people of all classes bought medicines for their minor ailments over the counter. This illustration shows an elegantly-appointed shop carrying a wide range of drugs. (National Library of Medicine)

alcohol, often devising their own variations on well-known remedies. In 1832, a druggist in the north of England advertised:

> His invaluable medicine BALSAM of HOREHOUND, for curing Coughs, Colds, Asthmas, Hooping [*sic*] Cough, Declines and Consumption, Also ... his truly valuable and never failing Medicine for the Cholera Morbus, or Vomiting and Purging; and also his excellent medicines for Worms; all of which medicines ... have obtained very high reputations, and can only be prepared by G. B. Reinhardt, as he is the sole possessor of his late Father's recipes.[5]

Druggists carefully composed their medicines to suit their customers. South African drug sellers sold Western remedies to their European customers and compounded medicines including indigenous herbs aimed at the black population.

An increasing demand for medical care worldwide allowed drug sellers to flourish. In Europe and North America, druggist's shops were found in every town and city. Successful traders established chains of stores. In England, Boots' chemist shops expanded from a single market stall in 1849 to over 300 branches by the 1900s.

There was tension among druggists and between doctors. European practitioners complained that pharmacists were stealing their business by prescribing for patients as well as selling them medicines over the counter. Pharmacists, trained in making up prescriptions, complained that chemists selling popular over-the-counter remedies in bulk undercut their prices. This prompted a movement to improve standards of education in pharmacy and the development of new training courses and qualifications at colleges and universities. While qualified pharmacists enjoyed some advantages—they alone had the right to sell dangerous drugs and poisons—they did never enjoyed a monopoly of trade. Throughout the century, anyone could set up a shop and sell medicines without any formal training.

These debates about competence were mirrored in India, where practitioners anxious to improve standards of care hit out at drug sellers with little knowledge of medicines. One writer complained that drug sellers had "ten to twenty pots, which have turmeric, tamarind paste, black pepper, and they begin dispensing medicines."[6] Prompted by these concerns, practitioners set up an indigenous pharmaceutical industry in India, mass-producing ayurvedic and unani medicines of a consistently high quality that were sold at set prices. As they purchased manufacturing machinery from the West, they also adopted the forms of medicine used in Europe and North America—pills and powders—and standardized the strength of medicines.

PATENT MEDICINES

The nineteenth century saw a boom in the market for proprietary or patent medicines. (The term is a misnomer, as the medicines were not protected by legal patents.) The exact composition of these remedies was a secret, known only to the manufacturer, and they were heavily marketed. These were usually self-prescribed, rather than recommended by a medical practitioner, and were bought over the counter from druggists, grocers, or through mail order. Patent medicines had been developed in Europe in the eighteenth century, but flourished in the nineteenth century with the development of the retail trade in medicines and in advertising.

Many remedies claimed to cure minor ailments and offered a cheap alternative to going to a doctor. Others were supposed to cure fatal diseases such as cancer, where doctors could offer little hope. Lydia Pinkham's Vegetable Compound, a mix of herbs and alcohol claimed to be a panacea —a cure-all. Advertisements claimed that the compound would:

> [C]ure the worst forms of Female Complaints, all Ovarian Troubles, Inflammation and Ulceration[,] Falling and Displacement of the Womb, and consequent Spinal Weakness, and is peculiarly adapted to the Change of Life. . . . It dissolves and expels tumors from the Uterus . . . Bloating, Flooding, Nervous Prostration, Headache, General Debility quickly yield to it. . . . It quickly removes . . . Dizziness, Faintness, sleeplessness, flatulency, melancholy or the "blues" and headache.[7]

The boom in sales of medicines was helped by a range of preparations aimed at people who were not ill, but who felt they need to protect or boost their health. Pills, potions, and powders promised health and vigor by cleansing the body, or stimulating the nerves, or building up the blood. Bile Beans and Beecham's Liver Pills promised robust health, while Bromo-phosoph was a "brain food" that would restore vitality. Tonics, often in the form of wine fortified with drugs, were particularly popular at the end of the century to combat the exhausting pace of modern life. Many patent medicines were presented as modern and based on scientific research. Lactopeptine claimed to contain "ptyalin, pepsin and pancreatine" to help digest starch, protein, and fats, respectively. Exotic foreign remedies were also popular. "Sequah's Prairie Water," a medicine reputedly based on Native American remedies, was sold across Europe in the 1890s.

By the late nineteenth century, patent medicines were sold around the world, from Europe and North America to colonies in Africa and Asia, where they were manufactured by local firms. In southern Africa, for example, European remedies were sold in stores, by mail order, and by traveling peddlers to Afrikaner farmers, Europeans, and Africans. Many patent medicines were popular with Africans, as they claimed, like indigenous remedies, not to cure disease but to strengthen the body and purify the blood. Bizarrely, "Dr. William's Pink Pills for Pale People" proved particularly popular among black Africans.

MEDICAL EXCHANGES

Knowledge of medicines traveled around the world in the nineteenth century. Western remedies were brought to Africa and Asia by practitioners and settlers in the new colonies; migrant workers from India and China took their own medicines to the Americas and Africa. In late nineteenth-century southern Africa, where European farmers, soldiers, and administrators worked alongside migrant workers from India and China, a rich mix of indigenous, Western, ayurvedic, and Chinese medicines were widely available. Such medical exchanges between different systems of medicine had a long history. Theriac or Venice treacle dated back to medieval times. It was a panacea, able to cure many diseases and counter poisons, and was reputed to contain as many as 70 ingredients, including the flesh of vipers. In the nineteenth century, unani *hakim*s in India were still importing and prescribing the medicine under the name "Treak farook."

With globalization, more and more doctors trained in different medical traditions came into contact and became aware of the remedies used in other medical systems. In India, ayurvedic and unani practitioners began to prescribe European medicines alongside their traditional remedies. In the early part of the nineteenth century, British doctors in India sought out local remedies as possible substitutes for expensive imported drugs. Over time, however, Western practitioners became skeptical about the efficacy of medicines used in other cultures.

MEDICINES AND PATIENTS

Patients were active consumers of medicine. In every culture, patients made their own medicines to treat everyday complaints using local plants and foodstuffs. When urbanization limited access to the wild plants that provided the raw materials for medicines, patients purchased ingredients or bought ready-made medicines. In Europe, even people who could afford to go to a doctor made use of homemade medicines. Whisky and hot water was a popular cure for colds; honey or jam dissolved in hot water soothed a tickly cough. Mustard added to a bath helped to warm patients suffering from chills and poultices made from all sorts of materials, including animal dung or old bread, were used to treat boils.

While Western practitioners took a conservative attitude toward medicines used in other cultures, their patients were happy to try alternative medicines if their usual drugs failed. In North America, many turned to alternative medicines such as homeopathy. Unorthodox systems were popular not only because they represented a more "natural" approach to healing, but because they were marketed as empowering ordinary people to become their own doctor. Kits of homeopathic and herbal medicines, along with books on their use, were sold by druggists. Settler families living a long way from towns and medical help turned to native herbal medicines, partly because they were easy to obtain, but also because it was generally believed that local remedies were particularly effective against local diseases. European farmers in South Africa were happy to try indigenous herbal remedies when their own remedies had failed. In Java, European settlers took local remedies for dysentery and used Chinese medicines to treat syphilis and diphtheria.

DRUG ADDICTION

The open market in medicines brought problems, as not only simple remedies, but poisonous or addictive drugs were readily available. Some medicines, such as opium, had a long history of both medical and recreational use. Opium was widely used in the Middle East, partly for pleasure and partly as a means of keeping healthy. In unani medicine, opium was classed as a cold dry medicine, and doctors particularly recommended it for older people and those living in damp climates as a means of preserving their health. Tea also shared this dual identity; it was a hot and humid drug but also a pleasant drink. In the West, doctors prescribed large qualities of opium-based drugs, such as laudanum (powdered opium dissolved in alcohol) to reduce pain, stop spasms, and promote sleep. The drug was cheap and widely sold by drug vendors. When the hypodermic syringe was developed in the 1860s, morphine came into general use for pain relief.

Many patent medicines containing opium were sold as treatments for aches and pains, minor ailments, and insomnia. Dr. Collis Browne's Chlorodyne, a popular remedy for diarrhea, contained opium. It was even included in medicines aimed at children. "Soothing syrups" were advertised as a way to calm teething children and crying infants. Working mothers regularly gave their children these medicines to ensure that they slept through the night or during the day while they were out at work. Enormous quantities of opium were consumed. In Britain, imports rose from 41,000 pounds in 1839 to 114,000 pounds in 1852. In the United States, the increase in opium imports was staggering: from 24,000 pounds in 1840 to over 500,000 pounds in the 1890s.

Not surprisingly, many people became addicted. With no laws against drug taking, in the late nineteenth century, the recreational use of morphine was widespread, socially acceptable, and even fashionable. Plans to treat addicts were devised, based on a gradual withdrawal or the substitution of alternative drugs including cocaine. This, of course, simply created a new form of addiction. By the end of the nineteenth century, there was a public outcry against the use of opium in Europe and North America. Laws were passed to control the sale of opium by pharmacists, and to stop the trafficking of the drug for recreational use. Newspapers mounted successful campaigns against the inclusion of opium in patent medicines, especially those intended for children.

NOTES

1. Oliver Wendell Holmes, "Currents and Counter-Currents in Medical Science," Address to Massachusetts Medical Society, in *Medical Essays 1842–1882* (Boston: Houghton Mifflin, 1892), pp. 202–203.

2. *British Pharmacopeia* (London, 1867), p. 123.

3. X. Marmier, *Lettres sur l'Algérie* (Brussels, 1852), pp. 71–72, quoted in Marie-Cecile Thoral, "Colonial Medical Encounters in the Nineteenth Century: The French Campaigns in Egypt, Saint Domingue and Algeria," *Social History of Medicine* 25 (2012), p. 621.

4. John Wilson, "On Chinese Pharmacy," *Pharmaceutical Journal and Transactions* 5 (1846), p. 567, quoted in Linda Barnes, *Needles, Herbs, Gods, and Ghosts: China, Healing and the West to 1848* (Cambridge, MA: Harvard University Press, 2005), p. 267.

5. *Wakefield and Halifax Journal*, November 16, 1832, quoted in Hilary Marland, "The Medical Activities of Mid-Nineteenth-Century Chemists and Druggists, with Special Reference to Wakefield and Huddersfield," *Medical History* 31 (1987), p. 433.

6. *Oudh Akhbar*, October 20, 1879, p. 3283, quoted in Seema Alavi, *Islam and Healing: Loss and Recovery of an Indo-Muslim Medical Tradition 1600–1900* (New York: Palgrave Macmillan, 2008), p. 253.

7. *The Sun*, December 1, 1905, p. 8, http://tsu.stparchive.com/Archive/TSU/TSU12011905P08.php.

CHAPTER 11

War and Medicine

The nineteenth century was an age of political and social upheaval. The desire for power and new territory, the emergence of new nations from older groups of states, old nations conquering new territory in Asia and Africa, and independent nations breaking away from their colonial masters all provided the catalysts for conflict. War changed radically during the nineteenth century. Around the world, weapons became deadlier: rifles replaced muskets, spears, and clubs, and killing became distanced and impersonal. In the West, war was industrialized. Armies became massive organizations with complex administrations to mobilize and support huge numbers of troops. Factories supplied weapons, ammunition, and food. The boundary between soldiers and civilians was blurred; civilians became increasingly conscripted into armies, provided medical care, and produced the goods that supported soldiers in the field.

War affected people's lives and health in many ways. For those involved in fighting, often hundreds or even thousands of miles from home, there was the risk of wounds or disease. Civilians were caught up in conflicts, forced to defend their homes or trapped in besieged towns, suffering from artillery bombardments or rifle fire. Far more were affected economically. For farmers able to sell their crops to the army, war was a time of prosperity; for civilians close to the battlefields, war could be a disaster. Soldiers in the field would take cattle and crops to feed themselves, and retreating armies destroyed foodstuffs to ensure they could not fall into the hands of the enemy, leaving civilians to go hungry. Not surprisingly, epidemics and famines frequently occurred in the aftermath of war.

WARS BETWEEN WESTERN POWERS

In Europe and the Americas, nations fought each other for power and territory. The nineteenth century saw frequent conflicts as the map of Europe was redrawn. The old Ottoman and Austro-Hungarian empires began to crumble, and the new nations of Italy and Germany were formed from coalitions of small states. In 1848, there were unsuccessful popular uprisings all over Europe against old rulers. These wars involved radically different types of conflicts, from set piece battles between huge armies (the Battle of Borodino in 1812, for example, involved around a quarter of a million troops) to guerilla warfare by Spanish civilians against occupying French forces during the Peninsular War of 1808–1813.

In the nineteenth century, wars became industrialized. Huge numbers of troops were delivered to the front lines by railroads and on steamships. They were supplied with weapons, ammunition, uniforms, and preserved and tinned food produced in factories. After 1854, the telegraph allowed rapid communications on the battlefield and brought news of war to homes within hours of the fighting. Weapons became more deadly. Muskets, accurate over relatively short distances and with a slow rate of fire, were replaced by high-velocity rifles. Artillery played a greater role in battles, while cavalry became redundant. Tactics changed, too; commanders abandoned the use of static formations of troops in favor of rapid maneuvers to attack defensive positions.

MILITARY MEDICAL SERVICES

Over the century, the medical care provided to soldiers steadily improved. Conscription—the compulsory enlistment of men into the armed services—was introduced during the Napoleonic Wars and continued thereafter in many European countries. As a result, a large proportion of the male population could expect to serve in the military at some point in their lives. While it was generally accepted that soldiers had to risk their lives when fighting, there was increasing public concern that they should be protected against disease and should receive good-quality medical care if hurt.

Soldiers and Disease

At the beginning of the century, armies suffered high levels of mortality even when not involved in fighting. Large barracks, where many soldiers lived, ate, and slept, provided a perfect environment for the spread of infectious diseases. From the 1850s, sanitary reforms, similar to those introduced in cities, were imposed on soldiers' accommodations. New barracks were built on healthier sites, away from swampy ground, with good drainage and ventilation and supplied with clean water. At the same time, new policies were introduced to improve soldiers' health. Regulations required soldiers to bathe regularly (initially at least every month) and to have their clothing laundered. Rations of alcohol were drastically curtailed, and soldiers were encouraged to drink beer rather than spirits. To reduce high levels of venereal disease, prostitutes visited by soldiers were required to undergo regular inspection and, if found to be infected, to enter hospitals for treatment. Vaccination against smallpox was made compulsory.

It was much more difficult to control disease when soldiers were on campaign. Camps were often set up quickly with little opportunity to dig latrines or secure clean water supplies. Officers lacked the time to enforce basic levels of personal hygiene among the rank and file. Typhoid fever was a constant scourge of armies in the nineteenth century, weakening Napoleon's forces in their attack on Russia in 1812 and causing huge casualties on both sides in the Crimean War of 1853–1856 and the American Civil War in 1861–1865.

BATTLEFIELD MEDICINE

The Organization of Care

Over the course of the century, the medical care provided to soldiers in the field was revolutionized. Haphazard and inadequate care was replaced by organized systems to rapidly evacuate soldiers through a hierarchy of medical posts where they received appropriate care. At Waterloo, the final battle of the Napoleonic Wars, fought on June 18, 1815, wounded soldiers received care at regimental medical posts. These temporary stations were set up just behind the lines. They had few staff, and during the battle, the supplies of medicines, dressings, and even clean water soon ran out. Soldiers with minor wounds walked, or were helped by comrades, to their regiment's medical post. The majority of the wounded remained on the field; at the end of the fighting, over 40,000 injured troops were spread over five square miles, and many waited for days to be discovered and given help. After the battle, wounded soldiers were cared for in temporary hospitals set up in nearby farms, villages, and towns. All available buildings—houses, churches, and stables—were pressed into service.

By the end of the century, a streamlined system of medical care for wounded soldiers had been developed, supported by more and better-trained medical staff. Mimicking industrial processes, the movement and treatment of wounded soldiers was broken down into a series of steps. When wounded, soldiers received first aid from their comrades; by the end of the century, all troops carried a field dressing in their uniforms. The injured soldiers were carried off the field by stretcher bearers to an aid post staffed by a medical officer. He re-dressed their wounds and carried out basic treatment to prepare the injured soldiers for the journey on to field hospitals away from the battlefield. These hospitals had a few hundred beds, a small staff, and basic equipment. Soldiers with minor wounds recuperated there, and then returned to the fighting. The more seriously wounded were moved further away to larger and better-equipped general hospitals. Although a vast improvement over the care provided to earlier generations of soldiers, the system was not perfect. During the journey between each post, often over bad roads, the soldier-patients were jolted, causing wounds to reopen, and some troops bled to death before reaching their destination.

Dealing with Wounds

More rapid evacuation of troops and quicker access to care undoubtedly saved lives. The treatment of battle injuries also improved radically, reflecting broader improvements in surgery. In the early decades of the nineteenth century, soldiers suffered from cuts inflicted by swords and lances and from wounds from cannon fire, shrapnel, and musket balls. Treatments were limited. Surgeons probed wounds to remove shrapnel; they stitched cuts and set broken bones. Most wounds became infected, so when faced with a badly mangled limb, surgeons usually chose to amputate. The survival rate for amputations was poor—between 10 percent and 25 percent of soldiers died following the operation. Amputating quickly—within a day after being wounded—increased a soldier's chances of survival; if they had to wait longer, the chances of dying from infection increased. By the mid-nineteenth century, treatment strategies remained the same, but wounded soldiers did have the benefit of anesthetics that allowed surgeons to operate more slowly and carefully. Later conflicts saw the introduction of improved techniques to control bleeding, using clamps, tourniquets, and elastic bandages. By the end of the century, surgeons had learned that efforts to remove bullets and shrapnel often introduced infection, so unless the object was in a dangerous position within the body, they simply dressed the wound and allowed it to heal.

Care was also better organized. At the siege of Sevastopol in the Crimean War, a Russian surgeon, Nikolai Pirogov, pioneered a system of triage or sorting. Instead of treating all officers first, then ordinary soldiers on a first-come, first-served basis, Pirogov divided the wounded into three categories. Those who were too badly wounded to survive were put to bed and received basic nursing care. Those with fairly minor wounds were given a number and asked to wait. Soldiers likely to live after surgery were given priority. Leo Tolstoy, the Russian writer, visited the hospital and described what he saw:

> You are assailed without warning by the sight and smell of forty or fifty amputees and critically wounded, some of them on camp beds, but most of them lying on the floor ... through the doorway on the left, that is the room in which wounds are bandaged and operations performed. There you will see surgeons with pale, gloomy physiognomies [faces], their arms soaked in blood up to the elbows, deep in concentration over a bed on which a wounded man is lying under the influence of chloroform, open-eyed as in a delirium and uttering words which are occasionally simple and affecting. The surgeons are going about the repugnant but beneficial task of amputation.[1]

Pirogov's system of triage was widely adopted and ensured that surgeons focused their efforts on the soldiers that could benefit from their care.

Mortality in War

Every war was different, in its length, intensity, and the types of weapons used, and consequently in the number of soldiers killed and the types of injuries they suffered. The muskets used in the Napoleonic Wars fired a large ball that caused terrible damage to flesh and bones. The high-velocity rifle bullets used in later conflicts caused less damage to the tissues, and as a result, the wounds healed better. The conditions in which troops lived and fought had a major impact on mortality. On Napoleon's retreat from Russia in the winter of 1812, over 350,000 French soldiers, around 95 percent of the army, died from cold and starvation. The total number of deaths caused by different conflicts varied widely. It is impossible to derive exact figures for the mortality caused by the Napoleonic Wars, fought between 1803 and 1815, but probably between 2.5 million and 3.5 million soldiers died. During the Crimean War, 25,000 British soldiers, 35,000 Turks, 100,000 French, and up to half a million Russians died.

Over the century, there was a clear trend in the proportion of deaths caused by wounds and disease. At the beginning of the century, soldiers were much more likely to die from disease than from injuries sustained in combat. During the Napoleonic Wars, the British lost 24 times as many soldiers to disease as to wounds. In the Crimea and the American Civil War, the ratio was five soldiers dead of disease to one from combat. In the Franco-Prussian War of 1870–1871, the Prussian army, with its well-organized medical services, lost 15,000 troops to disease and just 11,000 to wounds.

CIVILIANS AND WAR

Civilians suffered and died as a consequence of war, often in large numbers. In war zones, soldiers consumed local food supplies, disrupted trade, and brought infectious diseases so that epidemics and famines frequently followed war. An outbreak of plague the wake of the Russo-Turkish War of 1806–1812 killed one-third of the inhabitants of Bucharest in Romania. At least a million (and perhaps as many as three million) civilians died during the Napoleonic Wars as both a direct and indirect result of the conflict. Civilians were engaged in war in many ways: they worked in factories, supplying the materials used by soldiers, and they played an increasing role in providing medical care.

Civilian Nurses

In army hospitals, nursing care was provided by untrained orderlies and ward sergeants helped by soldiers' wives and camp followers. Civilians had traditionally helped to look after wounded soldiers following battles. In the aftermath of Waterloo, Belgian civilians helped to set up temporary hospitals and provided bedding and assistance to the wounded. Female civilian nurses began working in military hospitals in the 1850s. In response to reports of dreadful hospital conditions, in 1854, the British Secretary at War sent a party of female nurses, led by Florence Nightingale, to the Crimea.

Nightingale's impact on the British army's general hospital at Scutari (some 200 miles from the main Crimean battlefields) has become the stuff of legend. At the time, Nightingale was presented as a saintly figure, performing hands-on care and transforming Scutari from a death

Florence Nightingale (the central figure in this image) famously brought order to the chaotic conditions in the British military hospital at Scutari. This ward, staffed by male and female nurses is scrupulously clean and the windows allow in fresh air. (Library of Congress)

trap, where soldiers were neglected and left to die from wounds and disease. In fact, Nightingale (as even her family acknowledged) lacked the caring qualities of a nurse, but she was a brilliant administrator. She reorganized the hospital supplies and helped to instigate a massive clean-up. The other nurses kept order on the wards, reportedly scolding orderlies into making improvements, and distributing food and medicines. Their efforts had little effect on mortality, however—soldiers continued to die in huge numbers from typhoid, typhus fever, and dysentery. It was only when a sanitary commission discovered that the hospital's water supplies were contaminated by sewage that the death rates fell.

Female nurses also worked among French and Russian soldiers in the Crimea. French soldiers were cared for by nursing sisters from the Order of St. Vincent de Paul. In Russia, the Grand Duchess Elena Pavlova formed the Community of the Holy Cross, organizing teams of doctors and nurses to help Russian soldiers. The Crimean War set a pattern, and women formed a significant part of the medical workforce in later conflicts. In the American Civil War, women volunteered to serve as nurses, cooks, and cleaners for the Union army.

The Red Cross

Further civilian involvement in the care of soldiers came with the founding of the Red Cross. The movement was inspired by Henry Dunant, a Swiss businessman who witnessed the inadequate medical services provided to all combatants after the Battle of Solferino in 1859, one of the conflicts during the Italian War of Independence. Dunant wrote a pamphlet describing his experiences and concluded: "Would it not be possible, in time of peace and quiet, to form relief societies for the purpose of having care given to the wounded in wartime by zealous, devoted and thoroughly qualified volunteers?"[2] This was not a new idea—similar notions had been circulating since the end of the eighteenth century—but in the late 1850s, with growing concern for the welfare of soldiers, his ideas were swiftly put into practice. Over the next few decades, the Committee of the International Red Cross was formed in Geneva, and national Red Cross societies were formed throughout Europe, the Americas, the Ottoman Empire, and Japan. The new organization also drew up the first Geneva Convention in 1864, setting down rules for the treatment of sick and wounded soldiers and of civilian medical staff.

Initially, coordinating the civilian Red Cross Services with existing military medical services proved problematic. During the Franco-Prussian War, the French Red Cross Society worked separately from the army. While some of its volunteers undoubtedly helped many soldiers, its services were badly organized. The society sent out mobile field hospitals that were ill equipped, often over- or understaffed with untrained nurses, and rarely reached the battlefields when they were required. Civilians declared their homes to be Red Cross hospitals to escape the requirement to provide accommodation for soldiers, and society ladies set up hospitals as a means of proving their patriotism, regardless of where they were needed. By contrast, in Prussia, the work of Red Cross volunteers was closely coordinated with the army. The military medical services were highly organized, and Red Cross staff were used to complement the existing services. Red Cross nurses helped to staff hospitals and the hospital trains used to evacuate the wounded. They provided refreshments and manned re-dressing stations along the evacuation route. The Prussian approach provided the model for other national Red Cross societies in later conflicts.

War and Civilian Medicine

War is often portrayed as a laboratory, in which practitioners and administrators can experiment with new medical techniques and forms of organization that are later brought into civilian medicine.

There were certainly examples of civilian medicine drawn from war-time experience. In the nineteenth century, army ambulance services provided the model for civilian services. But the relationship between civilian and military medicine was complex. Much that was learned in wartime, such as new techniques to deal with bullet wounds, was simply not applicable to civilian life.

War had an important although indirect impact on civilian health by inspiring investments in infant welfare programs. Around the world, governments equated population with power: a large population provided men for the army and workers for industry. However, in the West, birth rates were falling, provoking fears that the population might shrink. There were also fears about the quality as well as the quantity of manpower. Large-scale inspection of recruits and conscripts revealed a worrying picture of the health of nations, revealing that many volunteers were unfit for service because they were too short, had flat feet, or had poor teeth. To ensure that the next generation of men would be strong and healthy, governments and charities set up schemes to improve the health of infants. Mothers were provided with free milk and were taught how to look after their children. Babies were weighed and monitored to ensure that they grew at the correct rate.

WARS BEYOND THE WEST

Outside Europe and North America, wars took many forms. There were short conflicts between different groups or tribes of indigenous people, or between indigenous people and foreign settlers, over access to land and other resources. There were civil wars between large groups within a single nation, like the Taiping Rebellion in China, which lasted for several years. With increasing global travel and conquest, European armies fought many wars overseas, seeking to control rebellions in established territories. Haiti broke away from French rule and became an independent republic in 1804, and Mexico, Brazil, Argentina, and Chile gained independence from their colonial masters in the 1810s and 1820s. Armies also fought overseas to gain new colonies in Asia, Africa, and the Pacific. In 1838 and 1856, the British fought the so-called "Opium Wars" to force the Chinese government to permit trading by European merchants. These wars took many forms: pitched battles between forces of hundreds of thousands of troops, sieges of cities, skirmishes, and guerilla wars.

There was no clear division between Western and non-Western in these conflicts. Often, the combatants were a mix of foreign and indigenous fighters. Māori joined with British forces to fight anti-British

Māori; the British army in India included large numbers of indigenous soldiers or *sepoys*. Non-Western armies, such as the imperial forces of Japan and China, adopted Western systems of command and weaponry. In other cultures, fighters used Western firearms alongside traditional weapons.

NON-WESTERN MILITARY FORCES

While wars between Western powers were usually fought with large bodies of well-trained and coordinated forces, the size of military conflicts in non-Western cultures varied radically. In India, the rulers of the Maratha Empire raised around 200,000 troops in the early nineteenth century to fight against the British East India Company. In the Satsuma Rebellion in Japan in 1877, an army of over 20,000 rebels, led by members of the traditional warrior class of *samurai*, fought against an imperial army of around 65,000 troops. By contrast, many disputes between indigenous peoples were relatively small scale. Among the Māori people of New Zealand, small groups of related people (*hāpu*) frequently engaged in conflicts. One *hāpu* could muster around 140 to 400 fighting men, but sometimes several *hāpu* allied to attack another group. In the Indian Wars in North America, most tribes had hundreds, rather than thousands of warriors, and large battles, such as Little Big Horn in 1876, involved perhaps 2,000 warriors (although it is difficult to arrive at a definite number).

When indigenous tribes unified under a single leader, they could support large and highly organized military forces. In the early nineteenth century, Shaka kaSenzangakhona, or Shaka Zulu, commanded an army of perhaps 15,000 troops, conquering an area of several thousand square miles in southern Africa. Shaka is often credited with inventing new tactics and introducing new weapons, and he undoubtedly developed the fighting capabilities of the Zulu tribes. Under his rule, Zulu warriors fought in named groups or "regiments" of 400 to 4,000 warriors, under a hierarchy of commanders. All young men had to serve in the king's army. They were called up for service at the age of 17 or 18, and they lived in a separate community, or barracks, associated with their fighting group or regiment. Each group had its own distinctive headdress, and carried cowhide shields of a different color. In the barracks, they went through a period of training, including exercises in the use of weapons and in military tactics.

In conflicts involving indigenous groups, the division between civilians and combatants was never hard and fast. In cultures such as the Māori and Zulu, all adult men were likely to be involved in warfare at some point. In popular uprisings, such as the Haitian Revolution of 1791–1804, a large proportion of the slave population took part in the fighting. Women supported warfare behind the lines by growing and carrying food to be eaten on campaign and by helping the wounded. In some cases, they fought alongside men. Indian women helped to fight against American cavalry by frightening the soldiers' horses. In the Taiping Rebellion, there were separate units of female fighters, while Māori women worked alongside male warriors building defensive structures.

WEAPONRY AND TACTICS

The risks of death and injury to warriors depended on the type of weapons they faced. In the early nineteenth century, wars between indigenous peoples were often fought with traditional weapons that had been in use for hundreds or thousands of years. Māori fought hand to hand with stone clubs (*mere* or *patu*). From the 1810s, they traded with passing ships for iron tools, such as billhooks, that they also used in combat. Traditionally, Zulu warriors fought using light throwing spears and small shields, but under Shaka's rule, they added heavier stabbing spears (*assegai*) and clubs to their armory. Native American peoples fought with bows and arrows from horseback. All these weapons were most effective at fairly close range and capable of causing serious cuts, broken bones, or death.

Traditional weapons had a strong symbolic function as well as a practical one. The Japanese *samurai* were traditionally allowed to carry two swords, and the Satsuma Rebellion was sparked when the modernizing imperial government attempted to deprive warriors of this sign of their status. In the conflict, the rebels fought mainly with guns and artillery; but during the final battle, warriors made a last symbolic charge using their swords.

By the middle decades of the century, the risks of death or serious injury were increased by the use of firearms such as muskets, rifles, and artillery. In most conflicts, both sides had guns, but the quality of firearms often had a decisive impact. In the Taiping Rebellion in China, the rebels had older, less powerful rifles, while the imperial armies had better rifles and modern artillery pieces, purchased from Europe. Zulu and Māori fighters acquired muskets, but they were often old, required a long time to reload, and frequently malfunctioned. As a result, their guns were much less effective than might be expected. The Māori began to acquire muskets in the early nineteenth century, and when first introduced they had a significant effect in combat, as coordinated volleys of fire killed large numbers and caused confusion. However, warriors quickly devised new tactics that reduced their effect. Guns were not fully integrated into Zulu ways of fighting. In battle, the Zulus used them rather like throwing spears, firing one shot, then continuing forward without attempting to reload. When they reached the enemy lines, they fought hand to hand with spears and clubs.

Fighters used an assortment of tactics. Many conflicts mirrored those of the West: in wars in India, China, and Japan, large armies fought battles in which one side set up defensive positions around a fort, city, or strategically important piece of ground, and the other attacked using artillery and infantry. The Chinese armies had traditionally mounted sieges, but they proved ineffectual when facing British and French ships and artillery during the Opium Wars. By contrast, the Indian Wars in North America involved a mix of battles and guerilla warfare that allowed small numbers of warriors to make best use of their mobility and limited weaponry to attack civilians or small groups of enemy combatants. While most battles were fought by soldiers on foot, cavalry forces took to the field in India, in northern China during the Nein Rebellion of 1851–1868, and in North America.

Indigenous people used elaborate fighting strategies, both defensive and offensive. Wars between Māori people usually took place around the community's *pā*, a defensive enclosure surrounded by fences, ramparts, and ditches. The local people would withdraw into the enclosure, with supplies of food and water, and defend the area against efforts to undermine or burn down the defensive walls. When firearms were introduced to Māori warfare, the *pā* was redesigned to absorb musket fire and to allow the defenders to fire out onto the enemy. Between 1845 and 1872, when facing British forces armed with modern artillery, Māori designers incorporated underground "bunkers" roofed with stones that allowed warriors to survive even heavy bombardments. At the Battle of Gate *Pā*, British troops entered the structure, believing all the fighters to be dead as a result of a fierce artillery bombardment. They fled in panic when Māori warriors suddenly appeared from their underground structures. Māori also devised completely new types of defensive structures to halt the progress of British troops—long lines of ditches and trenches, with redoubts. As soon as it became clear that the position could no longer be held, the Māori abandoned these positions to build new structures at other strategic points.

By contrast, the Zulu army used offensive tactics, splitting into three groups to encircle the enemy. This formation was called "the beast's horns." Young, mobile fighters moved around to the right and left,

The Zulu tribes had highly trained and disciplined warriors, who fought using elaborate military tactics. This group of warriors display the distinctive coloured shields and headdresses associated with different sub-groups of the army, and carry spears. (Private Collection/The Stapleton Collection/The Bridgeman Art Library)

while the more experienced fighters remained in the center. Once in position, the warriors launched a rapid, coordinated attack. These tactics proved successful at the Battle of Isandlwana in 1879, when a Zulu army of around 20,000 warriors encircled and attacked a British army camp, killing large numbers of troops. From a defensive position, however, the British troops were able to make better use of their superior weaponry and defeat much larger forces of Zulu warriors. At Rorke's Drift, fought shortly after Isandlwana, around 140 British troops held off a force of 3,000–4,000 Zulu warriors.

Medicine

Fighting groups drawn from indigenous peoples rarely had organized medical services. The highly organized Zulu army had healers to provide supernatural medicines as a form of preparation and protection. Before going into battle, warriors went through a process of purification: they drank medicines to make them vomit; then they were sprinkled with water containing substances including human flesh, to give them power and make them invincible. After the battle, the surviving Zulus went through a further purification process. Wounded Zulu warriors, like fighters from other cultures, had to find their own care. They walked or crawled or were carried away from the battlefield by comrades or family members. Many died from wounds on the field. Those who made it back to safety were treated by healers. Grasses, moss, and herbs were used to clean wounds and prevent infection. Zulu healers sewed up large wounds using sinews, but could do little for bones shattered by high-velocity bullets. In the years after the Zulu wars, travelers reported meeting veterans of the conflicts with multiple large scars, proving that at least some survived their injuries.

European troops serving overseas had the benefit of organized medical care, but even the best medicine could do little in the face of exotic and unfamiliar diseases such as yellow fever, to which troops had little or no immunity. Soldiers died in vast numbers. During the Indian Mutiny of 1857, the British army lost 9,467 soldiers; 586 were killed in the conflict, but 8,881 died from disease. The French lost 36,000 of their 39,000 soldiers sent to fight in Haiti in 1802–1803 to disease. Disease affected not only troops fighting in unfamiliar climates. Thousands of civilians and fighters died during an outbreak of plague spread through disruption to trade routes during the Muslim Rebellion of 1862–1877 in China.

MORTALITY IN NON-WESTERN CONFLICTS

Mortality in wars outside the West varied enormously. In a small skirmish, a handful of warriors might be injured and none killed. Rebel armies tended to suffer high mortality as they fought to the last. During the Satsuma Rebellion, around 18,000 of a total force of 22,000 rebel troops were killed or wounded. By contrast, the Japanese government army of 65,000 soldiers lost 6,000 killed and 10,000 wounded. Sieges of towns were very destructive. During the battle of Nanking in the Taiping Rebellion, 100,000 inhabitants died as fighting and fire swept through the city. During the Anglo-Boer War of 1899–1902, thousands of civilians were trapped alongside British troops in the besieged towns of Ladysmith, Mafeking, and Kimberley. Many were killed by shelling from the Boer artillery, and all suffered from the severe food shortages. The Boers besieging Ladysmith cut off the town's water supply, forcing the inhabitants to drink polluted water and causing outbreaks of typhoid and dysentery. Toward the end of the war, large numbers of Boer civilians, mainly women and children, were interned in over 100 concentration camps to prevent them from providing aid to the Boers' guerilla campaign. The camps were crowded and unsanitary, with inadequate shelter and food. Diseases, including measles and pneumonia, spread quickly. At least 28,000 women and children and around 20,000 black people died in the camps.

Several factors helped to reduce the death toll from conflicts between indigenous people. Wars were usually short, because agricultural societies could not grow and store enough supplies to feed a large force of warriors for long periods. In addition, their fighting men were also farmers, and fighting had to stop during planting and harvesting seasons. In some conflicts between indigenous people, the rules of war were designed to avoid wholesale slaughter and to limit the number of deaths. Although the Māori people engaged in frequent conflicts, they had extremely elaborate strategies to reduce the number of casualties. *Taua muru* conflicts were far more common than full-scale wars. These conflicts were a means by which one group sought redress or punished another group, but without outright war. Satisfaction could be achieved without bloodshed, by plundering food stores or destroying crops. Rituals, such as performing a *haka* (a war dance), or brandishing weapons replaced actual fighting. Muskets became part of this ritualized fighting: warriors would exchange symbolic volleys of fire, or fire into the ground to prove their readiness to attack, without causing any injury.

Full-scale Māori wars involved up to several hundred warriors, with women and slaves to support them. Even in these conflicts, there were clear rules of engagement. In order to achieve a victory with limited bloodshed, chiefs sent out warnings before launching an attack, or agreed before the battle not to kill more than a certain proportion of the defenders. Fighting stopped at dusk to allow the defenders to come out of the *pā to* forage for food and water. When one side sensed that they were likely to lose, they used peacemakers to find a resolution. This might involve giving up land and moving away from the area, or presenting the victors with gifts such as canoes or clothing. The victors took prisoners or slaves, some of whom were killed and eaten. The rules of engagement were not always observed. A missionary, writing in 1845, noted:

> The wars of the tribes are . . . generally conducted with moderation, and in accordance with established rules: this may arise partly from superstitious grounds; but when some act of more than usual atrocity has been committed by one party [i.e., the rules are broken by one side] it seems like a signal to proceed to acts of the greatest barbarity. But these cannot be regarded as mere acts of wanton cruelty; they are perpetrated with a view to intimidate the opposite party.[3]

In conflicts between Zulu tribal groups, there was some element of ritual, and the disputes caused relatively few casualties. By contrast, the battles between British and Zulu forces were extraordinarily violent, as the Zulu warriors pressed on with their attacks. One Zulu described how, during a battle:

> We never got nearer than 50 paces to the English, and although we tried to climb over our fallen brothers we could not get very far ahead because the white men were firing heavily close to the ground into our front ranks, while the "by and bye" [artillery] was firing over our heads into the regiments behind us ... Some of our men had their arms torn right off by [shells]. The battle was so fierce that we had to wipe the blood and brains of the killed and wounded from our faces, arms, legs and shields after the fighting.[4]

At the Battle of Isandlwana, around 1,300 of the 1,750 British defenders were killed along with around 1,000 Zulu warriors. At Rorke's Drift, the British suffered only 14 casualties, but the encounter ended with 350 Zulus dead and perhaps another 500 wounded Zulus massacred, in revenge for previous encounters. By March 1879, the huge death toll from repeated battles had decimated and demoralized the Zulus, who could no longer put a large army into the field.

NOTES

1. Leo Tolstoy, *The Sebastopol Sketches* (London, 1986), pp. 44, 47–48, quoted in Orlando Figes, *Crimea: The Last Crusade* (New York: Penguin Books, 2010), p. 298.

2. Henry Dunant, *A Memory of Solferino* (Geneva: International Committee of the Red Cross, 1986), quoted in John F. Hutchinson, *Champions of Charity: War and the Rise of the Red Cross* (Boulder, CO: Westview Press, 1996), p. 18.

3. Octavius Hadfield, "System of Government among the New Zealand Tribes," manuscript, Grey Collection, Auckland Public Library, quoted in Angela Ballera, *Taua, "Musket Wars," "Land Wars" or Tikanga? Warfare in Māori Society in the Early Nineteenth Century* (New York: Penguin Books, 2003), p. 71.

4. Account of Chief Zimena, *Natal Mercury*, 1929, quoted in Ian Knight, *The Anatomy of the Zulu Army from Shaka to Cetshwayo 1818–1879* (Mechanicsburg, PA: Stackpole Books, 1995), p. 220.

CHAPTER 12

Institutions

While a one-to-one consultation between a fee-paying patient and an independent practitioner was by far the most common form of medical encounter, care provided through institutions became more frequent around the world in the nineteenth century. Institutions can be defined as organizations or structures developed for some social purpose. In the case of medicine, the range of institutions was very broad: they were responsible for organizing and delivering care to the sick, disease prevention, medical research, and training medical practitioners. Institutions were able to work in ways that individual practitioners could not. Large-scale projects, such as cleaning up the urban environment by instituting street cleaning or installing citywide drainage, required collective planning and financing. Only well-funded institutions could afford to buy new and expensive medical technologies, such as X-ray machines and operating theater equipment.

The growth in the range and numbers of medical institutions in the nineteenth century was driven by rapid and widespread social change. The movement of workers from the countryside to cities, factories, and plantations created a class of people who lacked family support in times of illness or injury. In rapidly growing and often unsanitary cities and towns, there was a need for measures to control and prevent disease. New welfare and medical institutions also reflected changing expectations of health services. Medicine was no longer a luxury available only to those able to pay: increasingly, governments acknowledged that they had a responsibility to ensure that their populations were not exposed to disease, while charities helped the poor to find care when they fell ill.

MEDICAL INSTITUTIONS IN THE WEST

In Europe and North America, institutions played a prominent part in providing medical services, especially in opening up access to high-quality medical care to all social classes. Churches and charities had a long tradition of providing care through hospitals and other institutions, and they continued and even increased these activities throughout the nineteenth century. However, much of the growth in the number of medical institutions and their expanding range of activities was due to the entry of the state into the provision of medical services. This brought huge new investments in hospitals, welfare programs, and especially public health reforms.

The Funding of Institutions

Churches and charities had traditionally organized care for the poor and sick, and they continued to play a leading role in this work throughout the nineteenth century. Protestant and Catholic churches collected money ranging from small donations at church services to major endowments of land or property to provide free treatment for poor patients in hospitals or in their own homes. Hospitals, dispensaries, and clinics catering to the poor and run by secular and religious charitable bodies were also funded through public donations. Toward the end of the century, these charities pioneered new services, such as welfare programs providing advice, medical care, and food to poor mothers and children, and schemes to educate midwives.

Donors gave money to these institutions for several reasons. There was a strong humanitarian or religious impulse to help people who could not afford to pay for treatment. Medical services also had a social or moral purpose. The hard-working poor or members of religious congregations were more likely to be given care than the improvident and impious. Education on hygiene not just served to control disease, but also incorporated a message about the benefits of order and thrift. The donors also benefited; by contributing to medical charities, they demonstrated their generosity and concern for those less well off than themselves.

Over the course of the century, central and local government bodies began to provide medical and welfare services and programs of disease prevention and control funded through taxes. A growing number of institutions also provided medical services in return for fees. By the end of the century, wealthy patients were able to pay for treatment in hospitals, nursing homes, and clinics. Various forms of prepayment or insurance helped to spread the cost and opened up these services to a wider population.

HOSPITALS

Hospitals have a very long history. From medieval times, hospitals run by Christian churches had offered the old, the sick, and pilgrims a place to stay. Originally, hospitals offered only limited medical care, as they were primarily places of care and hospitality rather than of cure. Hospitals began to acquire their modern character in the late eighteenth century, gradually becoming centers for high-quality, modern medical treatment, staffed by well-trained practitioners and treating patients suffering from serious injuries and illnesses.

At the beginning of the nineteenth century, hospitals were confined to large towns and cities. A few were very large; the *Allgemeines Kranenhaus* in Vienna, opened in 1784, had 2,000 beds, but most

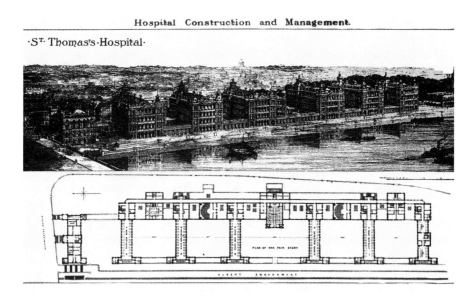

St. Thomas' Hospital, London, opened in 1871 on the River Thames, was one of the first institutions built on the pavilion plan, with long wards opening off a central corridor to prevent cross infection between different groups of patients. (National Library of Medicine)

institutions had accommodation for fewer than 100 patients. Hospitals were modeled on large country houses, with grand entrances (which usually housed the institution's offices), wings containing the patient's rooms or wards, and courtyards where patients could take exercise.

Over the century, the number of hospitals grew; by 1900, every town of any size had a hospital, while cities had several, and their average size also increased. Hospital design was transformed in an effort to combat the possible spread of infection. New hospitals were laid out using the pavilion plan. Large wards were housed in "pavilions"— buildings well separated from each other and laid out in such a way that staff and patients never passed through a ward to get to any other part of the hospital, thus avoiding any possibility of carrying contamination from one ward to another. The wards themselves were long and narrow, with many large windows that could be opened to provide a flow of fresh air to blow away bad smells and germs. Walls, floors, and furnishings were made of impermeable materials that could be kept scrupulously clean.

In the early part of the century, only certain types of cases were admitted to hospitals. The rules of the Infirmary in Huddersfield, a town in the north of England, declared:

> No person be admitted ... who is able to pay for medical aid ... no apprentices or servants ... no soldier[s] ... no woman advanced in pregnancy, no child under six years (except in particular cases, as fractures, cutting for the stone, amputations, couching, or where some other surgical operation may be required) or persons disordered in their senses, subject to epileptic fits, suspected to have the smallpox, measles, itch, or other infectious distemper, having habitual ulcers, syphilis ... or those suspected to be in a consumption, or an incurable or dying state.[1]

Charitable hospitals preferred to take in sick or injured adults likely to recover with a few weeks' rest and care and who would then return to work. Curing such cases boosted the institution's reputation and established its role in serving the local economy by helping to restore men and women to the workplace. This in turn helped to attract more funding.

The exclusive admissions policies of some general hospitals drove the creation of other hospitals. Specialist hospitals were founded to treat children, to care for patients suffering from fever and other infectious diseases, and for pregnant women to deliver their babies. Governments and charities funded the care of patients suffering from chronic diseases and requiring long-term care. With the development of medical knowledge, specialist hospitals or departments within general hospitals were also founded to treat particular conditions, such as diseases of the skin or of the ear, nose, and throat.

Over the century, hospitals became centers for the treatment of the most serious cases of illness and injury. An increasing number of patients were admitted for surgery, as the introduction of anesthesia and antisepsis allowed surgeons to treat severely injured patients and to operate for a greater number of conditions, such as stomach ulcers and appendicitis. Operating theaters became a crucial part of the hospital, developing from spaces designed to allow students to observe operations (sometimes crammed into lofts) to suites of rooms carefully designed to provide the best environment for surgery. Wooden floors and plastered walls were replaced with sterile glass and tile, and simple tables were replaced by special operating tables. Better lighting and equipment to sterilize instruments was installed. To deal with the increased number of surgical cases and patients suffering from acute illness, hospitals employed more and better-trained nurses. Over the century, nurses' work shifted from domestic care—cooking meals and keeping the ward tidy—to a more medical role, closely monitoring their patients and performing simple medical tasks as well as keeping patients comfortable and ensuring a high level of cleanliness.

For much of the century, hospitals treated the poor. In return for receiving free care, patients were expected to express their gratitude to the institution and its donors. Some were used as teaching material for medical students. Patients were subjected to a strict regime: there were timetables for meals, regular ward inspections, few entertainments, and little freedom to move around. Patients grumbled that an obsession with fresh air meant that wards were cold and drafty. In extreme cases, they rebelled. Lepers in a hospital in Lima, Peru, marched out to the viceroy's palace, protesting that the hospital's chief doctor was using them as guinea pigs for a new treatment.

Rich patients were formally excluded from charitable hospitals, and in any case, they did not want to be cared for alongside the poor. Instead, they were treated in their own homes, even undergoing surgery there. By the late nineteenth century, however, it was clear that hospitals offered much higher standards of care than were possible in a domestic setting. Private hospitals, private wards within general hospitals, and nursing homes were established to cater to middle- and upper-class patients able to pay for treatment.

Relatively few patients were admitted to hospitals; much larger numbers were treated as outpatients at hospitals, clinics, and dispensaries. In the 1890s, the large London teaching hospitals treated at least

10 times more outpatients than inpatients admitted to the wards—over 100,000 outpatients each year. Outpatient departments and dispensaries dealt mainly with patients suffering from minor illnesses, such as respiratory complaints and stomach upsets. Nurses and doctors (often junior members of hospital staff) offered basic treatments and prescribed simple medicines. Patients were seen on a first-come, first-served basis and, despite the very basic standard of care, were willing to stand or sit in line for hours to receive free treatment.

PREVENTATIVE MEDICINE AND PUBLIC HEALTH

While hospitals and other institutions offering treatment to the sick were funded by a mix of religious, charitable, and government support, the field of public health was dominated by the state. From the 1830s, across Europe and the Americas, governments developed increasingly extensive policies to protect the populations from the threat of disease, usually based on temporary measures mounted in response to epidemics. Generally, central government departments set policy and municipal and regional agencies were responsible for putting it into practice. Governments in different countries engaged with public health and disease prevention to varying degrees. Some, like the United States, largely left responsibility for health in the hands of community or state authorities. In European nations, such as Britain, central government drove the public health agenda and helped to fund reforms. Progress was far from steady; an outbreak of disease often prompted communities to action, only for their enthusiasm to lapse as the danger passed. Nevertheless, public health programs grew in size and scope, driven by rising expectations that governments should protect their populations from disease.

The type of actions taken to prevent disease shifted over the century, reflecting changing medical knowledge. In the first half of the century, public health policies centered on sanitary reforms—large-scale projects to remove dirt from the urban environment by introducing street cleaning and refuse collection, and citywide schemes of drainage, sewage processing, and water supply. Charities backed up these projects through health education, teaching the poor (especially women) about the need to keep their bodies, clothes, and homes clean. From the 1870s, germ theory permitted a more targeted approach. State and local authorities set up isolation hospitals to care for people suffering from infectious diseases and to prevent the spread of disease through the community. In an age when infections are largely controlled by immunization and antibiotics, it is easy to forget that at the end of the century, in some European countries, the majority of hospital beds were provided for patients suffering from infectious diseases.

From midcentury, doctors and public health administrators became increasingly aware of the link between disease and low standards of living; people who lived on a poor diet, had inadequate housing, and were unemployed were much more likely to fall ill than those who enjoyed better living conditions. This knowledge underpinned the development of welfare programs. States became involved in supplementing the free medical care provided through charities, ensuring that the poor had access to doctors and to basic medical treatments. Pensions were introduced to save the elderly from falling into sickness and poverty, and state-run health insurance schemes gave working men access to basic medical primary care. The first scheme was launched in Germany in 1888 and was copied in many European countries. Contributions from government, employers, and individual workers were pooled to pay for care provided by designated doctors. Governments also provided free medical aid to certain groups. Schoolchildren were subjected to regular medical inspection, to identify problems with teeth and eyesight, illnesses, and infestation with parasites such as head lice. Infants were targeted by government welfare programs that monitored their growth and provided assistance to mothers to ensure that their children grew into healthy adults.

INSTITUTIONS AND THE MEDICAL PROFESSION

Institutions played an increasingly important part in the lives and careers of medical practitioners during the nineteenth century. Doctors in Europe and North America trained in medical schools and universities, where they spent several years attending lectures, dissecting bodies, developing practical skills in laboratories, and observing practice on hospital wards. During their studies, as well as acquiring knowledge, students absorbed the ethos of the profession—the ethics and behavior expected of a doctor—and made contacts with their peers and with more senior practitioners.

In many (though not all) countries, separate institutions oversaw the training offered by medical schools, to ensure that practitioners trained in different institutions reached an acceptable level of competence. In Britain, this role was performed by the General Medical Council, formed in 1858. In the United States, there was much less oversight, and standards of medical teaching were largely left to market forces. Ambitious students paid more for the best teaching; students who chose to attend

schools offering less rigorous training for lower fees were less likely to
gain access to prestigious posts.

Institutions played an important role in building a medical career.
Over the course of the century, newly qualified doctors increasingly
began work in hospitals or dispensaries as junior staff, gaining experience in diagnosis and treatment. Most doctors then left institutional
work to take up practice in the community, but the most ambitious
climbed through a hierarchy of hospital posts, hoping to become a con-
sultant or surgeon. Hospital posts were hard to come by, and some
determined young practitioners solved the problem by starting their
own small specialist hospitals as a way to build their expertise and gain
a reputation. A few practitioners went on to study and work in research
institutions. In Europe, these were mostly funded by governments, but
the Pasteur Institute, one of the most prestigious institutions, was
funded by public donations made in recognition of Louis Pasteur's
work on vaccines to prevent disease.

INSTITUTIONS OUTSIDE THE WEST

Institutions played a less prominent role in medicine outside the West.
Before the nineteenth century, medical care was provided by religious
institutions and by hospitals supported by wealthy individuals.
Practitioners at the courts of rulers in Asia trained small numbers of
students. In the nineteenth century, as in Europe and North America,
population growth and urbanization created a need for new institutions to offer care to members of a mobile population. Rulers and rich
merchants were inspired to revive traditional institutions, to found
new institutions modeled on traditional lines, and to establish
Western-style institutions. Colonial governments and charities introduced Western institutions, such as hospitals, dispensaries, and medical schools. Western institutional care was not always popular with
local populations; the most successful were those where care was
adapted to the local culture.

TRADITIONAL WELFARE IN CHINA

During the eighteenth and nineteenth centuries, while state involvement in medicine gradually increased in Europe and North America,
in China the role of the imperial government in health care declined.
During medieval times, the state had appointed government doctors,
set examinations for all practitioners, and countered epidemics by
organizing the distribution of free medicines to the poor and setting

up hospitals to care for the sick. The government gradually withdrew from these activities from the sixteenth century, and the gap was filled in part by charities set up by wealthy individuals, who wished to display their generosity and concern for social order as set out in Confucian teachings. In the nineteenth century, the need for such care increased, as the upheavals of the Taiping Rebellion, the famines of 1877–1879, and the movement of people from the countryside to the cities created migrants and refugees who lacked the family networks that usually provided support and care to the sick.

A variety of charitable institutions offered different forms of care. In the city of Tianjin, for example, wealthy merchants paid for orphanages and a hospital. The hospital developed from an institution to help ailing travelers and, by the nineteenth century, had become a sort of nursing home caring for the elderly. Donors also paid for the burial of corpses abandoned in the city streets. This was important for the physical and spiritual health of the community. Corpses could spread disease, and the spirits of the dead who did not receive full burial rites were believed to become "hungry ghosts" and cause disease among the living. As well as providing care and support, charitable institutions in China (like those in Europe) tried not to breed dependency and aimed to train the beneficiaries in correct ways of living.

> Throughout the ages, charities have been very concerned with providing food and clothing, considering this to be the highest good. However, these sorts of activities simply create a generation of lazy, apathetic people. How can we improve the simple and lazy nature of the Northerners and avoid bringing out their worst characteristics? ... Our task is to ensure that each and every individual has his own work and can rely on his own efforts to support himself.[2]

The Hall for Spreading Benevolence in Tianjin was a charity set up to provide a home for impoverished widows and their children and for young women sold as servants or concubines. To ensure that the women followed the Confucian precept of chastity, women, boys, and girls were strictly segregated within the accommodation. Women could go outside the institution only with a female escort. The male children of widows were trained in a trade; the young women had to work in the institution's textile workshop.

RELIGIOUS INSTITUTIONS AND HEALING

Religious foundations served as centers of medical care in many cultures. Hospitals were attached to Christian convents and monasteries, where monks and nuns provided medical care alongside spiritual aid to the sick poor. Buddhist monasteries also had a long tradition of offering care, and some became famous as centers of healing. In China, the Bamboo Grove Monastery in Xiaoshan City had a long tradition of treating women's illnesses. The monks there had acquired special knowledge of how to treat these conditions in the tenth century from a stranger—actually a Buddhist deity in disguise—who gave the monks a book of remedies. In the nineteenth century, a few monks who resided in the monastery continued to practice medicine and enjoyed a reputation for successfully treating menstrual disorders, problems associated with pregnancy, and slow labors. Accounts of their treatments circulated widely through books published by grateful clients. Unlike learned Chinese practitioners, they did not use the pulse to diagnose illness, but listened to a description of the patient's symptoms. They prescribed a range of secret medicines based on classical Chinese medicine and very similar to those described in standard medical texts, although some incorporated folk remedies and talismans.

The Bamboo Grove Monastery offered a form of healing similar to that provided by secular practitioners, but many religious institutions offered spiritual medicine. Buddhist and Hindu deities were believed to be capable of curing and preventing diseases and helping women to conceive and to have sons. Many of these gods were believed to have powers over particular diseases such as *T'ou-Shen Niang-Niang* and *Sitala*, the goddesses of smallpox in China and India, respectively. Those seeking help visited temples, monasteries, or pilgrimage sites associated with healing figures to pray, make offerings, or promise gifts should their wish be granted.

ADAPTING WESTERN INSTITUTIONS

Donors in Asia and Africa drew on both Western and traditional models when founding new institutions. Islamic cultures in North Africa had a long tradition of providing medical care through hospitals. Medieval *bismaristan* (or *maristan*) are often seen as the first true hospitals, as they had more medical personnel and placed a greater emphasis on curing patients than Christian hospices of a similar period. Islamic hospitals were traditionally funded by endowments of land; by the nineteenth century, these rarely provided enough income to support the institutions, and many had fallen into decay. While some hospitals remained open in Ottoman Turkey, none had survived in Iran. During the nineteenth century, wealthy members of society looked back to this tradition and funded new hospitals either by making new endowments or through donations. The hospitals were modeled on those in the West and aimed to offer high standards of medical care.

In India, there was a long history of charitable giving to beggars, pilgrims, and travelers. In the nineteenth century, this was translated into support for new, Western-style institutions offering medical care. In the second half of the century, many dispensaries were founded by local governments within Indian states to provide medical care to the poor, offering basic medical and surgical treatments. Over time, government support declined, and wealthy local citizens were encouraged to donate to these institutions. While the dispensaries were organized along Western lines, the care was adapted to the local culture. Some dispensaries employed both Western-trained doctors and unani *hakims*, thus allowing patients to choose the type of medical care they wished to receive. Hospitals offering only unani medical treatment were founded in the early twentieth century, as part of the more general revival and reform of unani medicine. The female rulers of Bhopal in India founded several hospitals, including one for women living in seclusion (*purdah*) with only female staff. As in the West, these dispensaries not only served poor patients, but provided valuable jobs for young Indian doctors, helping them to build their careers. For donors, the dispensaries provided a means for them to display their benevolence and a way of creating contacts with colonial administrators.

Adapting Care in Western Institutions

Western institutions that adapted care to the local culture proved very successful. Hospitals and dispensaries run by Christian missions flourished in China; by 1906, there were 241 dispensaries and 166 hospitals. Unlike Western institutions, in the Chinese hospitals the families of patients played an active and important role in treatment. Just as in an encounter with a traditional Chinese physician, relatives would accompany a patient seeking admission to the hospital, providing information on the course of the illness to help the doctor reach a diagnosis. A friend, servant, or family member accompanied each patient admitted to the hospital. They provided nursing and support to the patient, sleeping in the same room, preparing their food, and tending to their needs. They even accompanied patients into the operating theater. Compared to hospitals in the West, mission hospitals imposed few rules on their patients. They were free to sit up, move about, eat, talk, and even smoke as they wished.

The active participation of family members in hospital care was a mixed blessing. On the positive side, the support from relatives and friends helped to give Chinese patients (especially female patients) the confidence to seek help from Western doctors, and their labor allowed mission hospitals to care for large numbers of patients with very few staff. The Chinese Hospital in Shanghai had six wards for 30 patients, cared for by one missionary doctor and two Chinese assistants. However, family members also interfered with the course of treatment; sometimes they gave patients local remedies if they believed that the medicines provided by the mission doctors were inappropriate, and they often ignored the doctor's advice on diet.

Clinics offering free vaccination against smallpox were opened in many parts of Asia by colonial and indigenous governments, but the procedure received a very different reception in different countries. In Japan, vaccination was supported by local rulers and elite practitioners, and offers of free vaccination were readily accepted by the general population. The procedure was introduced to Nagasaki in 1849 and its use was spread by *ranpō* physicians—Japanese doctors trained in Western medicine. The practice was taken up by wealthy families, anxious to protect their own children against smallpox. They extended the benefits of vaccination to poorer families by funding vaccine clinics that attracted large numbers of children.

Similarly in China, the sponsorship of wealthy members of society ensured that institutions offering free vaccination attracted many clients. Vaccination was introduced to China in 1805, when a group of wealthy merchants and a surgeon working for the East India Company set up a clinic in Canton. The practice spread rapidly; between 1860 and 1911, 43 vaccination clinics were set up all over China. Initially intended for the poor, the clinics proved so popular that they opened their doors to all children. The procedure followed by Chinese clinics was similar to that in vaccine institutions in Europe, but was adapted to fit with Chinese theories that smallpox was caused by "fetal poison," left in the body of children after birth. In the West, children were vaccinated at any time of year and at any point on the arm or leg. In China, vaccination was offered only at favorable seasons, in spring and autumn. The cowpox matter was placed on the Lesser Yang circulation tract, where it was carried to the kidney and thus helped to remove the fetal poison from the body.

In India, a failure to take account of local sensibilities meant that the vaccination was only gradually accepted by the indigenous population. Inoculation—the practice of deliberately infecting children with smallpox in the hope that they would have a mild form of the disease—was widely used within the local population. Vaccination was

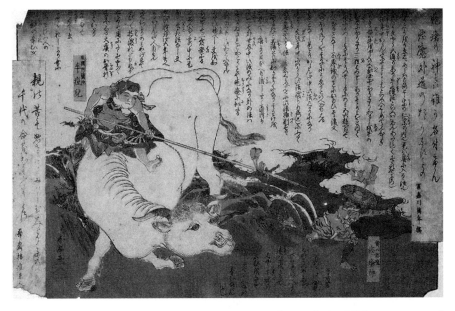

This handbill encouraged Japanese parents to have their children protected against smallpox using the new western technique of vaccination. The image, made in a traditional style, shows a child seated on a cow chasing away a smallpox demon. (Courtesy of Archives and Special Collections, Library and Center for Knowledge Management, University of California, San Francisco)

introduced to India in 1802, and European administrators assumed that the new, much safer procedure would quickly supersede inoculation. Their hopes were dashed. Vaccination proved unpopular because it did not fit with traditional practices. Whereas inoculation was practiced only at certain times of the year, and accompanied by prayers and special diets, vaccination was offered year-round, and vaccinated children were given no special treatment. Parents also resisted taking their infants to be vaccinated by unfamiliar practitioners employed by local governments. Hindus objected to a practice using vaccine that originated in cows—a sacred animal—and all respectable Indian families feared that their child might be vaccinated using material taken from the arm of a child from a lower caste.

Public Health

Around the world, Western medicine provided the model and the inspiration for public health initiatives. Many towns in China and North Africa had ancient systems of water supply and drainage as well as teams of night-soil men who collected excrement and other refuse to fertilize local farmland. However, as cities expanded, this infrastructure broke down. The population of Tehran in Persia (modern Iran) grew from a few thousand to around 200,000 in the nineteenth century. Travelers reported that:

> [S]treams of water in dirty ditches called *jubes*, run through the centre of the streets ... These ditches served at the same time for irrigation streams, drains and wash-tables, and in warm weather gave forth the most pestilential odour. Refuse of all sorts were thrown out in the streets, courtyards, or anywhere in the open.[3]

Similar conditions were reported from other cities in Asia and South America; drainage ditches were blocked with waste, water tanks and rivers were polluted, and cemeteries were overcrowded.

The nineteenth century saw renewed initiatives to keep cities clean and well supplied with water, modeled on Western sanitary reforms, with the aim of increasing the comfort of inhabitants and as a means of reducing disease. Local and central governments set up permanent bodies to oversee public health issues, and to organize street cleaning, better water supplies, drainage, and sewage. Later, like Western governments, they turned their attention to improving child health and regulating housing. Rural areas, with their more scattered population, tended to lag behind in public health reforms, even though houses in the countryside were often overcrowded and unsanitary.

ADOPTING WESTERN INSTITUTIONS

Western institutions were also transplanted wholesale into Asia and Africa by colonial governments. Given the importance of hospitals in the West, it is not surprising that colonial administrators and indigenous rulers sought to introduce similar centers for care. For example, in Sri Lanka, a British colony from 1815, the colonial authorities established government-funded hospitals and dispensaries to care for the sick poor in the cities, modeled on those in Europe. Provision was extended to provinces by local welfare societies, funded by a mixture of charity and government support. In Africa, hospitals were funded by Christian missions, rather than governments. In Iran, new hospitals were established by a range of Western agencies, including missionaries, foreign legations, commercial companies, and charities such as the Russian Red Cross.

In Asia, the Pacific, North Africa, and South America, colonial governments tried to spread scientific medicine to their populations and ensure a supply of doctors for the army by setting up institutions to train practitioners in Western medicine. The first medical schools in South America were set up in Brazil in 1808 by the Portuguese royal family at Rio de Janeiro and Salvador da Bahia. Sydney Medical School, the first in Australia, began teaching in 1883. In China, mission hospitals acted as centers for medical training. Textbooks were published in Chinese languages in the 1850s. Formal training in Western medicine was available from 1866 when the first medical school was opened. However the number of students trained in Western medicine was very small—there were only around 300 graduates by the end of the century.

The teaching of Western medicine also spread to independent states where it was seen as "progressive" and as a means of ensuring the health of the population. Western-style medical training was available in Egypt at the *Dar al-fonun* from 1852, under the leadership of French practitioners and using French textbooks translated into Arabic. In Japan, the government founded medical schools modeled on those in Germany. By 1900, there were 14 medical colleges that had trained roughly one-half of all practitioners working in the country. Through Japan, Western medicine was introduced to Taiwan and Korea. Not all Western medical schools succeeded. A medical school founded in Lima, Peru, in 1808 was based on the outdated teaching of the University of Leiden in the eighteenth century. Not surprisingly, the school was widely criticized, and it closed in 1834.

In India, the colonial authorities experimented with the teaching of ayruvedic and unani medicine alongside Western medicine. Faced with a shortage of practitioners, in 1822, the Native Medical Institute was founded in Kolkata by the British East India Company to train students to work as assistants within the Indian Medical Service. Students were taught anatomy, medicine, and basic surgery using European texts translated into Indian languages, but also ayurvedic and unani medicine. However, the initiative was short-lived, and the teaching of indigenous medicine was abandoned in 1835.

The Native Medical Institute was replaced by schools where the teaching was modeled on that of Europe. Like medical schools in France and other European countries, the Kolkata Medical College, founded in 1835, offered different grades of education. One group of students followed a standard curriculum, covering anatomy (including human dissection), theory and practice of medicine, pharmacy, chemistry, and materia medica. Lectures were given in English. Students in other classes studied a smaller range of subjects, with a greater emphasis on practical medicine, and were taught in Indian languages. Even though the curriculum followed that of Western medical schools, the content was adapted to the Indian context.

> It is ... incumbent upon [the medical teachers] to teach their pupils the nature of disease and the principles of treatment, as regarded practically from an Indian point of view ... Every Englishman, who has risen to the rank of a first-class practitioner in India, has learnt the necessity of unlearning many of the principles which he brought with him, and of cautiously adapting the rest of his store of knowledge to surrounding circumstances.[4]

Materia medica and pharmacy classes included teaching in the use of native medicinal plants.

Schools dedicated to teaching ayurvedic and unani medicine were not established until the late nineteenth century, as part of an effort to improve standards of medical knowledge and practice. Traditionally, ayurvedic and unani medicine had been taught on a very small scale. Rather than a large group of students attending lectures, a practitioner would train just a few students at a time, guiding their reading of classical texts and allowing them to observe the processes of diagnosis and prescription. From the 1880s, Indian practitioners set up unani medical schools, as part of a drive to improve the status of the system. From 1872, a four-year course in unani medicine was offered at the Oriental College in Lahore (in modern Pakistan). In 1889, teaching was also established in Delhi, India at the *Madrasa-e-Tibbia,* and in Hyderabad.

NOTES

1. "Rules for the Admission and Discharge of Patients," quoted in Deborah Brunton, ed., *Health, Disease and Society in Europe, 1800–1930: A Source Book* (New York: Manchester University Press, 2004), p. 25.

2. *Chongxin Tianjinfu zhi* (*Revised Gazetteer of Tianjin Prefecture*), 1898, quoted in Ruth Rogaski, "Beyond Benevolence: A Confucian Women's Shelter in Treaty-Port China," *Journal of Women's History* 8 (1997), p. 72.

3. James Fraser, *Travels and Adventures in the Persian Province on the South Banks of the Caspian Sea* (London, 1826), p. 158, quoted in Ebrahimnejad Hormoz, *Medicine, Public Health and the Qājār State: Patterns of Medical Modernization in Nineteenth-Century Iran* (Boston: Brill, 2004), p. 37.

4. "Medical Education: Bibliographical Record," *Indian Annals of Medical Science,* vol. 2 (1855), p. 723, quoted in Christian Hochmuth, "Patterns of Medical Culture in Colonial Bengal, 1835–1880," *Bulletin of the History of Medicine,* 80 (2006), p. 52.

CHAPTER 13

Disease, Healing, and the Arts

At first glance, medicine and the arts seem odd bedfellows; in the nineteenth century, medicine in the West was increasingly seen as a science. Nevertheless, medicine and the arts intersected at many levels. Images and objects used by practitioners in their work were designed to be not only functional, but also beautiful; or they were decorated in ways that were pleasing to the eye and increased their healing power. In stories, images, and music, writers represented the diseases that terrified them and celebrated the healers who conquered them. As a result, the arts mirrored medicine in the nineteenth century—the new diseases that moved around the globe, the illness bred in the slums of growing cities, the power of new medical knowledge and practices, and the changing consumption of medical services.

IMAGES AND MEDICAL KNOWLEDGE

Around the world, practitioners made use of a wide range of objects and images to convey information about the body in their practice and to teach students. While some were provided strictly technical data, such as an X-ray plate, many others combined the practical and the aesthetic.

Western Medical Images

In the West, anatomical images had a long history of being more than purely practical. From the Renaissance, images of skeletons and dissected bodies were portrayed in a naturalistic manner, as if still alive. Skeletons appeared to look at skulls, like Hamlet in William Shakespeare's play, pondering on death. Dissected figures were drawn holding up their own skin to allow the viewer to examine the muscles and organs beneath. In the nineteenth century, beauty was sacrificed to utility. Complex backgrounds for anatomical figures disappeared as did all elements of the individuality of the dissected body such as the face, hair, and clothing.

At the same time, anatomical images began to reflect doctors' belief that disease affected particular organs or tissues. A new genre of images appeared, showing disembodied diseased organs such as a lung or kidney. Illustrators aimed for clarity; images were hand tinted or printed in color to show alterations to the appearance of the body parts caused by disease. Alternatively, the organs were shown injected with different colored waxes, to highlight different structures.

As surgery became more important within Western medicine, artists were employed to draw illustrations of different stages of an operation, such as the amputation of the leg. Images were also used to record different wounds and injuries. John Bell, a Scottish surgeon with considerable artistic abilities, produced a series of drawings of soldiers suffering from different types of wounds inflicted during fighting in the Crimean War. During the American Civil War, photography was used to record soldiers' injuries and the results of successful amputations. Although these images were intended simply as a record of the work of army doctors, they have a compelling quality and have been exhibited as artworks.

Asian Medical Images

In Asia, images and text often gave a pleasing appearance as well as conveyed technical information. In Tibetan medicine, which included elements of unani medicine alongside Chinese and ayurvedic ideas, practitioners used bloodletting charts. These gave practical information on where and when to let blood to treat various conditions, but they also incorporated images of gods and animals in complex and beautiful designs. Chinese medical texts included simple drawings of patients suffering from conditions such as skin diseases. Often rather stylized, the drawings showed the whole patient, rather than focus on portraying the symptoms in detail. Instead, the disease was described in the accompanying text, and words and image were laid out in a sympathetic and pleasing way. Books on acupuncture showed the points where the needles were to be inserted, in order to treat certain conditions. Sometimes, the charts were plain and very functional, showing the front and back of the whole body or a part of the body, such as an ear. In other works, acupuncture points and channels were illustrated using realistic paintings of figures, shown standing and with some of their clothing removed to reveal the relevant part of the body. The images shared the page with text describing the uses of the acupuncture points. Similar aesthetic considerations dictated the presentation of medicinal plants in Chinese texts. Drawings provided an accurate representation of the shape, the texture, and sometimes the color of fruits, flowers, and leaves alongside the associated text.

Chinese practitioners also made use of three-dimensional images. Carved ivory figurines of a woman lying on a couch were given to elite female patients, who could not expose their bodies to practitioners, so that they could indicate where they felt pain. The ivory figures were simple, but realistic. The women appeared to recline in natural positions in their carrying boxes, with calm facial expressions and elaborate carved hairstyles.

In nineteenth-century China, it was not acceptable for male doctors to see the bodies of their elite female patients, only to hold their wrist to feel the pulse. Women used these ivory figures to mark where they felt pain. (SSPL/Getty Images)

In Japan, traditional forms of visual media were used to help popularize vaccination, a new practice introduced from the West. Smallpox patients often had images of the warrior *Tametomo* defeating the smallpox demon hung in their rooms to aid recovery. To help popularize smallpox vaccination, a Japanese practitioner, Dr. Ryusai Kuwata, commissioned a woodcut in a similar style. This showed a child seated on a white cow, chasing away a smallpox demon with a spear. Text laid out around the image explained the new practice and urged parents to have their children vaccinated.

A remarkable set of images that bridge East and West were produced by Lam Qua, a Chinese painter trained in Western art. Between 1836 and 1855, he was commissioned by Peter Parker, an American medical missionary, to paint a series of over 100 portraits of patients suffering from huge tumors and growths that were subsequently removed at the Canton Mission Hospital. Parker took the paintings back to the United States to explain the work of the mission and to raise funds. Unlike anatomical drawings in the West, these were genuine portraits; while the images were dominated by distortion of the body caused by the tumor, they also showed the sitter's face and body and revealed something of their character.

ART AND SPIRITUAL MEDICINE

In the West, the objects and instruments used in scientific medicine were designed to be purely functional, with little or no consideration for decoration or aesthetic qualities. For example, at the beginning of the century, surgical instruments might have handles made of attractive wood, but they were otherwise quite plain: with the advent of antiseptic surgery, they were made entirely of metal that could be sterilized. By contrast, the objects associated with Western and non-Western spiritual medicine were often produced with great skill and elaborately decorated, in part to give them a pleasing appearance, but mainly to enhance their healing powers.

Outside the West, healers were often people of great knowledge and power who had a particular role and status within their society. In many cultures, healers wore special clothing or carried objects that marked them out. Tibetan practitioners were immediately recognizable by their elaborately decorated clothing and hats. Among North American indigenous peoples, medicine men wore clothing that was painted, embroidered, or beaded with images of stylized animals or symbols. Healers also carried special objects. In many African cultures, healers carried special bags or containers for medicines, decorated in particular styles using materials including shells, beads, and metal. Others had decorated staffs or rattles used in healing ceremonies to communicate with the spirit world. In some cultures, healers wore masks. Among the Inuit of Canada, shamans wore masks representing the contorted features of a healing spirit.

HEALING OBJECTS

Divination was often used by healers to diagnose illnesses caused by supernatural forces—ghosts, spirits, or witches. Diviners threw small objects on the ground or a mat. As supernatural forces dictated where and how each object came to rest, healers discovered the cause of disease by interpreting their positions. Objects used for divination ranged from simple, natural objects such as shells, stones, or seeds, to carved and decorated objects made of wood or bone. These took the form of decorated plaques or sometimes small animal figures, as particular spirits were associated with certain animals. The divining objects were kept in and thrown from special containers. In some cultures, these were simple baskets or gourds; in others, the bowls or containers were elaborately carved.

In many African cultures, two- or three-dimensional figures were used in medicine and are now highly prized for their artistic qualities. For African healers, the figures served to collect and hold supernatural power that could then be used to cure, prevent, or cause illness or injury. Figures were made of wood, bone, or clay, and were often produced by professional carvers. They acquired their powers by being rubbed with medicinal substances, or by having medicines attached to or placed inside the figure, and through ceremonies. In some cases, they had to be activated by further ceremonies; the figures used by Yoruba healers would be "woken up" by having metal objects such as nails hammered into them, or by setting off small explosions using gunpowder. Some medical figures were very simple. In Yoruba culture, *sigidi* figures were roughly shaped from clay mixed with medicines. When activated by ceremonies, they developed a spirit that could be controlled by a healer to cause illness or even to kill. Other figures, such the *minkisi* (singular *nkisi*) used by people in the Congo were carved from wood. They looked toward the sky, and had partially opened mouths as if about to speak. Some figures were quite plain, others elaborately decorated, with carved representations of chief's hats or headdresses and painted or decorated with fabric and feathers. *Minkisi* figures stored power from the spirits of the dead that was used to protect against illness or injury or to cause illness to strike other individuals. They were also used in rituals to protect warriors going into battle.

In many cultures, statues of pregnant or breastfeeding women, or women holding small children, were used to treat infertility and to help ensure a safe and speedy birth. The images were often highly stylized, emphasizing the belly, breasts, and female facial features. Among the Ashanti people, for example, women who wanted to conceive carried a wooden doll called an *akua mma*. The dolls had a simple, rudimentary body and limbs but large, carefully carved flat circular faces, narrow eyes, and curved brows, all features associated with Ashanti ideals of beauty.

African medicine figures linked the natural and supernatural worlds. In many religions, deities were believed to influence the lives and health of the living. Highly decorated images or figures of gods and deities associated with medicine, such as *Yakushi Nyorai*, the Buddha of healing, or deities linked to diseases such as cholera, were placed in Hindu and Buddhist temples. There, people offered prayers, food, and incense and requested the gods to protect them from disease or to cure them of their ailments. In China, carved figures of the Medicine King, often shown with a tiger and dragon, were given to temples by donors. The figures were made with a small cavity to contain a piece of paper with the name of the donor and a request for help.

Spiritual or supernatural healing often involved some form of ceremony. Music, in the form of drumming, chanting, and singing, played an important role in calling up or driving away spirits, or sending healers into trance states where they could contact the spirit world. Native American peoples carried out elaborate Thirst or Sun Dances, to seek healing for a sick person or to give thanks for a cure. In a large, specially built lodge, communities came together to dance, sing, blow through bone whistles, drum, and pray for four days. In parts of China, ceremonies were held each year to protect the community from disease. In southern China, communities held festivals to seek the protection of Marshal Wen against epidemics. For several days, parades were held that included drummers and people dressed as Marshal Wen and his entourage. In this form, the deity left his temples and patrolled the streets, chasing away any ghosts or evil spirits that might bring disease. At the end of the festival, there was a feast, and the disease demons were enticed on to a decorated bamboo and paper boat, fitted out with paper furnishings, tools, and food. This was towed out on to a river or the sea and set on fire. During the festival, actors performed plays, puppet plays, and operas that portrayed the chasing away of demons and ghosts. Such ceremonies were also held during outbreaks of disease, in an effort to expel the illness from the community. In eastern China, the Five Emperors were invoked to give protection against disease. Images of the emperors, shown as fierce and ugly figures with blue or black faces, red hair, and military costumes, were worshipped in temples.

Images were also widely used to prevent disease by chasing away demons or spirits from homes. In Japan, wooden or pottery models of *Shoki* the "Demon Queller," a rather plump warrior with a fierce expression, were hung up to frighten away demons. In China, plaques painted with frightening demon faces and in the Nicobar Islands in the Indian Ocean, "scare devils"—wooden figures with wings, sometimes wearing Western dress—were used for the same purpose. In North Africa, people wore charms or jewelry with representations of eyes to deflect the malign influence of the "evil eye" that was believed to cause illness.

Containers used to store or to give medicines to patients were often highly decorated. The decoration was a means of imparting power to the medicines. Among North American peoples, bowls used to make up medicines or to give remedies to the sick were carved with animal symbols to give the medicine additional power. In Tanzania, plain gourds or calabashes were used to store foodstuffs, but calabash containers for medicine were decorated and had elaborately carved stoppers. Medicine containers were also made of special materials; antelope horn was used in Africa to make small vessels that were decorated with carvings of spirits and decorated with feathers. Carved rhino horn containers were used in Tibetan medicine. In other cultures, including China and Japan, decoration was used on medicine containers both to show the value of the contents and to present a pleasing appearance. Expensive medicines were stored in elaborately decorated chests or in decorated porcelain jars. In Japan, *inrō*—small cases made of beautifully carved and painted wood or lacquer—were used for carrying medicines or snuff.

In Europe and parts of Africa, images of Christian saints and God were the focus for requests for healing or for protection from disease. In Ethiopia, priests from the Orthodox Church produced long scrolls to cure or prevent disease. Made from a long strip of parchment cut to the same length as the patient's body, the scrolls were covered with images of kings and prophets from the Old and New Testament and abstract designs, often incorporating eyes, to represent God or angels. Texts offered prayers and requested divine help for the owner of the scroll. Similar texts and images were also written on small pieces of parchment that were folded up and worn as amulets to prevent disease.

Paintings of saints, showing important events from their lives, were found in every Catholic church in Europe and the Americas. In the Eastern Orthodox Church, painted icons with stylized images of the Virgin and Christ were often heavily encrusted with silver or gold and precious stones. In the Western Catholic Church, figures of the saints and of the Virgin Mary stood in elaborately carved and painted chapels. In times of crisis, such as an epidemic, these images were the focus of prayers and were carried around a town or village to drive away the disease. Images were also left in churches as a sign of gratitude by people whose prayers had been answered. These votive objects took the form of small models of the part of the body that had been healed, such as a hand or eye, or paintings depicting the illness or injury and the intercession of a saint.

PRACTITIONERS AT WORK

Portraits of formally trained medical practitioners are found all around the world as both two-dimensional images and three-dimensional figures. Images of non-Western practitioners usually showed them at work, treating patients. In China, for example, there were many images of male doctors taking the pulse of a female patient. Similar scenes were depicted by Japanese *netsuke*, miniature sculptures used to attach objects to the belt of a kimono. These images present the doctor in a sympathetic light, but others criticized or made fun of learned doctors. In Japan, cartoons depicted incompetent doctors carrying out eye surgery likely to render the patient blind, or practitioners trying to cure patients with impossible complaints such as a woman who wants to have her neck shortened. For Europeans traveling to the colonies, healers were part of a strange and exotic world, and they commissioned paintings of ayurvedic practitioners at work, being consulted by patients and carrying out eye surgery.

In the West, the work of surgeons was celebrated in paintings epitomizing their new status as heroes of medicine. Thomas Eakin's paintings *The Gross Clinic* (1875) and *The Agnew Clinic* (1889) and Adalbert Seligmann's painting *Theodor Billroth Operating* (1899) all show distinguished surgeons in control of the operating theater. All are engaged in teaching, passing on their skills and knowledge to audiences of students. (It has been suggested that the artists drew on religious paintings when designing their work, with the surgeon as a Christ-like figure surrounded by acolytes.) The paintings were extremely realistic, showing the anaesthetized patient and surgical instruments (*The Gross Clinic* aroused controversy because it showed a very small amount of blood).

The paintings reflect the development of surgical technologies in the use of ether or chloroform anesthetics and the shift to wearing special clothing. While Samuel Gross and his assistants wore ordinary street clothes, Billroth and his assistants were shown in surgical gowns, although they did not have masks or gloves.

PORTRAITS OF PRACTITIONERS

In the West, huge numbers of portraits of doctors were produced in the nineteenth century: as paintings, as printed images, and in fiction. The rising number of images reflected the shifting social status of medical men. For centuries, only wealthy individuals could afford to commission artists to paint portraits of themselves and family members. In the nineteenth century, professional men such as doctors could also afford painted or photographic portraits.

Doctors chose to be portrayed as learned gentlemen, usually soberly dressed, with a serious facial expression. Some were shown with objects linked to their careers including books, papers, or even medical instruments. Alexander Wood, a Scottish physician, chose to remind viewers of his role in the development of the hypodermic syringe: in his portrait he holds an early syringe. The relatively low costs of photography allowed the creation of group portraits, reflecting the increasing importance of institutions in the careers of doctors and nurses. Medical and nursing students frequently owned class photographs, providing a permanent reminder of the school or hospital where they had trained. Group photographs of the staff of a hospital ward or surgical team reinforced the importance of working in a team.

DOCTOR AS HERO OR VILLAIN

Portraits of practitioners also appeared in novels and paintings for a general audience. Doctors appeared as heroes, dedicated to caring for their patients regardless of reward, or as villains using their knowledge to advance themselves financially or socially. The novelist Anthony Trollope presented a sympathetic portrait of the general practitioner in *Doctor Thorne* (1858). The title character was not a brilliant scholar, but he faithfully served the local community. Trollope accurately portrayed the social tensions within medicine in mid-nineteenth-century Britain. The hero of the title is a provincial general practitioner who does not think it beneath him to dispense medicines and treat poorer clients as well as the local gentry. This gets him into a dispute with the established elite practitioners in the area. In this and other novels,

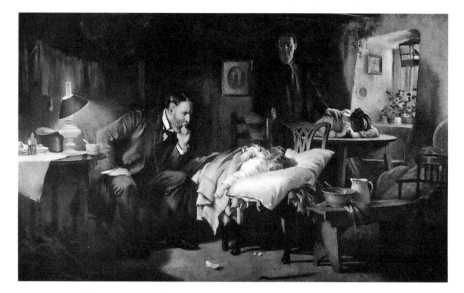

Luke Fildes' painting *The Doctor* presents a sympathetic image of a caring practitioner watching over a poor child, and reflected the high regard for the medical profession in late-nineteenth century Britain. (National Library of Medicine)

Trollope shows the reader what he thinks of elite physicians by giving them ludicrous names such as Dr. Omnicrom Pie, Dr. Mewdew, and Dr. Fillgrave.

A similarly positive image of the doctor was provided by Luke Fildes's painting *The Doctor* (1890). The painting shows the ideal doctor, watching over a sick child in a poorly furnished room. Here the doctor is hard working (dawn is breaking, so the doctor has spent at least part of the night with his patient), and selfless (the poorly furnished interior suggests that he is not likely to be paid well for his efforts). Fildes was not the only artist to produce such positive images of practitioners; there was a genre of paintings of humanitarian doctors showing their compassion by their care for the living and respect for the dead.

Many portraits of doctors were much less respectful. Right through the century, cartoons portrayed medical men as greedy and incompetent, more concerned with their fees than ensuring that their patients recovered. Late-nineteenth-century cartoonists also poked fun at women doctors: they were either so glamorous that male patients fell in love with them, or rather masculine and unattractive. In Gustav Flaubert's *Madame Bovary* (1856), the doctor Charles Bovary is overambitious and lacking insight. Dr. Bovary is an *officier de santé*, a second grade of practitioner trained in a medical school but without taking a full degree course. Nevertheless, attempting to prove that he is abreast of recent medical developments, Bovary treats a local man's club foot by cutting the tendon—an operation far beyond his abilities. The wound becomes infected, and a more qualified doctor has to be called in to amputate the limb. His real downfall is not his medical ambition, but his choice of an unsuitable wife. Emma sees marriage to Bovary as a step up the social ladder, but quickly becomes discontented with her dull life and dull husband, and she embarks on a series of affairs, runs up debts, and finally commits suicide.

Overambition was also the cause of the downfall of Tertius Lydgate, one of the main characters in George Eliot's *Middlemarch* (published in serial form in 1871–1872). Lydgate is anxious to pursue medical research through the observation of cases in a small, provincial hospital he has helped to establish. His career suffers as he spends more time on research than on the day-to-day work of treating patients, and his downfall is accelerated by his marriage to a self-centered young woman more concerned with social status than with professional reputation. Lydgate is forced to abandon his research and become a practitioner at a fashionable resort in order to make money.

A more extreme fate was meted out to the title character in Mary Shelley's *Frankenstein* (1818). It reveals a deep concern about doctors' knowledge of the human body. The hero, Dr. Victor Frankenstein, is a brilliant scientist who builds a "creature" from human body parts and brings it to life using electricity. (Shelley was making use of the discovery that electrical impulses ran along nerves, made in the 1790s.) Frankenstein's hideous creation is unable to integrate with society and wreaks a horrible revenge on its creator by murdering members of Frankenstein's family. In Robert Louis Stevenson's novella *The Strange Case of Dr. Jekyll and Mr. Hyde* (1886), research also proves fatal to its medical protagonist in a work that explores the tensions between outward Victorian respectability and inward uncontrolled passions. Dr. Jekyll, a respectable practitioner, develops a potion that he hopes will suppress the occasional evil urges that he struggles to control. Instead, the potion transforms him into Mr. Hyde, a cruel and violent man. At first, Jekyll is able to reverse the transformation, but increasingly Hyde takes over. At the end of the novel, Jekyll/Hyde commits suicide.

Sir Arthur Conan Doyle's stories of Sherlock Holmes neatly encapsulated the ambivalent views of medical men. Conan Doyle was trained as a doctor, but turned to writing and, from 1886, produced a very successful series of stories featuring the detective Sherlock Holmes and his companion Dr. John Watson. The character of Holmes was inspired by Dr. Joseph Bell, one of Conan Doyle's teachers at medical school. Bell was a brilliant diagnostician, able to draw conclusions from apparently trivial features of the patient's appearance. Holmes approached his cases in the same manner. In "The Adventure of the Norwood Builder," Holmes instantly deduced that a client is a bachelor, a solicitor, a Freemason, and an asthmatic from his untidy clothes, the legal papers that he carried, a charm on his watch-chain, and his labored breathing. Holmes is a complex character, lacking in empathy. His friend and sometimes accomplice Watson is far more sympathetic and displays more feeling, but is less insightful.

PATIENTS

Writers and artists also presented varying images of patients and practitioners. Many novels contained semi-comic characters obsessed with their health and petrified of falling ill. Mr. Woodhouse, the father of the heroine in Jane Austen's *Emma* (1815), spends much of the novel worrying about the effects of diet, temperature, and climate on his own health and that of his family and friends. Although Mr. Woodhouse's concerns are exaggerated for comic effect, he does reflect how middle- and upper-class people pursued good health by carefully monitoring their lifestyle and were willing to pay a practitioner for advice on preventing ill health as well as treating disease. The theme of the power of the paying patient over their practitioners continued through the century. Cartoons in magazines such as *Punch* portrayed fickle upper-class patients changing their doctors when offered a diagnosis they did not like, and working-class patients and children showing little respect for the profession.

The patient did not have the whip hand all the time. The introduction of anesthetics aroused concern that doctors would take advantage of their helpless patients to carry out unnecessary or experimental surgery. The contrast between the powerful surgeon and the helpless patient was graphically represented in Henri Gervex's painting *Before the Operation* (1887). In a striking and disturbing image, a partially clad and anesthetized female patient is exposed to the gaze of a number of fully dressed doctors.

THE IMPACT OF DISEASE

In the West, art, literature, and music all dealt with diseases, particularly those that aroused fear among the public. Disease was rarely portrayed in simplistic ways; authors and artists offered changing and sometimes contradictory views of the same condition.

Cholera, a disease that arrived in Europe for the first time in 1830 and spread terror through the population, was the subject of many images. Colored engravings showed the horrific effects of cholera: attractive women became withered, blue corpses; people collapsed in the street, struck down with cramps and vomiting. Émile Loubon, a French painter, conveyed the fear that reached all sections of society in his *Emigration pendant l'epidemie de cholera a Marseille en 1850 (Migration during the Cholera Epidemic at Marseilles in 1850)*. The painting shows carriages, carts, and people on foot fleeing the city for the healthier countryside. Cholera was also the subject of cartoons, in which the disease appears as a person, dressed in strange, often oriental clothes, recalling the origin of the epidemics in India. Other cartoons satirized the ineffectual efforts of local authorities to deal with the emergency.

Disease was portrayed in novels as a way of analyzing social ills and drawing attention to the social conditions of the poor. In his novels and magazine articles, Charles Dickens exposed the dreadful living conditions in the rapidly growing slums of London and the diseases that bred there, ready to escape and infect the wealthy and respectable residents. In a famous passage in *Bleak House* (1852), a fictitious slum district called "Tom-all-alone" is portrayed as a person spreading infection.

> There is not a drop of Tom's corrupted blood but propagates infection and contagion somewhere. It shall pollute, this very night, the choice stream ... of a Norman house, and his Grace will not be able to say Nay to the infamous alliance. There is not an atom of Tom's slime, nor a cubic inch of any pestilential gas in which he lives, not one obscenity or degradation about him, not an ignorance, not a wickedness, not a brutality of his committing, but shall work its retribution, through every order of society, up to the proudest of the proud, and to the highest of the high ... Tom has his revenge.[1]

Dickens was warning his middle-class readers of the dangers of failing to help the poor of society, leaving them ill housed, ill fed, and diseased. In *Bleak House*, the diseases emanating from the slums claim two victims. Jo, the crossing-sweeper who lives in Tom-all-alone, dies of an unnamed disease, probably a respiratory illness. His death stands in for that of all poor people; Dickens ends the scene with the stinging rebuke "And dying thus around us, every day." Esther Summerson, a middle-class woman, catches smallpox from Jo and is left permanently disfigured.

Smallpox also causes the death of the title character of Émile Zola's *Nana* (1880). Nana is a courtesan, a prostitute with a string of upper-class lovers, who rises from the gutter to fame and fortune. At the end of the novel, smallpox robs her of her beauty and her life. Zola links the disease with Nana's roots in poverty, and describes it returning her body to its social as well as its physical origins. Her dead body is described as:

> [A] charnel–house, a heap of pus and blood, a shovelful of putrid flesh. The pustules had invaded the whole face, so that one pock touched the next. Withered and sunken, they had taken on the greyish colour of mud, and on that shapeless pulp . . . they already looked like mould from the grave . . . Venus was decomposing. It was as if the poison she had picked up in the gutters, from the carcasses left there by the roadside, that ferment with which she had poisoned a whole people, had now risen to her face and rotted it.[2]

The most common cause of death for much of the nineteenth century was tuberculosis. It was frequently depicted in art and in opera, but in a strange, contradictory way. Tuberculosis sufferers were usually women, and the disease highlighted their feminine characteristics—they were frail, beautiful, and passive, their pale skin contrasting with their red lips. The disease was believed to heighten creativity (many writers suffered from TB) and was associated with sexual indulgence. The realities of the horrible death from tuberculosis—the pain, fever, and racking cough—were glossed over. In Giuseppe Verdi's *La Traviata* (first performed in 1853 and based on the novel *La Dame aux Camélias* of 1852) the heroine, Violetta, is an archetypal victim of tuberculosis. Her sexual availability (she is a courtesan) and her hedonistic lifestyle, filled with parties, gambling, and excitement, are signs that her unnamed illness is tuberculosis. Just as her lifestyle consumes money, diamonds, and lovers, the disease consumes her body and beauty. Violetta's passionate love for Alfredo, a student, takes her away from this life; but the disease cannot be halted, and she dies in the final scene.

La Traviata was written before the discovery in 1882 that tuberculosis was caused by a bacterium. Nevertheless, many of the features of the tuberculosis character and lifestyle remained in the public consciousness. Giacomo Puccini's opera *La Bohème* of 1896 is set in Paris in 1830 and the characters live in the cold, damp slum housing now understood to be linked to tuberculosis. Mimi, the heroine, works as an embroiderer, and she is already suffering from the disease when she meets Rodolfo. He is attracted to her fragile appearance and pale skin, those archetypal signs of the disease. Mimi later takes up with a wealthy protector—repeating the old association between tuberculosis and sex—but later leaves him and is reunited with Rodolfo just before her death.

Mental illness also featured in nineteenth-century literature. In Charlotte Brontë's *Jane Eyre* (1847), the mad and violent Bertha Rochester is portrayed as an object of fear, confined to the attics of Thornfield Hall. Brontë reflects medical and popular views of the causes of mental illness by linking her madness to heredity (Bertha's mother was also insane), to alcohol, and to race—Bertha was born in the West Indies. A more kindly view of the mad was provided by Dickens (and others) who described the inmates of asylums. In "A Curious Dance around a Curious Tree," published in the magazine *Household Words* in 1852, Dickens praises the humane treatment of patients in St. Luke's Asylum in London. In his description of a dance (dances were often held in asylums, as a means of encouraging patients to display "normal" behavior), he presents the inmates as slightly comical and endearing, rather than alarming.

In 1859, the wave of popular concern over the wrongful incarceration of women in lunatic asylums by family members seeking to control their money was also reflected in popular fiction. In Wilkie Collins' *The Woman in White* (serialized in 1859–1860), two women are wrongly locked away in private asylums. Anne Catherick is hidden away because she knows a guilty secret that might lead to a scandal. Laura Fairlie is locked up to get control of her money. In Mary Elizabeth Braddon's *Lady Audley's Secret* (1862), the plot of wrongful confinement is given a different twist. In the novel, the beautiful wife of Lord Audley is revealed to be a social climber who has abandoned her child, faked her own death, bigamously married Lord Audley, and then murdered her first husband to cover up her crimes. When her acts are discovered, rather than have her arrested, a doctor is called in and he diagnoses madness brought on by stress as the cause of her criminal behavior. Lady Audley ends her life in a private asylum in France.

The Transforming Effect of Illness

The lasting impact of illness was a recurring theme in nineteenth-century novels. In Jane Austen's novel *Sense and Sensibility* (1811), the romantic, emotional Marianne Dashwood falls into a fever brought on by nervous strain when the man she loves abandons her. She survives her illness, but becomes calmer and less impulsive and marries the older, rather grave Colonel Brandon. In a parallel story in *Persuasion* (1818), the young and headstrong Louisa Musgrave falls from a harbor wall and sustains a serious head injury. This transforms her into a thoughtful woman who becomes engaged to the book-loving Captain Benwick. Austen was not the only author to use illness in this way. Susan Coolidge's heroine in *What Katy Did* (1872) suffers a fall and serious illness that turn her from a boisterous tomboy into a calm and considerate young woman.

Novels did not faithfully reflect the incidence of disease. A complaint called "brain fever" appeared frequently in nineteenth-century literature. It was a genuine medical condition, identified as a form of inflammation, causing headaches and delirium, brought on by physical or mental stress. There is no data to suggest that it was particularly common or alarming, but for novelists it provided a dramatic device to emphasize the depth of emotional feeling. Emily Brontë had Catherine Linton in *Wuthering Heights* develop brain fever when forced to reject Heathcliff, and Gustav Flaubert described Emma Bovary suffering from the same condition when abandoned by her lover.

NOTES

1. Charles Dickens, *Bleak House* (New York: Oxford University Press, 1996), pp. 654, 657.

2. Émile Zola, *Nana*, trans. George Holden (New York: Penguin, 1972), p. 470.

Glossary

Amulet—An object worn to protect against disease.

Antiseptic—A substance used to kill bacteria on skin, in wounds or on instruments. Antiseptic surgery refers to a method of surgery that uses antiseptics to kill bacteria and thus prevent infection.

Aseptic—Free of disease-causing bacteria or other agents. Aseptic surgery refers to a strategy of operating in a bacteria-free environment to avoid infection.

Ayurvedic medicine—A system of medicine used in India from ancient times. Health reflects a balance of three *doṣas*; disease is the result of an imbalance of these.

Bloodletting—The practice of removing a controlled amount of blood from the body by various methods. Bloodletting was used in Western, unani, ayurvedic, and some forms of folk medicine.

Chinese medicine—A system of medicine practiced in China from ancient times that understood disease to be caused by a disruption to the flow of *qi* or blood (*xue*) within the body.

Dais—Traditional midwives working in India and Asia.

Divination—A means of diagnosing disease, especially if caused by supernatural forces, used in many systems of folk medicine.

Doṣas—Three substances (*vāta, pitta, kapha*) within the body that influence health and disease in ayurvedic medicine.

Endemic—An infection present within a population at all times.

Epidemic—A large number of cases of a disease breaking out within a population. Between outbreaks, epidemic diseases may be wholly or largely absent.

Folk medicine—Systems of medicine that make use of a range of treatments to cure specific diseases, not underpinned by an overarching theory of how the body works in health and disease.

Hakims—Learned practitioners trained in unani medicine.

Humors—Four fluids within the body that are understood to determine health and disease in unani medicine.

Jinn—A spirit capable of causing disease, found in North Africa.

Miasma—Bad air arising from rotting organic materials, responsible for causing or helping to spread diseases.

Pandemic—An outbreak of infective diseases that spreads over a large area or even around the world.

Qi—The energy or force distributed through the body, understood to be responsible for health and disease in Chinese medicine.

Unani medicine—A system of medical knowledge based on Greek and Islamic ideas, practiced in India and North Africa. In unani medicine, four humors are believed to determine whether the body is healthy or diseased.

Vaids—Learned practitioners trained in ayurvedic medicine.

Western medicine—The system of medical knowledge developed in Europe and North America. In Western or scientific medicine, disease is located in the solid organs and tissues of the body.

Bibliography

Abugideiri, Hibba. *Gender and the Making of Modern Medicine in Colonial Egypt.* Burlington, VT: Ashgate, 2010.

Alavi, Seema. "Unani Medicine in the Nineteenth-Century Public Sphere: Urdu Texts and the *Oudh Akhbar.*" *Indian Economic and Social History Review* 42 (2005): 101–129.

Alavi, Seema. *Islam and Healing: Loss and Recovery of an Indo-Muslim Medical Tradition 1600–1900.* New York: Palgrave Macmillan, 2008.

Alpen, Jan Van, and Anthony Aris. *Oriental Medicine: An Illustrated Guide to the Asian Arts of Healing.* London: Serindia Publications, 1995.

Anderson, Robin L. "Public Health and Public Healthiness, São Paulo, Brazil, 1876–1893." *Journal of the History of Medicine and Allied Sciences* 41 (1986): 293–307.

Anderson, Stuart, ed. *Making Medicines: a Brief History of Pharmacy and Pharmaceuticals.* London: Pharmaceutical Press, 2005.

Anderson, Warwick. "Geography, Race and Nation: Remapping 'Tropical' Australia, 1890–1930." *Medical History* 44, supplement S20 (2000): 146–159.

Apple, Rima D. "Constructing Mothers: Scientific Motherhood in the Nineteenth and Twentieth Centuries." *Social History of Medicine* 8 (1995): 161–178.

Apple, Rima D., ed. *Women, Health and Medicine in America.* New York: Garland Publishing Inc., 1990.

Arnold, David. *Colonizing the Body. State Medicine and Epidemic Disease in Nineteenth-Century India.* Berkeley: University of California Press, 1993.

Arnold, David, ed. *Imperial Medicine and Indigenous Societies*. New York: Manchester University Press, 1988.

Arnold, David, ed. *Warm Climates and Western Medicine: The Emergence of Tropical Medicine, 1500–1900* Atlanta, GA: Rodopi, 1996.

Attewell, Guy. *Refiguring Unani Tibb: Plural Healing in Late Colonial India*. Hyderabad, India: Orient Longman, 2007.

Bala, Poonam. *Imperialism and Medicine in Bengal: A Socio-Historical Perspective*. Newbury Park, CA: Sage Publications, 1991.

Bala, Poonam. *Medicine and Medical Policies in India: Social and Historical Perspectives*. Lanham, MD: Lexington Books, 2007.

Baldwin, Peter. *Contagion and the State in Europe 1830–1930*. New York: Cambridge University Press, 1999.

Ballara, Angela. *Taua, "Musket Wars," "Land Wars" or Tikanga? Warfare in Māori Society in the Early Nineteenth Century*. New York: Penguin Books, 2003.

Banerjee, Madhulika. *Power, Knowledge, Medicine: Ayurvedic Pharmaceuticals at Home and in the World*. Hyderabad, India: Orient BlackSwan, 2009.

Barnes, Linda L. *Needles, Herbs, Gods, and Ghosts: China, Healing and the West to 1848*. Cambridge, MA: Harvard University Press, 2005.

Barry, Lorelle, and Catharine Coleborne. "Insanity and Ethnicity in New Zealand: Maori Encounters with the Auckland Mental Hospital, 1860–1900." *History of Psychiatry* 22 (2011): 285–301.

Belich, James. *The Victorian Interpretation of Racial Conflict: The Maori, the British, and the New Zealand Wars*. Montreal: McGill-Queen's University Press, 1989.

Bell, Leland V. *Mental and Social Disorder in Sub-Saharan Africa: The Case of Sierra Leone, 1787–1990*. New York: Greenwood Press, 1991.

Benedict, Carol. *Plague in Nineteenth-Century China*. Stanford, CA: Stanford University Press, 1996.

Benton, Edward H. "British Surgery in the South African War: The Work of Major Frederick Porter." *Medical History* 21 (1977): 275–290.

Berg, Manfred, and Geoffrey Cocks, eds. *Medicine and Modernity: Public Health and Medical Care in Nineteenth- and Twentieth-Century Germany*. Washington, DC: German Historical Institute, 1997.

Bivins, Roberta E. *Acupuncture, Expertise, and Cross-Cultural Medicine*. New York: Palgrave in association with Centre for the History of Science, Technology and Medicine, University of Manchester, 2000.

Black, Jeremy. *War and the World: Military Power and the Fate of Continents 1450–2000*. New Haven, CT: Yale University Press, 1998.

Bordin, Giorgio, and Laura Polo D'Ambrosio. *Medicine in Art*. Translated by Jay Hyams. Los Angeles: J. Paul Getty Museum, 2010.

Branca, Patricia. *Women in Europe since 1750*. London: Croom Helm, 1978.

Bray, R. S. *Armies of Pestilence: The Effects of Pandemics on History*. Cambridge: Lutterworth Press, 1996.

Brunton, Deborah, ed. *Health, Disease and Society in Europe, 1800–1930: A Source Book*. New York: Manchester University Press, 2004.

Brunton, Deborah, ed. *Medicine Transformed: Health, Disease and Society in Europe, 1800–1930*. Manchester: Manchester University Press in association with the Open University, 2004.

Burnett, John. *Plenty and Want: A Social History of Diet in England from 1815 to the Present Day*. London: Scolar Press, 1979.

Burnett, Kristin. *Taking Medicine: Women's Healing Work and Colonial Contact in Southern Alberta, 1880–1930*. Vancouver: UBC Press, 2010.

Busfield, Joan. *Men, Women and Madness: Understanding Gender and Mental Disorder*. London: Macmillan Press Ltd., 1996.

Bynum, W. F, and Roy Porter, eds. *Companion Encyclopedia of the History of Medicine*. New York: Routledge, 1993.

Bynum, W. F., et al. *The Western Medical Tradition, 1800 to 2000*. New York: Cambridge University Press, 2006.

Carter, Eric D. *Enemy in the Blood: Malaria, Environment, and Development in Argentina*. Tuscaloosa: University of Alabama Press, 2012.

Chang, Che-chia. "The Therapeutic Tug of War: The Imperial Physician-Patient Relationship in the Era of Empress Dowager Cixi (1874–1908)." PhD thesis, University of Pennsylvania, 1998.

Cooter, Roger, ed. *In the Name of the Child: Health and Welfare, 1880–1940*. New York: Routledge, 1992.

Cullen, Christopher. "Patients and Healers in Late Imperial China: Evidence from the *Jinpingmei*." *History of Science* 31 (1993): 99–150.

Cunningham, Andrew, and Bridie Andrews, eds. *Western Medicine as Contested Knowledge*. New York: Manchester University Press, 1997.

Curtin, Philip D. *Death by Migration: Europe's Encounter with the Tropical World in the Nineteenth Century*. New York: Cambridge University Press, 1989.

De Barros, Juanita. "Dispensers, *Obeah* and Quackery: Medical Rivalries in Post-Slavery British Guiana." *Social History of Medicine* 20 (2007): 243–261.

De Barros, Juanita, Steven Palmer, and David Wright, eds. *Health and Medicine in the Circum-Caribbean, 1800–1968*. New York: Routledge, 2009.

Derickson, Alan. *Black Lung: Anatomy of a Public Health Disaster*. Ithaca, NY: Cornell University Press, 1998.

Dickens, Charles. *Bleak House*. London, 1852–1853; reprint, New York: Oxford University Press, 1996.

Digby, Anne. *Diversity and Division in Medicine: Health Care in South Africa from the 1800s*. Oxford: Peter Lang, 2006.

Digby, Anne. "Self-Medication and the Trade in Medicine within a Multi-Ethnic Context: A Case Study of South Africa from the Mid-Nineteenth to Mid-Twentieth Centuries." *Social History of Medicine* 18 (2005): 439–457.

Digby Anne, et al. *Crossing Colonial Historiographies: Histories of Colonial and Indigenous Medicines in Transnational Perspective*. Newcastle upon Tyne: Cambridge Scholars, 2010.

Dixon, Laurinda S., ed. *In Sickness and in Health: Disease as Metaphor in Art and Popular Wisdom*. Newark: University of Delaware Press, 2004.

Ebrahimnejad Hormoz, ed. *The Development of Modern Medicine in Non-Western Countries: Historical Perspectives* New York: Routledge, 2008.

Ebrahimnejad, Hormoz. *Medicine, Public Health and the Qājār State: Patterns of Medical Modernization in Nineteenth-Century Iran.* Boston: Brill, 2004.

Echenberg, Myron. *Africa in the Time of Cholera: A History of Pandemics from 1817 to the Present.* New York: Cambridge University Press, 2011.

Elvin, Mark, and Liu Ts'ui-jung. *Sediments of Time: Environment and Society in Chinese.* Cambridge: Cambridge University Press, 1998.

Engels, Frederick. *Condition of the Working Class in England in 1844.* Reprint, London: George Allen & Unwin, 1943. (Originally published 1845.)

Ernst, Waltraud. *Mad Tales from the Raj: The European Insane in British India, 1800–1858.* New York: Routledge, 1991.

Ernst, Waltraud, ed. *Plural Medicine, Tradition and Modernity, 1800–2000.* New York: Routledge, 2002.

Evans, Richard J. *Death in Hamburg: Society and Politics in the Cholera Years, 1830–1910.* New York: Oxford University Press, 1987.

Fick, Carolyn E. *The Making of Haiti: The Saint Domingue Revolution from Below.* Knoxville: University of Tennessee Press, 1990.

Figes, Orlando. *Crimea: The Last Crusade.* New York: Penguin Books, 2010.

Fildes, Valerie, Lara Marks, and Hilary Marland, eds. *Women and Children First: International Maternal and Infant Welfare, 1870–1945.* New York: Routledge, 1992.

Flint, Karen. *Healing Traditions: African Medicine, Cultural Exchange and Competition in South Africa, 1820–1948.* Athens: Ohio University Press, 2008.

Floor, Willem. *Public Health in Qajar Iran.* Washington, DC: Mage Publishers, 2004.

Furth, Charlotte. "Blood, Body and Gender. Medical Images of the Female Condition in China." *Chinese Science* 7 (1986): 43–66.

Furth, Charlotte. "Concepts of Pregnancy, Childbirth and Infancy in Ch'ing Dynasty China." *Journal of Asian Studies* 46 (1987): 7–32.

Gabriel, Richard A., and Karen S. Metz. *A History of Military Medicine.* Vol. 2. New York: Greenwood Press, 1992.

Gallagher, Nancy Elizabeth. *Medicine and Power in Tunisia, 1780–1900.* New York: Cambridge University Press, 1983.

Garton, Stephen. *Medicine and Madness: A Social History of Insanity in New South Wales, 1880–1940.* Kensington, NSW: New South Wales University Press, 1988.

Genshiro, Hiruta. "Japanese Psychiatry in the Edo Period (1600–1868)." *History of Psychiatry* 13 (2002): 131–151.

Gilman, Sander L. *Disease and Representation: Images of Illness from Madness to AIDS.* Ithaca, NY: Cornell University Press, 1988.

Gilman, Sander L. "Lam Qua and the Development of a Westernized Medical Iconography in China." *Medical History* 30 (1986): 57–69.

Good, Charles M., Jr. *The Steamer Parish: the Rise and Fall of Missionary Medicine on an African Frontier.* Chicago: University of Chicago Press, 2004.

Gordon, David. "A Sword of Empire? Medicine and Colonialism in King William's Town, Xhosaland, 1856–1891." *African Studies* 60 (2001): 165–183.

Greenspan, Robert E. *Medicine: Perspectives in History and Art.* Alexandria, VA: Ponteverde Press, 2006.

Grell, Ole Peter, Andrew Cunningham, and Robert Jütte, eds. *Health Care and Poor Relief in 18th and 19th Century Northern Europe.* Burlington, VT: Ashgate, 2002.

Handler, Jerome S. "Slave Medicine and Obeah in Barbados, circa 1650 to 1834." *New West Indian Guide* 74 (2000): 57–90.

Hanson, Marta E. *Speaking of Epidemics in Chinese Medicine: Disease and the Geographic Imagination in Late Imperial China.* London: Routledge, 2011.

Hardiman, David, ed. *Healing Bodies, Saving Souls: Medical Missions in Asia and Africa.* New York: Rodopi, 2006.

Hardy, Anne. *The Epidemic Streets: Infectious Disease and the Rise of Preventative Medicine, 1856–1900.* New York: Oxford University Press, 1993.

Hardy, Anne. "Rickets and the Rest: Child-Care, Diet and the Infectious Children's Diseases, 1850–1914." *Social History of Medicine* 5 (1992): 389–412.

Harrison, Barbara. *Not Only the "Dangerous Trades": Women's Work and Health in Britain, 1880–1914.* London: Taylor & Francis, 1996.

Harrison, Mark. *Climates and Constitutions: Health, Race, Environment and British Imperialism in India, 1600–1850.* Oxford: Oxford University Press, 1999.

Harrison, Mark. "Differences of Degree: Representations of India in British Medical Topography, 1820–c1870." *Medical History* 44, supplement S20 (2000): 51–69.

Harrison, Mark. *Disease and the Modern World: 1500 to the Present Day.* Cambridge: Polity, 2004.

Harrison, Mark, Margaret Jones, and Helen Sweet, eds. *From Western Medicine to Global Medicine: The Hospital beyond the West.* New Delhi: Orient BlackSwan, 2009.

Helmstadter, Carol, and Judith Godden. *Nursing before Nightingale, 1815–1899.* Farnham, Surrey: Ashgate, 2011.

Henley, David. *Fertility, Food and Fever: Population, Economy and Environment in North and Central Sulawesi, 1600–1930.* Leiden: KITLV Press, 2005.

Hepler, Allison L. *Women in Labor: Mothers, Medicine, and Occupational Health in the United States, 1890–1980.* Columbus: Ohio State University Press, 2000.

Hillam, Christine, ed. *The Roots of Dentistry.* London: British Dental Association, 1990.

Hillier, S. M., and J. A. Jewell, eds. *Health Care and Traditional Medicine in China, 1800–1982.* Boston: Routledge & Kegan Paul, 1983.

Hochmuth, Christian. "Patterns of Medical Culture in Colonial Bengal, 1835–1880." *Bulletin of the History of Medicine* 80 (2006): 39–72.

Hodgson, Barbara. *In the Arms of Morpheus: The Tragic History of Laudanum, Morphine, and Patent Medicines.* Buffalo, NY: Firefly Books, 2001.

Hokkanen, Markku. *Medicine and Scottish Missionaries in the Northern Malawi Region 1875–1930: Quests for Health in a Colonial Society.* Lewiston, NY: Edwin Mellen Press, 2007.

Homei, Aya. "Birth Attendants in Meiji Japan: The Rise of a Medical Birth Model and the New Division of Labour." *Social History of Medicine* 19 (2006): 407–424.

Hopkins, Donald R. *The Greatest Killer: Smallpox in History.* Chicago: University of Chicago Press, 2002.

Howard, Martin R. *Wellington's Doctors: The British Army Medical Services in the Napoleonic Wars.* Staplehurst, UK: Spellmount, 2002.

Hutcheon, Linda, and Michael Hutcheon. *Opera: Desire, Disease, Death.* Lincoln: University of Nebraska Press, 1996.

Hutchinson, John F. *Champions of Charity. War and the Rise of the Red Cross.* Boulder, CO: Westview Press, 1996.

Jackson, Mark, ed. *The Oxford Handbook of the History of Medicine.* New York: Oxford University Press, 2011.

Jankovic, Vladimir. *Confronting the Climate: British Airs and the Making of Environmental Medicine.* New York: Palgrave Macmillan, 2010.

Jannetta, Ann. *The Vaccinators: Smallpox, Medical Knowledge, and the "Opening" of Japan.* Stanford, CA: Stanford University Press, 2007.

Jennings, Eric T. "Curing the Colonizers: Highland Hydrotherapy in Guadeloupe." *Social History of Medicine* 15 (2002): 229–261.

Jolly, Julius. *Indian Medicine.* Kashikar: Munshiram Manohartat Publishers Pvt. Ltd., 1977.

Jones, Margaret. *The Hospital System and Health Care: Sri Lanka, 1815–1960.* New Delhi: Orient Blackswan, 2009.

Katz, Paul R. *Demon Hordes and Burning Boats: The Cult of Marshal Wen in Late Imperial Chekiang.* Albany: State University of New York Press, 1995.

Kaur, Amarjit. "Indian Labour, Labour Standards, and Workers' Health in Burma and Malaya, 1900–1940." *Modern Asian Studies* 40 (2006): 425–475.

Keller, Richard C. *Colonial Madness: Psychiatry in French North Africa.* Chicago: University of Chicago Press, 2007.

Kiple, Kenneth F. *Plague, Pox and Pestilence: Disease in History.* London: Weidenfeld & Nicolson, 1997.

Knight, Ian. *The Anatomy of the Zulu Army from Shaka to Cetshwayo 1818–1879.* Mechanicsburg, PA: Stackpole Books, 1995.

Lange, Raeburn. *May the People Live: A History of Maori Health Development 1900–1918.* Auckland: Auckland University Press, 1999.

Leavitt, Judith Walzer. *Brought to Bed: Childbearing in America, 1750 to 1950.* New York: Oxford University Press, 1986.

Leavitt, Judith Walzer, and Ronald L. Numbers, eds. *Sickness and Health in America: Readings in the History of Medicine and Public Health.* Madison: University of Wisconsin Press, 1978.

Leung, Angela Ki Che. "Organized Medicine in Ming-Qing China: State and Private Medical Institutions in the Lower Yangzi Region." *Late Imperial China* 8 (1987): 134–166.

Leung, Angela Ki Che. " 'Variolation' and Vaccination in Late Imperial China, ca. 1570–1911." In *Vaccinia, Vaccination, Vaccinology: Jenner, Pasteur and Their Successors,* edited by Stanley A. Plotkin and Bernardino Fantini, 65–71. Paris: Elsevier, 1996.

Leung, Angela Ki Che, and Charlotte Furth, eds. *Health and Hygiene in Chinese East Asia: Policies and Publics in the long Twentieth Century.* Durham, NC: Duke University Press, 2010.

Li, Shang-Jen. "Discovering 'The Secrets of a Long and Healthy Life': John Dudgeon on Chinese Hygiene." *Social History of Medicine* 23 (2009) 21–37.

Lomax, Elizabeth M. R. *Small and Special: The Development of Hospitals for Children in Victorian Britain.* London: Wellcome Institute for the History of Medicine, 1996.

Lossio, Jorge. "British Medicine in the Peruvian Andes: The Travels of Archibald Smith M.D. (1820–1870)." *História, Ciências, Saúde-Manguinhos* 13 (2006): 833–850.

Low-Beer, Daniel, Matthew Smallman-Raynor, and Andrew Cliff. "Disease and Death in the South African War: Changing Disease Patterns from Soldiers to Refugees." *Social History of Medicine* 17 (2004): 223–245.

Lux, Maureen K. *Medicine That Walks: Disease, Medicine and Canadian Plains Native People, 1880–1940.* Toronto: University of Toronto Press, 2001.

MacLeod, Roy, and Milton Lewis, eds. *Disease, Medicine and Empire: Perspectives on Western Medicine and the Experience of European Expansion.* New York: Routledge, 1988.

Macpherson, Kerrie L. *A Wilderness of Marshes: The Origins of Public Health in Shanghai, 1843–1893.* New York: Oxford University Press, 1987.

Marland, Hilary. "The Medical Activities of Mid-Nineteenth-Century Chemists and Druggists, with Special Reference to Wakefield and Huddersfield." *Medical History* 31 (1987): 415–439.

Matthee, Rudi. *The Pursuit of Pleasure: Drugs and Stimulants in Iranian History, 1500–1900.* Princeton, NJ: Princeton University Press, 2005.

Mazars, Guy. *A Concise Introduction to Indian Medicine.* Translated by T. K. Gopalan. Delhi: Motilal Bandarsidass Publishers Private Ltd., 2006.

McCandless, Peter. *Slavery, Disease, and Suffering in the Southern Lowcountry.* Cambridge: Cambridge University Press, 2011.

McCrea, Heather L. "Diseased Relations. Epidemics, Public Health and State Formation in Nineteenth-Century Yucatan, Mexico." PhD thesis, State University of New York, Stony Brook, 2002.

McIvor, Arthur J., and Ronald Johnston, eds. *Miners' Lung: A History of Dust Disease in British Coal Mining.* Aldershot, UK: Ashgate, 2007.

McKeown, Thomas. *The Modern Rise of Population.* London: Edward Arnold, 1976.

McNeill, William H. *Plagues and Peoples*. New York: Penguin Books, 1979.

Mead, Karen. "Beneficent Maternalism: Argentine Motherhood in Comparative Perspective, 1880–1920." *Journal of Women's History* 12 (2000): 120–145.

Meegama, S. A. *Famine, Fevers and Fear: The State and Disease in British Colonial Sri Lanka*. Dehiwela: Sridevi, 2012.

Melling, Joseph, and Bill Forsythe, eds. *Insanity, Institutions and Society, 1800–1914*. New York: Routledge, 1999.

Mercier, Jacques. *Art That Heals: The Image as Medicine in Ethiopia*. New York: Museum for African Art, 1997.

Messner, Angelika C. "On 'Translating' Western Psychiatry into the Chinese Context in Republican China." In *Mapping Meanings: The Field of New Learning in Late Qing China*, edited by Michael Lackner and Natascha Vittinghoff, 639–658. Leiden: Brill, 2004.

Mills, James. "A History of Modern Psychiatry in India, 1858–1947." *History of Psychiatry* 12 (2001): 431–458.

Mooney, Graham, and Jonathan Reinarz, eds. *Permeable Walls: Historical Perspectives on Hospital and Asylum Visiting*. New York: Rodopi, 2009.

Moscucci, Ornella. *The Science of Woman: Gynaecology and Gender in England, 1800–1929*. New York: Cambridge University Press, 1993.

Nash, Linda. *Inescapable Ecologies: A History of Environment, Disease, and Knowledge*. Berkeley: University of California Press, 2006.

Ng, Beng-Yeong. "Hysteria: A Cross-Cultural Comparison of Its Origins and History." *History of Psychiatry* 10 (1999): 287–301.

Ng, Vivien W. *Madness in late Imperial China: From Illness to Deviance*. Norman: University of Oklahoma Press, 1990.

Numbers, Ronald L., and Darrel W. Amundsen, eds. *Caring and Curing: Health and Medicine in the Western Religious Traditions*. New York: Macmillan Publishing Company, 1986.

Opp, James. *The Lord for the Body: Religion, Medicine, and Protestant Faith Healing in Canada, 1880–1930*. Montreal: McGill-Queen's University Press, 2005.

Palmer, Steven. *From Popular Medicine to Medical Populism. Doctors, Healers and Public Power in Costa Rica*. Durham, NC: Duke University Press, 2003.

Parle, Julie. *States of Mind: Searching for Mental Health in Natal and Zululand, 1868–1918*. Scottsville, South Africa: University of KwaZulu-Natal Press, 2007.

Parle, Julie. "Witchcraft or Madness? The Amandiki of Zululand, 1894–1914." *Journal of Southern African Studies* 29 (2003): 105–132.

Pati, Biswamoy, and Mark Harrison, eds. *Health, Medicine and Empire Perspectives on Colonial India*. London: Sangam Books, 2001.

Peltier, Leonard F. *Orthopedics: A History and Iconography*. San Francisco: Norman Publishers, 1993.

Pernick, Martin S. *A Calculus of Suffering: Pain, Professionalism, and Anesthesia in Nineteenth-Century America*. New York: Columbia University Press, 1985.

Pooley, Siân. " 'All We Want Is That Our Children's Health and Lives Should Be Regarded': Child Health and Parental Concern in England, c.1860–1910." *Social History of Medicine* 23 (2010): 528–548.

Porter, Roy, ed. *The Faber Book of Madness.* Boston: Faber and Faber, 1991.

Porter, Roy. *The Greatest Benefit to Mankind: A Medical History of Humanity from Antiquity to the Present.* London: Fontana Press, 1997.

Porter, Roy, and Mikulás Teich, eds. *Drugs and Narcotics in History.* New York: Cambridge University Press, 1995.

Porter, Roy, and David Wright, eds. *The Confinement of the Insane: International Perspectives, 1800–1965.* Cambridge: Cambridge University Press, 2003.

Powell, Margaret, and Masahira Anesaki, eds. *Health Care in Japan.* New York: Routledge, 1989.

Rampton, David. "The Doctors' Plot: Some Classic Nineteenth-Century Novels Revisited." *Modern Language Studies* 22 (1992): 57–66.

Reid, Janice. *Sorcerers and Healing Spirits: Continuity and Change in an Aboriginal Medical System.* Canberra: Australian National University Press, 1983.

Rogaski, Ruth. "Beyond Benevolence: A Confucian Women's Shelter in Treaty-Port China." *Journal of Women's History* 8 (1997): 54–90.

Rogaski, Ruth. "From Protecting Life to Defending the Nation: Tianjin 1859–1953." PhD thesis, Yale University, 1996.

Rogaski, Ruth. *Hygienic Modernity: Meanings of Health and Disease in Treaty-Port China.* Berkeley: University of California Press, 2004.

Russett, Cynthia Eagle. *Sexual Science: The Victorian Construction of Womanhood.* Cambridge, MA: Harvard University Press, 1989.

Sadowsky, Jonathan. *Imperial Bedlam: Institutions of Madness in Colonial Southwest Nigeria.* Berkeley: University of California Press, 1999.

Satya, Laxman D. *Medicine, Disease and Ecology in Colonial India: The Deccan Plateau in the 19th Century.* New Dehli: Manohar, 2009.

Scheid, Volker. *Currents of Tradition in Chinese Medicine, 1626–2006.* Seattle, WA: Eastland Press, 2007.

Schwieso, Joshua John. " 'Religious Fanaticism' and Wrongful Confinement in Victorian England: The Affair of Louisa Nottidge." *Social History of Medicine* 9 (1996): 159–174.

Scull, Andrew. *Most Solitary of Afflictions: Madness and Society in Britain 1700–1900.* New Haven, CT: Yale University Press, 1993.

Selin, Helaine, ed. *Medicine across Cultures. History and Practice of Medicine in Non-Western Cultures.* Boston: Kluwer Academic Publishers, 2003.

Sellers, Christopher C. *Hazards of the Job: From Industrial Disease to Environmental Health Science.* Chapel Hill: University of North Carolina Press, 1997.

Sengoopta, Chandak. "The Modern Ovary: Constructions, Meanings, Uses." *History of Science* 38 (2000): 425–488.

Sheils, W. J., ed. *The Church and Healing: Papers Read at the Twentieth Summer Meeting and the Twenty-first Winter Meeting of the Ecclesiastical History Society.* Oxford: Blackwell, 1982.

Shorter, Edward. *History of Psychiatry: From the Era of the Asylum to the Age of Prozac*. New York: Wiley, 1997.

Showalter, Elaine. *The Female Malady. Women, Madness and English Culture, 1830–1980*. New York: Pantheon Books, 1985.

Sivaramakrishnan, Kavita. *Old Potions, New Bottles: Recasting Indigenous Medicine in Colonial Punjab, 1850–1945*. New Perspectives in South Asian History. Hyderabad, India: Orient Longman, 2006.

Speziale, Fabrizio, ed. *Hospitals in Iran and India, 1500–1950s*. Boston: Brill, 2012.

Stowe, Steven M. *Doctoring the South: Southern Physicians and Everyday Medicine in the Mid-Nineteenth Century*. Chapel Hill: University of North Carolina Press, 2004.

Sullivan, Lawrence E., ed. *Healing and Restoring: Health and Medicine in the World's Religious Traditions*. New York: Macmillan, 1989.

Summers, Ann. "Pride and Prejudice: Ladies and Nurses in the Crimean War." *History Workshop Journal* 16 (1983): 33–56.

Szonyi, Michael. "The Illusion of Standardizing the Gods: The Cult of the Five Emperors in Late Imperial China." *Journal of Asian Studies* 56 (1997): 113–135.

Szreter, Simon. "The Importance of Social Intervention in Britain's Mortality Decline c. 1850–1914: A Re-interpretation of the Role of Public Health." *Social History of Medicine* 1 (1988): 1–37.

Taithe, Bertrand. *Defeated Flesh Welfare, Warfare and the Making of Modern France*. Manchester: Manchester University Press, 1999.

Thoral, Marie-Cecile. "Colonial Medical Encounters in the Nineteenth Century: The French Campaigns in Egypt, Saint Domingue and Algeria." *Social History of Medicine* 25 (2012): 608–624.

Ueyama, Takahiro. *Health in the Marketplace: Professionalism, Therapeutic Desires, and Medical Commodification in Late-Victorian London*. Palo Alto, CA: Society for the Promotion of Science and Scholarship, 2010.

Unschuld, Paul U. *Medicine in China: A History of Ideas*. Berkeley: University of California Press, 2010.

Unschuld, Paul U. *Medicine in China: A History of Pharmaceutics*. Berkeley: University of California Press, 1985.

Unschuld, Paul U. *Medicine in China: Historical Artifacts and Images*. Translated by Sabine Wilms. New York: Prestel, 2000.

Valenčius, Conevery Bolton. *The Health of the Country: How American Settlers Understood Themselves and Their Land*. New York: Basic Books, 2002.

Vogel, Virgil J. *American Indian Medicine*. Norman: University of Oklahoma Press, 1970.

Waddington, Keir. *An Introduction to the Social History of Medicine: Europe since 1500*. Basingstoke, Hampshire: Palgrave Macmillan, 2011.

Wang, Hsiu-yun. "Stranger Bodies: Women, Gender, and Missionary Medicine in China, 1870s–1930s." PhD thesis, University of Wisconsin–Madison, 2003.

Warren, Adam. *Medicine and Politics in Colonial Peru: Population Growth and the Bourbon Reforms*. Pittsburgh, PA: University of Pittsburgh Press, 2010.

Watts, Sheldon. *Epidemics and History: Disease, Power and Imperialism*. New Haven, CT: Yale University Press, 1997.

Weindling, Paul, ed. *The Social History of Occupational Health*. Dover, NH: Croom Helm, 1986.

Wohl, Anthony S. *Endangered Lives: Public Health in Victorian Britain*. Cambridge, MA: Harvard University Press, 1983.

Wolff, Norma H. "The Use of Human Images in Yoruba Medicines." *Ethnology* 39 (2000): 205–224.

Worboys, Michael. *Spreading Germs: Disease Theories and Medical Practice in Britain, 1865–1900*. New York: Cambridge University Press, 2000.

Wu, Yi-Li. "Transmitted Secrets: The Doctors of the lower Yangzi Region and Popular Gynecology in Late Imperial China." PhD thesis, Yale University, 1998.

Wu, Yi-Li. *Reproducing Women: Medicine, Metaphor, and Childbirth in Late Imperial China*. Berkeley: University of California Press, 2010.

Wujastyk, Dominik. *The Roots of Ayurveda: Selections from Sanskrit Medical Writings*. New York: Penguin Books, 2003.

Wynbrandt, James. *The Excruciating History of Dentistry: Toothsome Tales and Oral Oddities from Babylon to Braces*. New York: St. Martin's Press, 1998.

Young, Theron Kue-hing. "A Conflict of Professions: The Medical Missionary in China, 1835–1890." *Bulletin of the History of Medicine* 47 (1973): 250–272.

Zola, Émile. *Nana*. Translated by George Holden. Paris, 1880; reprint, New York: Penguin, 1972.

Index

Abscesses, 118, 121, 130
Accidents, 9, 12, 112, 113, 115, 143
Acclimatization, 10, 107
Acupuncture, 20, 32, 119, 122, 131, 145, 203
Advice books, 54–55, 59, 72
Africa, West, 10
Agriculture, 2, 7, 9, 102, 106, 183
Agricultural hazards, 12, 102, 106, 113
Air, and health, 11, 105–6, 111–12
Alcohol, 11, 37, 69, 91, 92, 107, 109, 124, 125, 140, 147, 162, 164, 171
Alternative medicine. *See* unorthodox medicine
Ambulances, 177
American Civil War, 171, 174, 175, 202
Amputation, 125, 126, 128, 131, 172, 173, 202, 211
Amulets, 43, 72, 92, 207
Anatomical images, 202, 204

Anatomy, 26, 27, 62, 199
Anesthetics, 62, 77, 157, 172, 189, 209, 212. *See also* chloroform; ether; local anesthetics; nitrous oxide
Anglo-Boer War. *See* Boer war
Animal products in medicines, 154, 155, 159
Antisepsis, 77, 128, 189
Apprenticeship, 161
Argentina, 66, 177
Armies, 171, 174, 176, 177, 178–79
Asepsis, 128
Aspirin, 158
Ashanti, 206
Asylums, 42, 138–41, 215; admission to, 140, 141, 149; colonial, 148–50; treatment in, 137–38, 140, 149; wrongful incarceration in, 142–43
Austen, Jane, 212, 215, 216
Australia, 3, 9, 10, 11, 12, 67, 78, 88, 96, 147, 199
Austria-Hungary, 93, 170

Ayurvedic medicine, 22–24, 32, 43,
    55, 56, 60, 68, 69, 70–71, 74, 75,
    89, 91, 104–5, 121, 124, 146, 154,
    155, 160, 163, 165, 199, 200, 202,
    208; diagnosis, 22; diet, 22, 23,
    56; drugs, 22, 154–55, 163, 165;
    understanding of illness in, 22,
    74, 76, 89, 104, 121, 146, 154, 155;
    practitioners, 23, 118, 123, 160,
    165, 200, 208; supernatural
    disease in, 22; training, 23, 160,
    199, 200; treatments, 22–23,
    70–71, 91, 121
Aztec medicine, 28, 59

Babies. *See* infants
Bacteria, 6, 8, 75, 77, 84, 90–91, 94,
    128, 214
Bamboo Grove Monastery, 194
Barbados, 49
Barracks, 14, 171, 178
Battlefield medicine, 171–73
Battles, 170, 180, 179, 183, 184. *See
    also* individual conflicts
Beard, George, 143
Behring, Emil von, 75–76
Bell, John, 202
Bell, Joseph, 211–12
Beri-beri, 3, 113
Birth. *See* childbirth
Bismaristan, 144, 194
Blackwell, Elizabeth, 64
Bladder stones, 118, 119, 124, 125
Blood loss, control of, 119,
    126, 129, 172–73
Bloodletters, 13, 118, 122
Bloodletting, 22–23, 59, 74, 91, 106,
    109, 118, 119, 121–22, 125, 131,
    138, 202
Boer wars, 182–83
Bolivia, 29
Bones, broken, 13, 59, 119,
    120, 126, 131
Bonesetters, 13, 74, 118
Borodino, Battle of, 170

Braddon, Mary Elizabeth, 215
Brain, 136, 146, 147, 155
Brazil, 80, 177, 199
Breastfeeding, 59, 68–69, 206
Britain, 2, 6, 8, 65, 66, 67, 79, 80, 87,
    93, 112, 142, 166, 190, 191, 209
Bronchitis, 8, 84, 112
Brontë, Charlotte, 215
Brontë, Emily, 216
Buddhism, 43–44, 55, 194, 206
Bullets, 120, 173, 182
Burials, 42, 93, 95, 112, 147, 193
Burma, 9
Butler, Josephine, 66

Canada, 3, 9, 80, 84, 205
Cancer, 57, 98, 114, 125, 129, 164
Caribbean, 9, 49, 63, 68, 110
Cataracts, 41, 124, 125, 131
Catholic church, 36, 38, 39, 40, 42, 45,
    186, 207, 208
Cautery, 119, 122, 125
Central America, 28, 46
Cesarean section, 62, 125
Charities, 10, 13, 15, 63, 65, 66, 79, 96,
    138, 177, 186, 188, 190, 191, 193,
    194–95, 198
Chiarugi, Vincenzo, 137
Chickenpox, 73
Childbirth, 54, 55, 56, 58, 60–63, 64,
    68, 76, 77, 126, 127, 141, 144, 159,
    196, 206
Childhood diseases, 73–76, 77, 80, 95
Children, 22, 42, 44, 58, 59, 67, 71–80,
    85, 108, 130, 137, 166, 167, 191,
    193, 196, 204
Chile, 177
China, 2, 7, 9, 12, 41, 42, 52, 53, 62, 64,
    68, 69, 71, 72, 76, 86, 87, 88, 92, 95,
    96, 108–9, 112, 124, 131, 144, 152,
    153, 160, 161, 165, 177, 178, 179,
    180, 182, 192–93, 194, 195, 196, 197,
    199, 207; religion in, 44–45, 206
Chinese medicine, 18–21, 31, 32, 33,
    41, 52, 54–55, 64, 69, 73, 91, 112,

121, 122, 144, 145, 153–54, 160,
194, 202; acupuncture, 20, 32,
119, 122, 131, 145, 203; blood,
54, 55, 56, 89; cold damage, 19,
88; diagnosis, 21, 194, 195; diet,
20, 55, 92; drugs, 20, 153–54,
160, 165, 166, 194; illness,
understanding of, 18–19, 73,
88–89, 91, 103–4, 145–46;
moxibustion, 20, 122, 145;
pestilential qi, 19, 33, 88, 91, 92,
104, 112; practitioners, 20–21,
53, 62, 118, 154, 160, 194, 195,
203, 208; qi, 18, 20, 54, 55, 56,
119, 145, 154, 160; reproduction
in, 54–55; supernatural diseases,
18, 42, 54, 69, 71, 76, 89; training,
20; treatment, 20–21, 68, 91;
warm factor, 19, 88; yin/yang,
18, 52, 54, 104, 145, 154
Chloroform, 62, 127, 129, 157
Cholera, 8, 11, 12, 22, 37–38, 43, 45,
72, 84, 86–88, 89, 90, 91, 92,
93–94, 95, 98, 99, 108, 113, 213
Christianity, and medicine, 9, 35–42,
49, 59, 186, 187, 193, 194, 207–8.
See also Protestant, Catholic
Civilian medicine, 176–77, 178
Civilians, 174–77
Cleanliness. *See* hygiene
Climate, and health, 9–11, 103–9,
145, 212
Clinics, 39, 77, 186, 187, 189, 196
Clothing, 4, 6, 52, 58, 72, 92, 105, 109,
136, 144, 171, 204, 209
Club foot, 77, 130, 211
Cocaine, 127, 157, 166
Collins, Wilkie, 215
Congo, 60, 86, 89, 205
Conjure, 48–49
Convulsions, 70, 71, 76, 77
Coolidge, Susan, 216
Corvisart, Jean, 26
Costa Rica, 118
Countryside. *See* rural

Cowpox, 75, 96, 196
Crimean War, 40, 171, 173,
174–75, 202
Cuba, 63
Curanderos, 33, 46, 59

Dais, 61, 62
Daoism. *See* Taoism
Darwin, Charles, 28
Death rates. *See* mortality
Deaths, 69, 73, 76–77, 79,
87–88, 97, 98; in war, 173–74,
179–80, 183, 184
Degeneration, 137, 141
Deities: healing, 43, 44–45, 46, 55, 93,
194, 202, 206; sending disease,
44, 45, 46, 76, 89, 92–93, 147, 206
Demons, 89, 145, 197, 204, 206, 207
Dentistry, 127, 131–33
Diarrhea, 46, 70, 71, 77, 87, 92, 99,
154, 159, 166
Dickens, Charles, 213, 215
Diet, 2–4, 38, 52, 55, 56, 59, 70–71, 72,
74, 78, 85, 91, 99, 103, 104, 107,
109, 130, 141, 143, 154, 191, 197,
212. *See also* food
Diphtheria, 73, 75–76, 166
Dirt, 6, 8, 88, 90, 91, 94, 104, 111–12,
175, 190, 198
Disease, 8, 11–12, 72–74, 83–91, 171,
182, 212–15; causation, 88–91;
infectious, 11–12, 52, 72–76,
78–79, 84–85, 86–88, 92–99, 171,
174, 190, 191; in specific
environments, 10–11, 84, 89,
90: movement of, 11–12, 73,
85–88, 95; prevention of, 14, 80,
92–99, 171, 192; transmission of,
85, 89–93, 111. *See also*
individual diseases
Disinfection, 93, 94, 128
Dispensaries, 39, 40, 65, 77, 131, 186,
189, 190, 192, 195, 198
Dissection, 26, 95, 191, 199
Divination, 30, 44, 48–49, 147, 205

Diviners, 29, 46, 47, 118, 147, 205
Dix, Dorothea, 142
Doyle, Sir Arthur Conan, 211
Drainage, 9, 190, 197, 198
Drug addition, 166–67
Drug sellers, 21, 25, 74, 160–63, 166
Drugs, 151–61, 163, 166–67;
    ayurvedic, 22, 74, 154–55, 163;
    Chinese, 20, 153–54, 160, 165,
    166, 194; folk, 29, 92, 158–60;
    mineral, 154, 155, 159; plant, 29,
    31, 151–52, 154, 155, 157, 159,
    160, 165, 200; trade in, 151–52;
    unani, 74, 155, 163; Western, 74,
    138, 155–58
Dudgeon, John, 108
Dufferin Fund, 63, 65
Dunant, Henry, 176
Dysentery, 9, 91, 106, 108, 113, 155,
    175, 182

Eakins, Thomas, 208
Ear diseases, 113, 189
Edinburgh, 65
Education, 57–58, 63, 66, 80
Egypt, 32, 59, 63, 64, 88, 199
Electricity, 138, 143, 211
Elephantiasis, 109
Eliot, George, 211
Emotions, 54, 69, 137, 145
Endemic, 8, 84
England, 38, 80, 90, 138,
    162, 163, 188
Enteric fever, 11
Environment: and disease, 94, 103–7,
    109, 112; and health, 107–109,
    110–13; and hazards, 101–3
Epidemics, 8, 76, 84, 86, 88, 89, 91, 92,
    95, 119, 174, 190, 192, 206–7;
    control of, 44–45, 98–99, 206,
    207, 208
Epilepsy, 57
Ether, 126, 129, 157
Ethiopia, 207
Evil eye, 61, 62, 71, 76, 207

Exercise, 23, 37, 55, 56,
    58, 92, 138, 154
Ex-voto. *See* votive objects
Eye diseases, 36, 119, 124, 131, 191

Factories, 2, 3, 9, 12, 52, 58, 72, 73, 80,
    112, 114, 115, 170, 174
Famine, 2, 71, 84, 102–3, 174, 193
Farming. *See* agriculture
Fashion, 52
Fetal poison, 68, 73, 196
Fever, 22, 46, 71, 78, 84, 86, 88, 91, 95,
    106, 107, 108, 109, 122, 155, 158,
    159, 214, 215
Fildes, Luke, 210
Finland, 92, 103
Flaubert, Gustav, 210, 216
Folk medicine, 13, 17, 28–31, 32, 59,
    75, 109–110, 118, 122, 157,
    158–60, 161; medicines, 158–60;
    practitioners, 29–31, 91, 118,
    125, 161; spiritual medicine,
    29–30; training, 31, 161;
    treatment, 17, 28, 29, 75, 91–92,
    121, 122, 146
Food, 2–4, 37, 54, 55, 56, 58, 69, 70,
    71, 72, 74, 84, 92, 102, 104–5, 109,
    165, 174, 175, 179, 180, 182, 183,
    186, 195, 206. *See also* diet
France, 36, 39, 65, 79, 80, 199, 215
Franco-Prussian War, 40, 174, 176
Freud, Sigmund, 143
Funerals. *See* burials

Germ theory, 90–91, 190
Germany, 77, 80, 137, 140,
    170, 191, 199
Gervix, Henri, 212
Ghana, 47
Ghosts, 29, 44, 46, 54, 89,
    145, 193, 206
Ginseng, 152, 160, 161
Global trade, 3, 9, 12, 86, 103, 151–52,
    164–65, 177
Global travel, 9–12, 17, 86, 101, 165

Gods. *See* deities
Governments, 79–80, 95, 111, 115, 119, 138–39, 148, 177, 179, 182, 186–87, 188, 190, 191, 192–93, 195; and public health, 14–15, 80, 93–94, 96–97, 98–99, 196, 198; and welfare, 66, 79–80, 177, 191
Graveyards, 7, 42, 48, 112

Haffkine, Waldemar, 98
Hahnemann, Samuel, 28
Haiti, 48, 177, 182
Hakimas, 64
Hakims, 24, 25, 118, 160, 165, 195
Hawaii, 12, 48, 85
Headache, 10, 57, 122, 143, 216
Health education, 59, 65, 79, 186, 190
Health, promoting, 4, 111, 164
Heart disease, 98
Heinroth, J. C., 137
Herbalism, 28, 37, 158, 165
Herbalists, 14, 29, 31, 58, 59, 74
Heredity, 90, 106, 136, 215
Hindu religion, 22, 45, 61, 75, 86, 97, 194, 197, 206
Hoffmann, Felix, 158
Holmes, Oliver Wendell, 156
Homeopathy, 28, 37, 158, 165
Hong Kong, 88, 90
Hospitals, 14, 27, 40, 41, 62, 63, 65, 66, 69, 74, 127, 128, 130–31, 136, 144, 187–90, 191, 192, 193, 194, 195, 198, 204, 209, 211; childrens', 77–79, 188; design of, 187–88; isolation, 93, 94, 188, 190; military, 172, 174–75, 176
Housing, 7, 10, 99, 109, 110, 113, 191, 198, 213, 214
Hydropathy, 28, 110–11
Hygiene, 4–9, 23, 37, 43, 58, 59, 63, 65, 79, 92, 93, 98, 171, 188, 189, 190
Hysteria, 55, 57, 127, 143, 147

Ibn Sina (Avicenna), 23
Iceland, 63
Immunity, 72, 73
Immunization, 95–98
India, 2, 3, 4, 7, 9, 10, 12, 22, 23, 25, 32, 41, 59, 61, 63, 64, 65, 75, 80, 86, 87, 88, 89, 90, 93, 94, 96, 97, 98, 103, 106, 108, 109, 113, 124, 131, 148, 152, 161, 163, 165, 178, 180, 194, 195, 196, 199, 200, 213
Indian Mutiny, 182
Indian Ocean, 207
Indian Wars (North America), 178, 180
Indiki, 147, 148
Indonesia, 102, 108
Industry: and war, 170, 172
Infant welfare. *See* welfare
Infants, 58, 60–63, 67, 68–71, 79, 125, 177, 188, 191
Infection, 60, 77, 120, 124, 125, 126, 127–28, 129, 130, 173, 190, 211, 213
Infertility, 55, 56, 57, 206
Influenza, 12, 32, 84, 85, 90
Injuries, 9, 11–12, 59, 61, 62, 64, 72–73, 77, 113, 114, 119–20, 125, 129, 190, 215
Inoculation, 75, 95–96, 97, 119, 196, 197
Iran, 60, 61, 68, 71, 194, 198
Ireland, 2, 36, 39, 84, 90
Isandlwana, Battle of, 181, 184
Islam, 5, 27, 29, 42–43, 86
Islamic medicine, 25, 194
Italy, 38, 77, 140, 170

Japan, 44, 86, 95, 96, 102, 131, 144, 145, 176, 178, 180, 196, 199, 204, 207, 208
Jaundice, 22, 68
Java, 3, 63, 166
Jenner, Edward, 99
Jex-Blake, Sophia, 65
Jinn, 43, 89

Kazakhstan, 29
Kenya, 30
Koch, Robert, 90, 91, 94
Korea, 199
Kraepelin, Emil, 142
!Kung, 46, 48
Kuwata, Ryusai, 204

Labor. *See* childbirth
Laboratories, 26, 27, 157, 191
Laborers, 9, 107, 108, 113, 115
Laennec, René, 20
Latin America, 9, 33, 46, 63, 79
Lifestyle: and health, 37, 38, 55, 56,
     57, 108–9
Lister, Joseph, 128
Literature: and medicine, 210–12,
     213–14, 215–16
Little Big Horn, Battle of, 178
Livingstone, David, 152
Local anesthetics, 127, 132
London, 3, 5, 7, 8, 39, 40, 78, 94, 126,
     187, 189, 213, 215
Loubon, Émile, 213

MacDowell, Ephraim, 126
Malaria, 12, 72, 86, 102,
     106, 107, 109
Malawi, 152
Malaya, 12, 63
Māori, 149, 150, 159, 177–78, 179, 183
Maori warfare, 178, 179, 180, 183
Materia medica. *See* pharmacopeias
Measles, 11, 12, 32, 73, 74, 85, 182
Medical figures, 54, 203, 205, 206
Medical images, 152, 201–4, 206, 207,
     209, 210, 213
Medical instruments, 26–27, 204
Medical practitioners, 14, 118–19,
     163, 165, 176, 187, 192, 208;
     learned, 14, 21, 24, 74, 119, 121,
     160, 163, 209–10. *See also*
     Ayurvedic medicine; Chinese
     medicine; folk medicine; unani
     medicine; western medicine

Medical systems, 13, 17, 18, 31, 32,
     64, 103, 118, 123, 152, 160. *See
     also* ayurvedic medicine;
     Chinese medicine; unani
     medicine; western medicine
Medicine King, 44, 206
Medicine man, 46, 47, 204
Medicines, 29, 55, 56, 58–59, 60, 64, 72,
     74, 91, 104, 110, 119, 120, 121, 124,
     130, 131, 151, 152, 161, 163–66,
     171, 175, 204, 205, 207, 209;
     herbal, 46, 49, 59, 92, 119, 125, 151,
     159, 166. *See also* drugs
Menopause, 54, 57
Menstruation, 54, 55, 57, 58, 194
Mental illness, 29, 42, 57, 136–37, 142,
     143, 215; causes, 136–37, 143–44,
     146, 149; moral therapy, 137–38;
     treatment, 137–41, 143, 144,
     145–46, 148–50; types, behavior,
     136, 142, 144, 146
Mentally ill: behavior of, 136–37,
     144–45, 146–47
Mercury, 91, 114, 152
Mexico, 28, 59, 92, 98, 177
Miasma, 8, 10, 31, 90, 106, 108, 111
Midwives, 21, 23, 25, 31, 60–63, 64,
     65, 68, 79, 186
Military medicine, 170–73
Mineral springs, 11, 110, 143
Mines, 9, 12, 72, 73, 80, 114
Mission hospitals, 40, 195–96, 198,
     199, 204
Missionaries, 9, 32, 41, 42, 144, 183;
     medical, 40–41, 204
Missions, medical, 40–41, 195, 196
Mitchell, Silas Weir, 143
Mongolia, 88
Morphine, 157, 166
Mortality, 61, 62, 72, 73, 75,
     76–77, 79, 84, 95, 96, 98–99,
     125, 128, 129; in war, 173–74,
     175, 182–83
Morton, William, 126
Mosquitoes, 12, 85, 106, 109

Mothers, 68, 69, 71, 72, 79, 177, 186, 191
Moxibustion, 20, 122, 145
Mumps, 32, 73
Muslim Rebellion, 182

Nanking, Battle of, 182
Napoleonic Wars, 170, 171, 173, 174
Nein Rebellion, 180
Nervous diseases, 57, 106, 136, 143–44, 147
Neurasthenia, 143
New Zealand, 3, 9, 10, 12, 46, 149, 150, 159
Ngoma medicine, 46, 47, 48
Nigeria, 30
Nightingale, Florence, 174–75
Nitrous oxide, 126, 132
Non-western medicine, 18, 33, 119–25, 131, 152–53, 192. *See also* ayurvedic medicine; Chinese medicine; folk medicine; unani medicine
Non-western wars, 177–78
North Africa, 7, 17, 23, 52, 76, 86, 89, 91, 106, 120, 122, 124, 131, 144, 197, 198, 207
North America, 3, 17, 25, 31, 40, 42, 48, 58, 61, 64, 65, 67, 68, 70, 71, 73, 75, 79, 84, 92, 103, 110, 113, 118, 122, 125, 131, 132, 135, 138, 143, 144, 148, 152, 155, 158, 159, 160, 163, 164, 165, 167, 177, 178, 180, 186, 191, 192, 204, 207; indigenous healers in, 46, 47, 204, 205; indigenous peoples, 31, 46, 60, 61, 68, 108, 109, 110, 120–21, 122, 131, 159, 164, 179, 204, 206, 207
Nurses, 79, 131, 174, 175, 176, 189, 190
Nursing, 38–40, 58, 59, 63–64, 78, 130, 174–75, 195
Nursing orders, 39, 42, 63, 175
Nursing homes, 187, 189, 193

Obeah, 49
Occupations: and health, 2, 9, 12, 14, 113–15

Ointment, 120, 155, 159, 160
Opera, 206, 214–15
Operating theatre, 64, 128, 131, 189, 195, 208
Operations. *See* surgical operations
Opium, 125, 156, 157, 161, 166–67
Opium Wars, 177, 180
Orthopedics, 77, 129–30
Ottoman Empire, 176

Pacific Islands, 12, 32, 85, 159
Pain: control of, 60, 121, 125, 126–27, 131, 132, 158, 160
Pakistan, 200
Pandemic, 84, 86, 93, 98
Parasites, 7, 86, 113, 155, 191
Paris, 3, 77, 126
Parker, Peter, 41, 204
Pasteur, Louis, 90, 98, 128, 192
Patent medicines, 4, 163–64, 166, 167
Patients, 21, 22, 28, 31, 32, 40, 41, 45, 53, 117, 126, 127, 128, 129, 155, 160, 165–66, 187, 188, 189, 190, 194, 195, 196, 202, 203, 204, 209, 212; with mental illness, 137, 139–40, 141, 142, 143, 144, 148–50
Pavlova, Grand Duchess Elena, 175
Pediatrics, 77–78
Peninsular War, 170
Persia, 61, 68, 198
Peru, 10, 106, 189, 199
Pharmaceutical industry, 157, 163
Pharmacopeias, 152–53, 156–57
Pharmacists, 161, 163, 167
Pharmacy, 160, 199, 200
Photography, 202, 209
Pilgrimages, 36, 55, 56, 89, 194
Pinel, Philippe, 137
Pirogov, Nikolai, 173
Plague, 86, 88, 90, 91, 92–93, 94
Plantations, 12, 72, 108, 113
Plants, 29, 31, 59, 151–52, 154, 155, 157, 159, 160, 165, 200, 203
Pneumonia, 8, 72, 84, 182

Polynesia, 48
Post, Justus, 107
Poultices, 58, 119, 120, 121,
    131, 155, 165
Prayer, 36, 37, 44, 49, 56, 59, 76, 96,
    109, 197, 206
Pregnancy, 54, 55, 56, 58, 194, 206
Priessnitz, Vincenz, 28
Prescriptions, 160, 161, 200
Protestant religion, 36, 37, 38, 39, 40,
    41, 186
Prussia, 176
Psychiatry, 141–42
Psychotherapy, 143, 145
Puberty, 54, 57
Public health, 14–15, 93–95, 98–99,
    186, 190–91, 197–98
Puccini, Giacomo, 214
Puerperal fever, 62

Qua, Lam, 204
Quarantine, 93–94
Quinine, 91, 107, 152, 157, 158

Race, 10, 85, 107–8, 149
Railroads, 9, 83, 170
Rats, 88, 90
Red Cross, 176, 198
Religious orders, 39, 42, 63
Respiratory diseases, 8, 77,
    78, 84, 105, 108, 112, 114, 159,
    190, 213
Rheumatism, 78, 131
Rickets, 8, 71, 78, 111, 130
Rituals, 5, 29, 31, 32, 45, 46, 47, 49, 63,
    66, 93, 147, 160, 183, 206
Romania, 174
Rorke's Drift, Battle of, 181, 184
Ross, Ronald, 109
Rural, 2, 4, 6, 7, 10, 11, 92, 98, 106,
    137, 193, 198, 213
Rush, Benjamin, 136, 138
Russia, 86, 87, 93, 95, 171, 173
Russo-Turkish War, 174
Rwanda, 125

Samoa, 32
Samurai, 178, 179
Sanitary measures, 93–94, 95, 98, 109,
    171, 190, 198
Satsuma Rebellion, 178, 179, 182
Scarlet fever, 73
Scotland, 90
Seasons: and health, 22, 84, 103,
    104–5, 108, 109, 121
Seligman, Adalbert, 208
Settlers, 10, 106, 107, 108, 109, 111,
    165, 166, 177
Sewerage, 9, 112, 190
Shaka Zula, 178, 179
Shamans, 21, 29, 46, 47, 92, 205
Shelley, Mary, 211
Ships, 9, 14, 84, 85, 152, 170
Sierra Leone, 148
Simpson, James Young, 126
Sims, James Marion, 126
Sitala, 45, 96, 97, 194
Skin complaints, 78, 111, 120–21, 131,
    155, 189, 202
Slaves, 48, 49, 69, 72, 107–8, 179, 183
Sleeping sickness, 11, 86, 109
Smallpox, 11, 12, 14, 37, 64, 73, 75, 76,
    80, 85, 89, 90, 91, 95–98, 160, 171,
    194, 196; deities, 44, 45, 76, 196,
    204, 213, 214
Smith, Archibald, 10, 110
Smoke pollution, 8, 111–12
Snow, John, 94
Soldiers, 10, 11, 84, 108, 111, 132,
    170–74, 176, 178–84; wounded,
    171–73, 179
Solferino, Battle of, 176
Sorcery, 29, 48–49, 59, 146. *See also*
    witchcraft
South Africa, 9, 49, 88, 103, 166
Southern Africa, 28, 30, 31, 46, 48,
    102, 109, 120–21, 147, 162, 164,
    165, 178
South America, 3, 10, 46, 63, 79, 85,
    88, 152, 157, 198, 199
Spas, 11, 111, 143

Spells, 44, 48
Spirits, 43, 44, 46, 47, 48, 71, 76, 89,
    109, 146, 147, 160, 193, 204, 205,
    206, 207
Spiritual healers, 13, 46–48, 74, 76,
    118, 131
Spiritual medicine, 13, 32, 43–48, 49,
    76, 93, 94, 181, 204, 206
Springs. *See* mineral springs
Sri Lanka, 194
States. *See* governments
Stevenson, Robert Louis, 211
Stomach complaints, 28, 71,
    73, 114, 190
Supernatural diseases, 29, 43, 44, 45,
    46, 47, 48, 49, 54, 61–62, 68, 71,
    76, 89, 145, 146–47, 160
Surgeons, 57, 62, 64, 77, 126, 128, 130,
    172–73, 192, 208–9
Surgery, 41, 63, 117–31, 172, 189, 195,
    199, 202
Surgical practitioners,
    118–19, 124, 125
Surgical techniques, 126, 128, 129,
    131, 209
Surgical operations, 122–25, 126, 127,
    129, 212
Sushruta, 104
Sweden, 80
Swellings, 28, 119, 121
Switzerland, 65
Syme, Joseph, 126
Syphilis, 85, 96, 140, 166. *See also*
    venereal disease

Taiping Rebellion, 2, 177,
    179, 182, 193
Taiwan, 199
Taoism, 44–45
Tanzania, 30, 207
Teeth, 131–33, 177, 191
Teething, 71
Temperature, 10, 11, 54, 68, 103, 104,
    105, 107–8, 113, 136, 154, 212
Tibetan medicine, 154, 202, 204, 207

Tikaders, 96
Tolstoy, Leo, 173
Tonics, 4, 121, 155, 164
Tooth extraction, 118, 119, 132
Toothache, 36
T'ou-Shen Niang-Niang, 44, 76, 194
Trollope, Anthony, 209
Tropical diseases, 11, 80, 109
Tuberculosis, 8, 11, 52, 72, 77, 84–85,
    90, 99, 111, 113, 214–15
Tumors, 41, 126, 129, 131,
    136, 140, 204
Tunisia, 94
Turkey, 152, 194
Typhoid fever, 8, 72, 89, 98, 99, 171,
    175, 182
Typhus, 84, 85, 175

Uganda, 86, 124, 125
Unani medicine, 23, 25, 31, 32, 51,
    55–56, 59, 64, 74, 89, 91, 92, 94,
    105, 118, 120, 121, 122, 123, 154,
    155, 160, 166, 199, 200, 202;
    diagnosis, 24; diet, 55; drugs,
    155, 160; humors, 23–24, 105;
    illness, understanding of, 23–25,
    89, 91, 105, 120, 154;
    practitioners, 24–25, 118, 160,
    165, 195, 200; revival, 25, 200;
    training, 24, 160, 199, 200;
    treatments, 24, 32, 74,
    121, 122, 195
United States, 3, 12, 37, 59, 86, 87, 95,
    106, 108, 142, 152, 159, 166, 190,
    191, 204
Universities, 27, 57, 64, 191
Unorthodox medicine, 28, 37, 158,
    165. *See also* herbalism;
    homeopathy; hydropathy
Urban life, 2, 12, 77, 84, 88, 92,
    111–12, 140, 193, 213
Urbanization, 5–6, 83–84, 192

Vaccination, 37, 64, 75, 80, 96–98,
    119, 171, 196–97, 204

Vaccines, 98, 192
Vaids, 23, 160
Valdés, José Manuel, 106–7
Venereal disease, 66, 171
Verdi, Giuseppe, 214
Virchow, Rudolf, 56
Virus, 85, 90, 95, 96
Vitamins, 3, 8, 71, 130
Votive objects, 36, 208

War, 79, 84, 169–84; wounds, 171–73, 174, 177
Warriors, 147, 178–81, 206; wounded, 179, 181–82
Water, 4–7, 14, 84, 86, 92, 94, 98, 111, 112–13, 171, 180, 183, 190, 197
Waterloo, Battle of, 132, 171, 174
Weapons, 170, 172, 173, 178, 179, 180, 183; injuries caused by, 172, 173, 177
Welfare, 65–66, 186, 191; infant, 65, 177
Wells, Horace, 132
West Africa, 10, 29, 148
West Indies, 3, 108
Western medicine, 17, 26–28, 31, 32, 33, 41, 51, 56, 59, 62, 63, 65, 73, 77–79, 91, 92, 94, 105–9, 111, 125–31, 135–44, 147, 155, 158, 170–77, 186–92, 197, 198, 200, 202–4, 208–16; anatomy in, 26, 27; criticisms of, 25, 33; diagnosis, 26; drugs, 155–58, 162, 163, 165, 166; illness, understanding of, 26, 89–91, 105–7, 126, 135–37; military medicine, 170–73; practitioners, 27, 58, 59, 62, 63, 155–56, 160, 165, 175, 190, 191, 192, 195, 196, 209–10; surgery, 32, 125–29;

training, 27, 62, 64–65, 130, 142, 160, 163, 191–92, 199–200, 208, 209, 210–11; treatments, 70, 75, 91, 137–38; women practitioners, 41, 63–65, 210. *See also* druggists; surgeons; surgery; orthopedics; pediatrics
Wet nurses, 69, 80
Whooping cough, 11, 32, 73, 74, 85
Wind, 103, 104, 106
Witchcraft, 29, 30, 48, 59, 68, 109, 147
Witchdoctors, 33, 42, 46, 49
Withering, William, 157
Women, 6, 12, 39, 45, 51–66, 69, 96, 114, 182, 183, 190, 193, 195, 206; and disease, 164, 194, 214–15; health, of, 44, 51–58, 136, 143; as patients, 22, 23, 41, 44, 54–56, 57–58, 69, 94, 127, 129, 136, 141, 143, 144, 147, 188, 194, 195, 203, 214, 215; as practitioners, 25, 41, 58–65, 175, 210; in war, 175, 179, 183, 184
Wood, Alexander, 209
Workplace, 9, 12, 57, 63, 72–73, 80, 188; hazards in, 84, 113–15
Wounds, 118, 119–20, 127, 159; in war, 171–73, 174, 182
Wright, Almoth, 98

Xhosa, 30, 31
X-rays, 27, 41, 202

Yellow fever, 11, 72, 85–86, 91, 102, 109, 182
Yoruba, 30, 205

Zola, Émile, 213
Zulu, 4, 48, 109, 178, 184; healers, 159, 182; warfare, 178–79, 180–82, 183–84

About the Author

DEBORAH BRUNTON was awarded a doctorate from the University of Pennsylvania in 1990 and is now Senior Lecturer in History of Medicine at the Open University in Milton Keynes in Britain. She has researched on public health, particularly smallpox prevention. She is the author of *The Politics of Vaccination: Practice and Policy in England, Wales, Ireland, and Scotland, 1800–1874* and contributed to and edited *Medicine Transformed: Health, Disease and Society in Europe, 1800–1930*.